wild Ocean

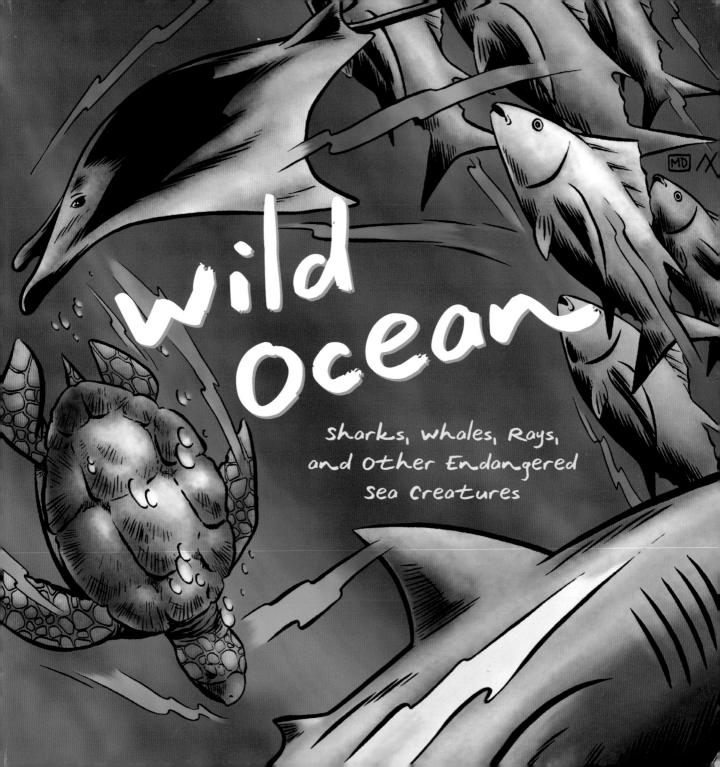

wild ocean

Sharks, whales, Rays, and Other Endangered Sea Creatures

Image use: p. 140: hawksbill sea turtle (Isabellebonaire/Dreamstime.com), hammerhead shark (Allnaturalbeth/Dreamstime.com); p. 141: albatross (Andreanita/Dreamstime.com), manta ray (Kkg1/Dreamstime.com); p. 142; blue whale (Jeremy Wee/Dreamstime.com), monk seal (Steven Oehlenschlager/Dreamstime.com); p. 143: whale shark (Krzysztof Odziomek/Dreamstime.com), seahorse (Alexandramp/Dreamstime.com); p. 144: bluefin tuna (Ugo Montaldo/Shutterstock.com), coral (Mychadre77/Dreamstime.com); p. 145: manatee (Naluphoto/Dreamstime.com), giant clam (Jonmilnes/Dreamstime.com); p. 150 (Tre' Packard/*pangeaseed.org* 2014).

Library of Congress Cataloging-in-Publication Data

Wild ocean (Fulcrum Publishing (Firm))
  Wild ocean : sharks, whales, rays, and other endangered sea creatures / edited by Matt Dembicki.
    pages cm
  Audience: 14.
  Summary: "The world's oceans represent the last wild frontier on Earth. While our understanding of life in the ocean is relatively basic, our actions are putting hundreds of species in danger. In this graphic anthology, Matt Dembicki, editor and an artist of the award-winning *Trickster* and *District Comics*, explores the adventures of twelve iconic endangered sea animals: hawksbill turtle, bluefin tuna, hammerhead shark, giant clam, manatee, blue whale, coral, albatross, whale shark, monk seal, manta ray, and seahorse. Produced in cooperation with the non-profit PangeaSeed, these gripping stories instill a passion to conserve our magnificent sea creatures. 8x8, 156 pages, color throughout, trade paper. PangeaSeed's mission is to contribute to the protection of sharks and the preservation of our oceans by taking responsible action, increasing public awareness, and providing education that encourages environmental activism and sustainable consumption choices"-- Provided by publisher.
  Includes bibliographical references.
  ISBN 978-1-938486-38-8 (paperback)
1. Marine animals--Conservation--Juvenile literature. 2. Endangered species--Conservation--Juvenile literature. I. Dembicki, Matt, editor of compilation. II. Title.
  QL122.2.W54 2014
  578.77--dc23
                              2014004451

Design by Fred Chao
Printed in the United States
0 9 8 7 6 5 4 3 2 1

Fulcrum Publishing
4690 Table Mountain Dr., Ste. 100
Golden, CO 80403
800-992-2908 • 303-277-1623
www.fulcrumbooks.com

From the Bottom of the Deep Blue Sea

Standing on the brink of the ocean, it's difficult to imagine that anything—even humankind—could affect this vastness. It's huge, powerful, and mysterious. When it flexes its muscles, the ocean can capsize fishing boats, batter ocean liners, and smash boardwalks—it has even pushed major metropolitan areas such as New York City to its knees. It also has the remarkable ability to filter human-made poisons that leak into its waters. But it can only be pushed so far. It's powerful but fragile, too. Constant oil spills, dumping of waste, and overfishing and wasteful practice have stretched the ocean's resilience to the point where, soon, it may not be able to bounce back. Many of its inhabitants, some of which look like creatures from distant planets, are dying out.

Humans, as stewards of Earth, have an obligation to preserve this resource: if not for a conscientious obligation to save other species, then to preserve our own—we simply need the food that it produces. This is not about politics. It's not a call for antibusiness environmentalism. Quite the contrary. It's an issue of altering behavior and turning toward our entrepreneurial spirit to find solutions to these problems so that current and future generations can enjoy the splendid aesthetics and bounty of the world's oceans.

Despite nearly daily reports that depict what appears to be an inevitable path toward a dying ocean, there is always hope. Little changes can lead to big ones. That's what we're trying to do with this comics anthology featuring 12 endangered sea animals. The stories here are meant to educate, inspire, and entertain. They present facts—often with a dash of fantasy—in a fun (and sometimes funny) way. Coupled with a dazzling array of artistic styles, the tales will stir your imagination and revive an appreciation for our wild ocean. And, just maybe, the collection might compel you to recycle more or make better consumer choices that will help preserve one of our planet's greatest natural treasures.

—Matt Dembicki

P.S. Part of the proceeds of this book will go to PangeaSeed, an international ocean-conservation organization that uses art to educate and spread the word about helping sea animals.

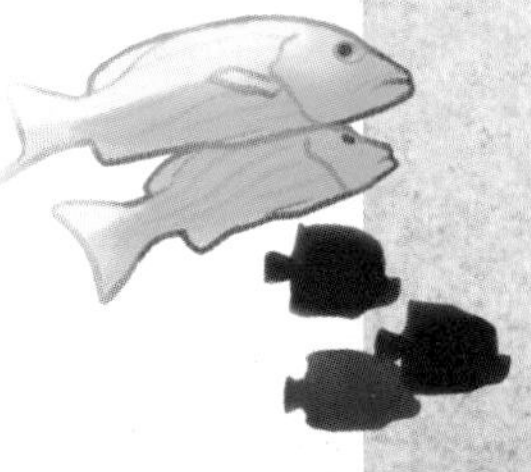

TORTUGA, THE ISLAND THAT SWIMS

BY JAY HOSLER

Gliding through the ocean, the hawksbill sea turtle has been a part of ocean ecosystems for more than 100 million years. The turtles—and their many passengers—must match their drive to survive against illegal egg and shell harvesting, habitat destruction, and climate change.

THE GALAPAGOS

BY MATT DEMBICKI

In the ongoing battle between desperate poachers and the vigilant rangers from the Galapagos Marine Reserve, the life of the hammerhead shark hangs in the balance. This story shows the cat-and-mouse game in which the sharks' survival becomes the ultimate prize.

THE RIME OF THE MODERN MARINER

BY ANDY K.

Inspired by Samuel Taylor Coleridge's "Rime of the Ancient Mariner," this piece of graphic fiction shows how the life of the ever-soaring albatross provides a sailor with a lesson of hope following a failed suicide attempt.

THE SHAPE OF THE FUTURE

BY MICHAEL COWGILL
ART BY TOM WILLIAMS

Although they are sometimes known by fearsome names such as "devil fish," manta rays are really docile creatures that migrate through the world's oceans. They also inspire some of the most exciting developments to impact transportation and construction design in years.

HAWAIIAN BLUES

BY DOVE MCHARGUE

Despite being the largest animal to ever roam the Earth, the blue whale was almost hunted to extinction in the 1900s. Through the prism of a young boy's imagination, the plight of a mother and baby whale mimics the relationship between the boy and his father.

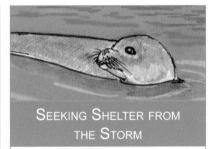

SEEKING SHELTER FROM THE STORM

BY TAMMY STELLANOVA

The once-numerous monk seal is critically endangered, with only 450 to 600 left living in the wild. This wordless story follows the path of a mother seal as she searches for a safe place to bear and raise her pup.

BUTANDING

BY PIERCE HARGAN

Although Philippine officials banned commercial fishing, as well as selling, importing, and exporting of whale sharks in 1998, hunting continues to endanger these, the largest fish in the world. In this story, the whale sharks, known locally as "butanding," encounter a lost fisherman, and live out a traditional folktale.

POSEIDON'S STEED

BY STEVE LOYA

With a chameleon-like ability to change colors to blend into their surroundings, the tiny, gentle seahorses are the subject of artwork through the ages, as well as concentrated efforts to protect them from possible extinction.

RAW POWER

BY JF FRANKEL

The bluefin tuna is at the top of the food chain in its ocean ecosystem. Just 50 years ago, it was called "horse mackerel" and tuna carcasses were used in cat food. Today, however, bluefin tuna flesh is a favorite in sushi restaurants, and the fish itself edges toward extinction.

ATOLLS OF THE MALDIVES

BY KEVIN PANETTA
ART BY PAULINA GANUCHEAU

The world's coral reefs, so massive that some can be seen from space, are also fragile and facing ever-increasing dangers from climate change and pollution. Explore a reef in the Indian Ocean through the eyes of a young butterflyfish, and meet some of the countless creatures that live there.

THE LADY OF THE SEA

BY PAT N. LEWIS

Basking in shallow, warm waters while they graze on aquatic plants, it's hard to imagine how manatees could ever have been mistaken for mermaids by sailors of long ago. Yet while these placid creatures might be the stars of many legends, the dangers driving them to extinction are very real.

THE LEGEND OF T. GIGAS!

BY BROOKE A. ALLEN

The giant clam, also known as *Tridacna gigas*, is often rumored to clamp down on and drown unsuspecting divers. Yet humans are actually the dangerous ones, harvesting these clams for their flesh and shells almost to the point of extinction.

3

Contents

FOREWORD

THE WORLD'S OCEANS REPRESENT the last wild frontier on Earth. While our understanding of life in the ocean is relatively basic, our actions are putting hundreds of species in danger.

Studies show that half of the species on the planet could disappear by the end of the century. In 2011, the International Union for Conservation of Nature (IUCN) designated a Red List of 620 threatened species of marine animals. Each and every one of these animals is in danger of becoming extinct. Each also provides an important reminder about why we humans need to change our behaviors and protect our oceans from pollution and overfishing.

Our planet's coral reefs, rain forests, and global fish stocks stand a very good chance of fully collapsing by mid-century. The mass extinction that would follow if this were to occur would harm us all.

Humanity is in dire need of a great revolution, a sea of change, in order to rethink the way we live, produce, and consume. We must see the underwater world through fresh eyes and realize the impact of our actions on the oceans and its incredible cast of characters while we still have the chance. It is time to reconnect with nature and be the change we want to see in the world.

To help achieve the necessary changes, PangeaSeed developed a project called Sea of Change: The Year of Living Dangerously in 2013. In collaboration with some of today's most talented and sought-after global artists, including Emek, Dave Kinsey, Kozyndan, Greg "Craola" Simkins, Tatiana Suarez, and Ken Taylor, we came up with an information campaign designed to shed light on the dangers facing marine life around the world.

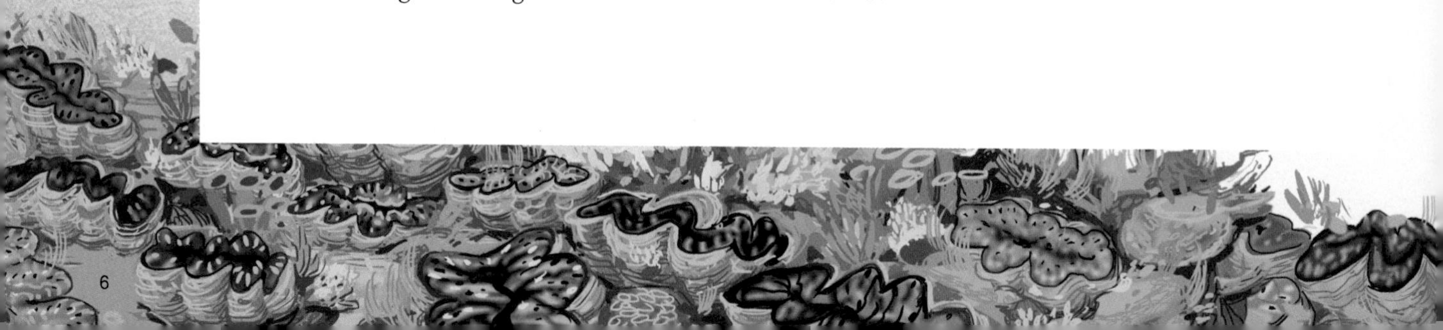

Wild Ocean is a natural extension of this worldwide education campaign. Working with Matt Dembicki, the editor and contributing artist behind the award-winning graphic novels *Trickster* and *District Comics*, we worked together to create a simple yet beautiful concept. We developed 12 compelling, illustrated stories to showcase 12 iconic endangered ocean animals:

- hawksbill turtle
- giant clam
- coral
- monk seal

- bluefin tuna
- manatee
- albatross
- manta ray

- hammerhead shark
- blue whale
- whale shark
- seahorse

Each gripping tale features the work of some of the most renowned graphic novelists and illustrators.

With projects such as *Wild Ocean*, we believe we can spark the activism that will turn into change, starting with individuals and spreading into communities. It's all part of the bigger picture of taking care of future generations and the natural world.

—Tre' Packard
PangeaSeed Founder and Managing Director

Tortuga, the Island That Swims

Story and Art by Jay Hosler

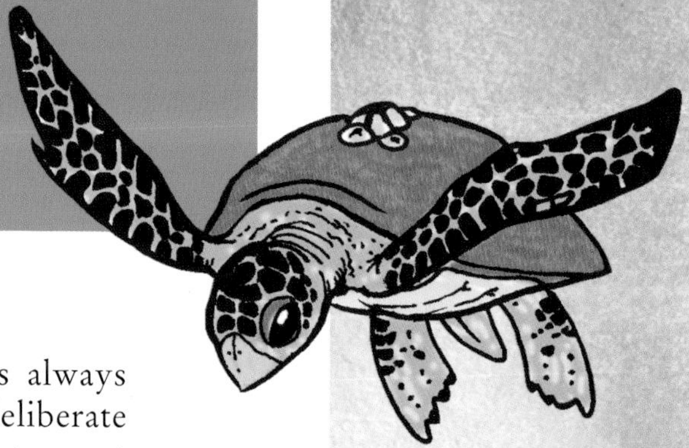

There's something about turtles that has always inspired my imagination. Their slow, deliberate movements and penetrating eyes suggest great wisdom to me. The hawksbill is no different. This beautiful animal soars through the water on winglike flippers, keeping a watchful eye on the ocean. Sea turtles have been important players in marine ecosystems for more than 100 million years, but in recent history humans have been responsible for many threats to their survival. The hawksbill has been hit particularly hard. Habitat destruction, illegal egg harvesting, climate change, and use of the hawksbill's shell to make "tortoise shell" jewelry have all had a devastating effect on hawksbill turtle populations.

And if the hawksbill disappears, its loss would be more than the devastating loss of another splendid animal. Hawksbill turtles often feed on sponges living in reefs, which can create space for animals that live on or near the seabed. Without these magnificent turtles, the succession—or healthy change—in some reefs may be permanently damaged.

This story focuses on a hawksbill turtle and the guests that live on her shell. Protecting the turtles also protects the guests that rely on these amazing creatures for their own survival—just another argument for finding a way to save the species so it can live another 100 million years, at least.

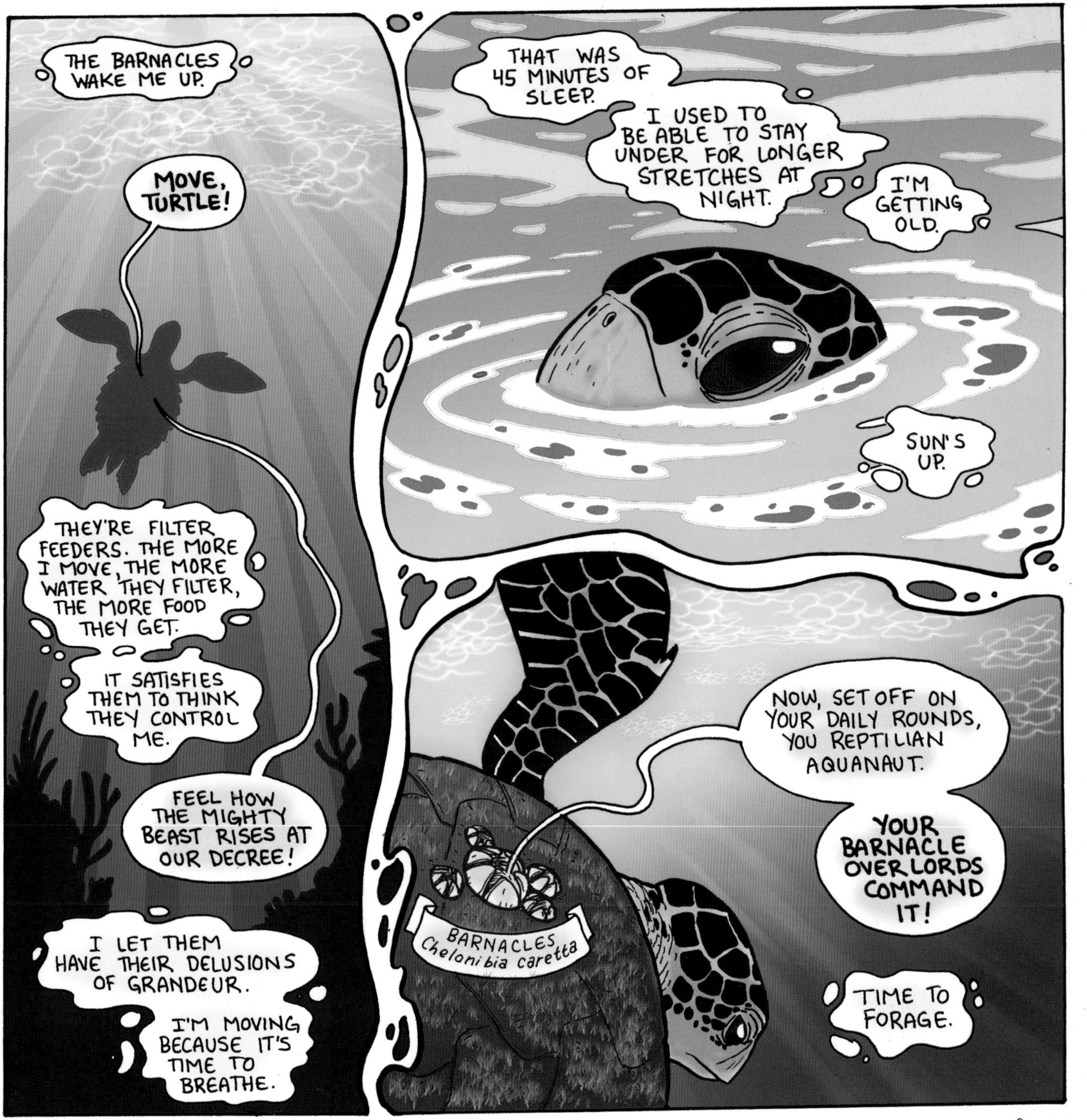
THE BARNACLES WAKE ME UP.
MOVE, TURTLE!
THEY'RE FILTER FEEDERS. THE MORE I MOVE, THE MORE WATER THEY FILTER, THE MORE FOOD THEY GET.
IT SATISFIES THEM TO THINK THEY CONTROL ME.
FEEL HOW THE MIGHTY BEAST RISES AT OUR DECREE!
I LET THEM HAVE THEIR DELUSIONS OF GRANDEUR.
I'M MOVING BECAUSE IT'S TIME TO BREATHE.
THAT WAS 45 MINUTES OF SLEEP.
I USED TO BE ABLE TO STAY UNDER FOR LONGER STRETCHES AT NIGHT.
I'M GETTING OLD.
SUN'S UP.
NOW, SET OFF ON YOUR DAILY ROUNDS, YOU REPTILIAN AQUANAUT.
YOUR BARNACLE OVERLORDS COMMAND IT!
BARNACLES
Chelonibia caretta
TIME TO FORAGE.

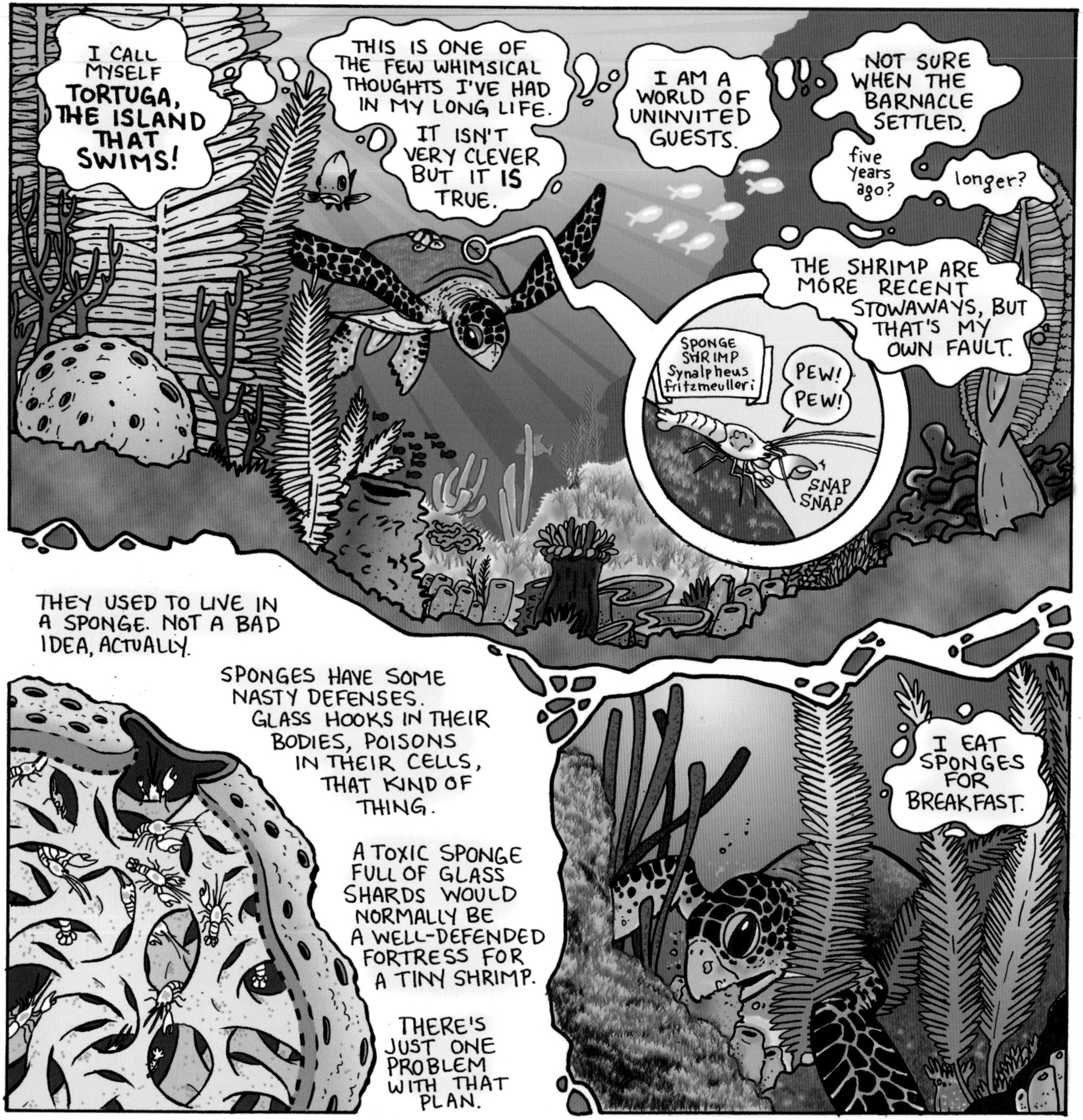
I CALL MYSELF TORTUGA, THE ISLAND THAT SWIMS!
THIS IS ONE OF THE FEW WHIMSICAL THOUGHTS I'VE HAD IN MY LONG LIFE.
IT ISN'T VERY CLEVER BUT IT IS TRUE.
I AM A WORLD OF UNINVITED GUESTS.
NOT SURE WHEN THE BARNACLE SETTLED.
five years ago?
longer?
THE SHRIMP ARE MORE RECENT STOWAWAYS, BUT THAT'S MY OWN FAULT.
SPONGE SHRIMP Synalpheus fritzmeulleri
PEW! PEW!
SNAP SNAP
THEY USED TO LIVE IN A SPONGE. NOT A BAD IDEA, ACTUALLY.
SPONGES HAVE SOME NASTY DEFENSES. GLASS HOOKS IN THEIR BODIES, POISONS IN THEIR CELLS, THAT KIND OF THING.
A TOXIC SPONGE FULL OF GLASS SHARDS WOULD NORMALLY BE A WELL-DEFENDED FORTRESS FOR A TINY SHRIMP.
THERE'S JUST ONE PROBLEM WITH THAT PLAN.
I EAT SPONGES FOR BREAKFAST.

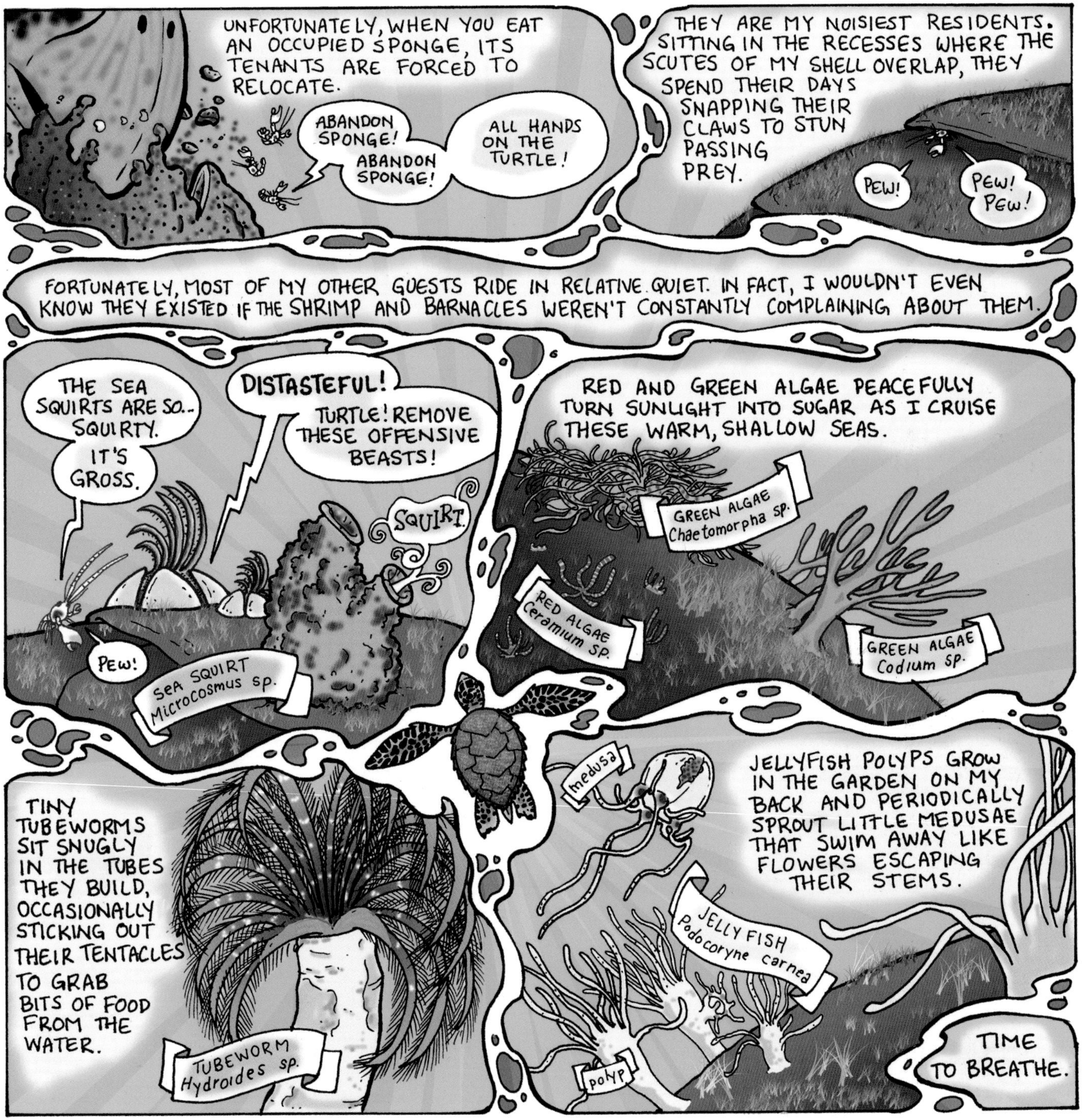
UNFORTUNATELY, WHEN YOU EAT AN OCCUPIED SPONGE, ITS TENANTS ARE FORCED TO RELOCATE.
ABANDON SPONGE! ABANDON SPONGE!
ALL HANDS ON THE TURTLE!
THEY ARE MY NOISIEST RESIDENTS. SITTING IN THE RECESSES WHERE THE SCUTES OF MY SHELL OVERLAP, THEY SPEND THEIR DAYS SNAPPING THEIR CLAWS TO STUN PASSING PREY.
PEW!
PEW! PEW!
FORTUNATELY, MOST OF MY OTHER GUESTS RIDE IN RELATIVE QUIET. IN FACT, I WOULDN'T EVEN KNOW THEY EXISTED IF THE SHRIMP AND BARNACLES WEREN'T CONSTANTLY COMPLAINING ABOUT THEM.
THE SEA SQUIRTS ARE SO... SQUIRTY.
IT'S GROSS.
DISTASTEFUL!
TURTLE! REMOVE THESE OFFENSIVE BEASTS!
SQUIRT.
PEW!
SEA SQUIRT Microcosmus sp.
RED AND GREEN ALGAE PEACEFULLY TURN SUNLIGHT INTO SUGAR AS I CRUISE THESE WARM, SHALLOW SEAS.
GREEN ALGAE Chaetomorpha sp.
RED ALGAE Ceramium sp.
GREEN ALGAE Codium sp.
TINY TUBEWORMS SIT SNUGLY IN THE TUBES THEY BUILD, OCCASIONALLY STICKING OUT THEIR TENTACLES TO GRAB BITS OF FOOD FROM THE WATER.
TUBEWORM Hydroides sp.
medusa
JELLYFISH POLYPS GROW IN THE GARDEN ON MY BACK AND PERIODICALLY SPROUT LITTLE MEDUSAE THAT SWIM AWAY LIKE FLOWERS ESCAPING THEIR STEMS.
JELLYFISH Podocoryne carnea
polyp
TIME TO BREATHE.

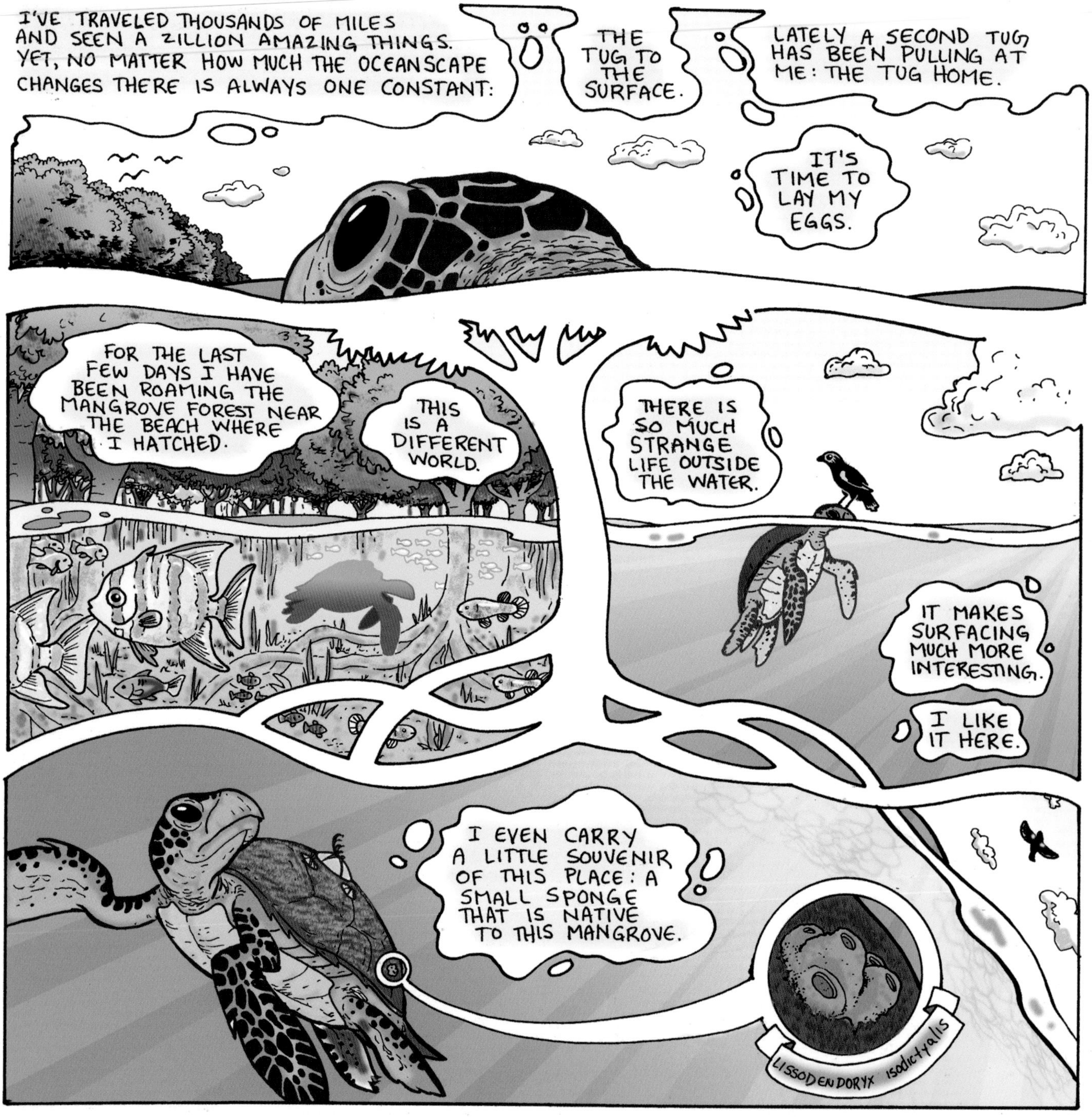
I'VE TRAVELED THOUSANDS OF MILES AND SEEN A ZILLION AMAZING THINGS. YET, NO MATTER HOW MUCH THE OCEANSCAPE CHANGES THERE IS ALWAYS ONE CONSTANT:
THE TUG TO THE SURFACE.
LATELY A SECOND TUG HAS BEEN PULLING AT ME: THE TUG HOME.
IT'S TIME TO LAY MY EGGS.
FOR THE LAST FEW DAYS I HAVE BEEN ROAMING THE MANGROVE FOREST NEAR THE BEACH WHERE I HATCHED.
THIS IS A DIFFERENT WORLD.
THERE IS SO MUCH STRANGE LIFE OUTSIDE THE WATER.
IT MAKES SURFACING MUCH MORE INTERESTING.
I LIKE IT HERE.
I EVEN CARRY A LITTLE SOUVENIR OF THIS PLACE: A SMALL SPONGE THAT IS NATIVE TO THIS MANGROVE.
LISSODENDORYX isodictyalis

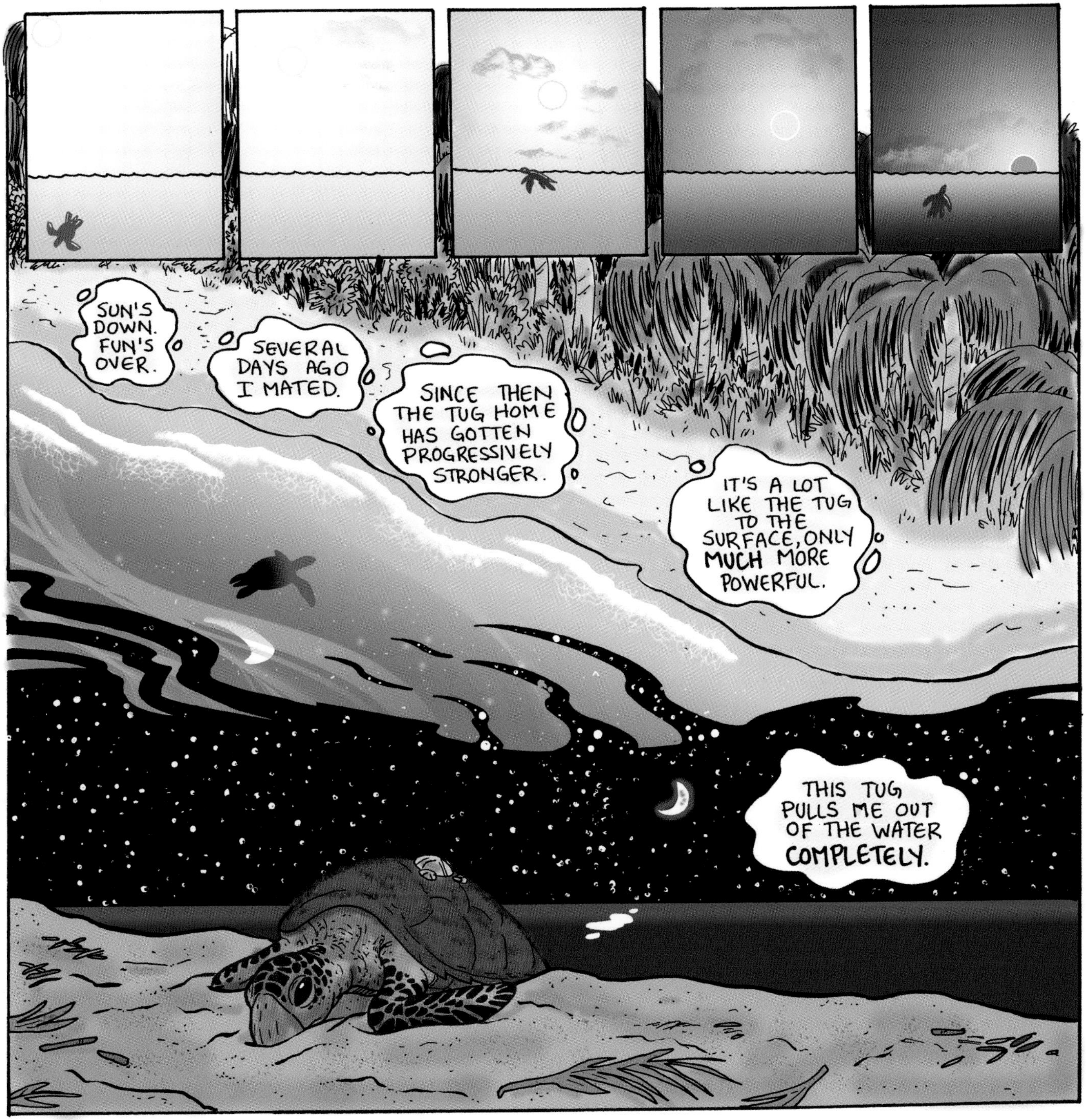
SUN'S DOWN. FUN'S OVER.
SEVERAL DAYS AGO I MATED.
SINCE THEN THE TUG HOME HAS GOTTEN PROGRESSIVELY STRONGER.
IT'S A LOT LIKE THE TUG TO THE SURFACE, ONLY MUCH MORE POWERFUL.
THIS TUG PULLS ME OUT OF THE WATER COMPLETELY.

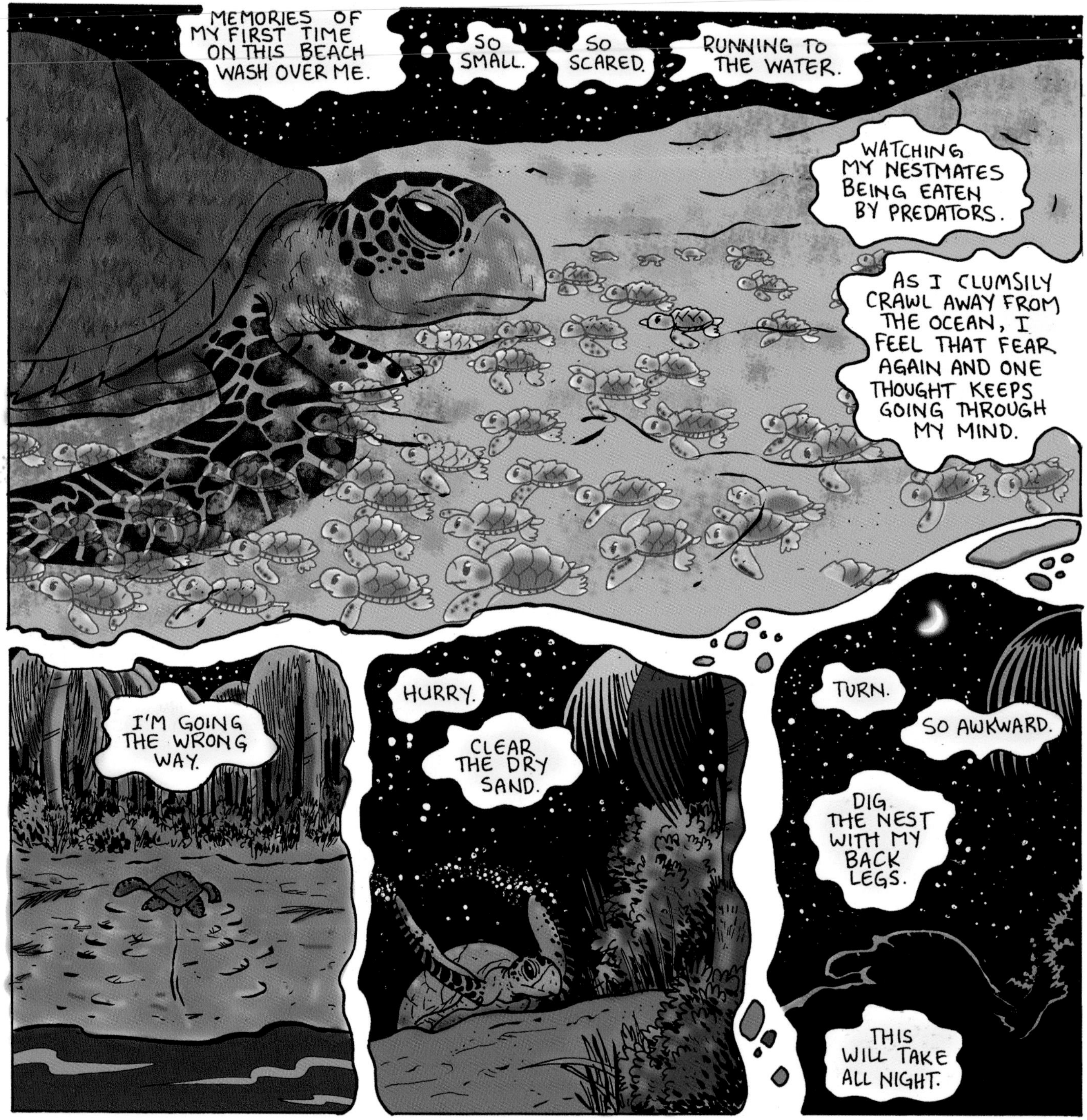
MEMORIES OF MY FIRST TIME ON THIS BEACH WASH OVER ME.
SO SMALL.
SO SCARED.
RUNNING TO THE WATER.
WATCHING MY NESTMATES BEING EATEN BY PREDATORS.
AS I CLUMSILY CRAWL AWAY FROM THE OCEAN, I FEEL THAT FEAR AGAIN AND ONE THOUGHT KEEPS GOING THROUGH MY MIND.
I'M GOING THE WRONG WAY.
HURRY.
CLEAR THE DRY SAND.
TURN.
SO AWKWARD.
DIG THE NEST WITH MY BACK LEGS.
THIS WILL TAKE ALL NIGHT.

THREE EGGS.

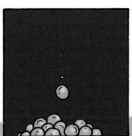

86

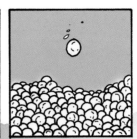

159

I FINISH COVERING MY EGGS AS THE SUN APPEARS.

I REACH FOR THE OCEAN AND THAT'S WHEN I SEE THEM.

PREDATORS.

LEAD THEM AWAY FROM THE EGGS.

SO SLOW.

TOO SLOW.

THEY HAVE ME.

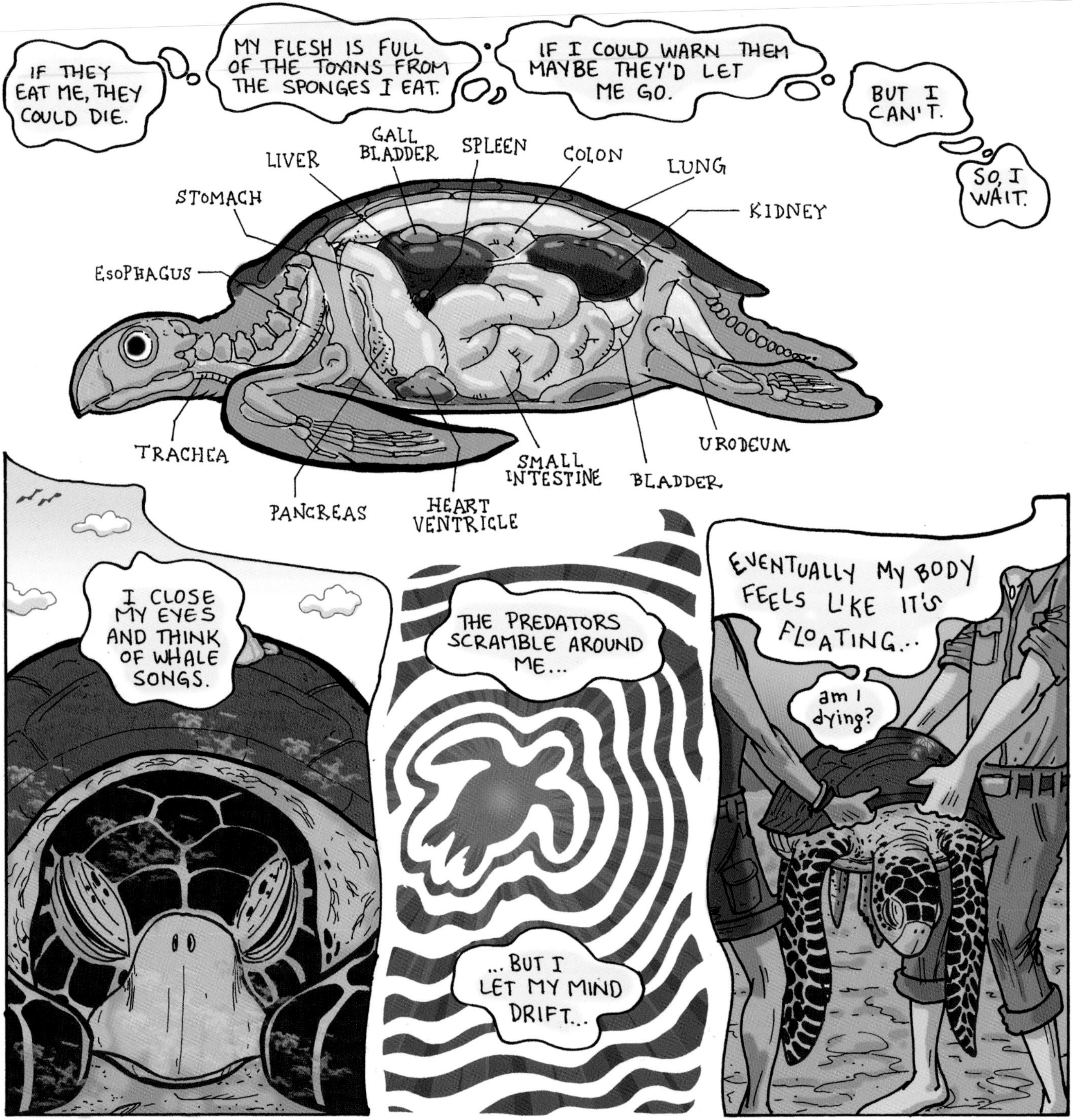

IF THEY EAT ME, THEY COULD DIE.
MY FLESH IS FULL OF THE TOXINS FROM THE SPONGES I EAT.
IF I COULD WARN THEM MAYBE THEY'D LET ME GO.
BUT I CAN'T.
SO, I WAIT.
GALL BLADDER
LIVER
SPLEEN
COLON
LUNG
STOMACH
KIDNEY
ESOPHAGUS
TRACHEA
UROGEUM
SMALL INTESTINE
BLADDER
PANCREAS
HEART VENTRICLE
I CLOSE MY EYES AND THINK OF WHALE SONGS.
THE PREDATORS SCRAMBLE AROUND ME...
...BUT I LET MY MIND DRIFT...
EVENTUALLY MY BODY FEELS LIKE IT'S FLOATING...
am I dying?

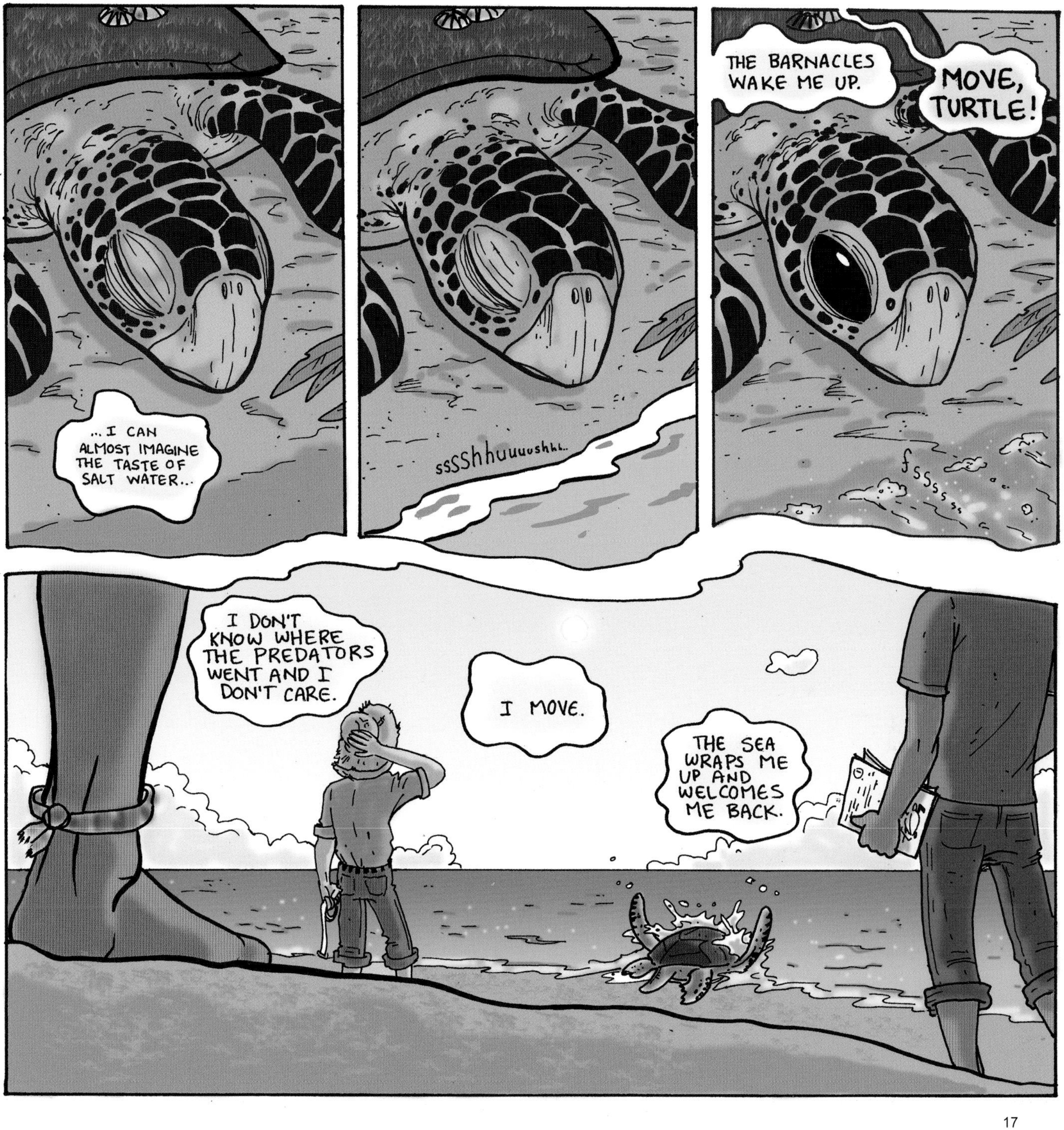
...I CAN ALMOST IMAGINE THE TASTE OF SALT WATER...
sssShhuuuushhh..
THE BARNACLES WAKE ME UP.
MOVE, TURTLE!
fsssssss
I DON'T KNOW WHERE THE PREDATORS WENT AND I DON'T CARE.
I MOVE.
THE SEA WRAPS ME UP AND WELCOMES ME BACK.

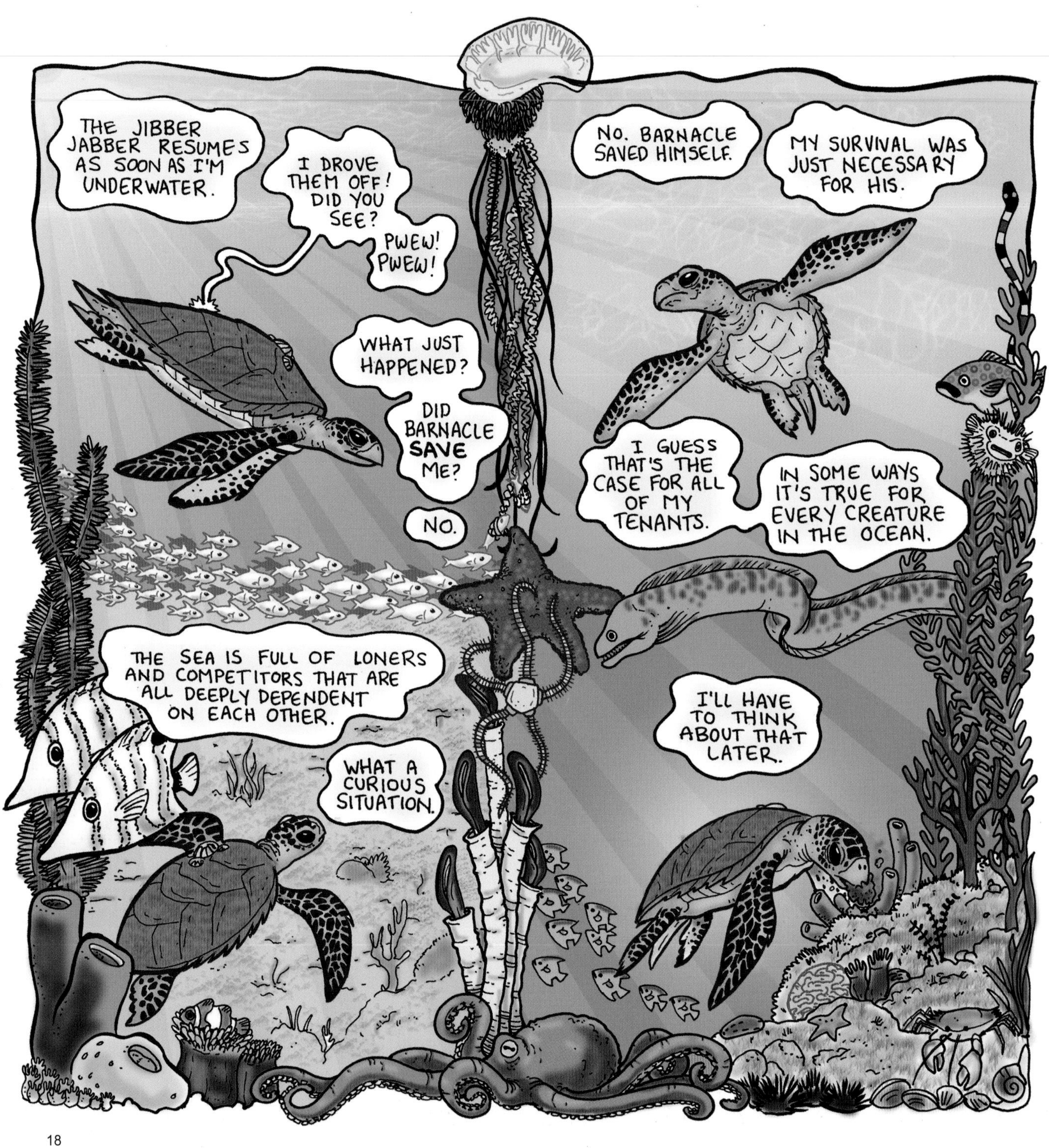
THE JIBBER JABBER RESUMES AS SOON AS I'M UNDERWATER.
I DROVE THEM OFF! DID YOU SEE?
PWEW! PWEW!
NO. BARNACLE SAVED HIMSELF.
MY SURVIVAL WAS JUST NECESSARY FOR HIS.
WHAT JUST HAPPENED?
DID BARNACLE **SAVE** ME?
NO.
I GUESS THAT'S THE CASE FOR ALL OF MY TENANTS.
IN SOME WAYS IT'S TRUE FOR EVERY CREATURE IN THE OCEAN.
THE SEA IS FULL OF LONERS AND COMPETITORS THAT ARE ALL DEEPLY DEPENDENT ON EACH OTHER.
I'LL HAVE TO THINK ABOUT THAT LATER.
WHAT A CURIOUS SITUATION.

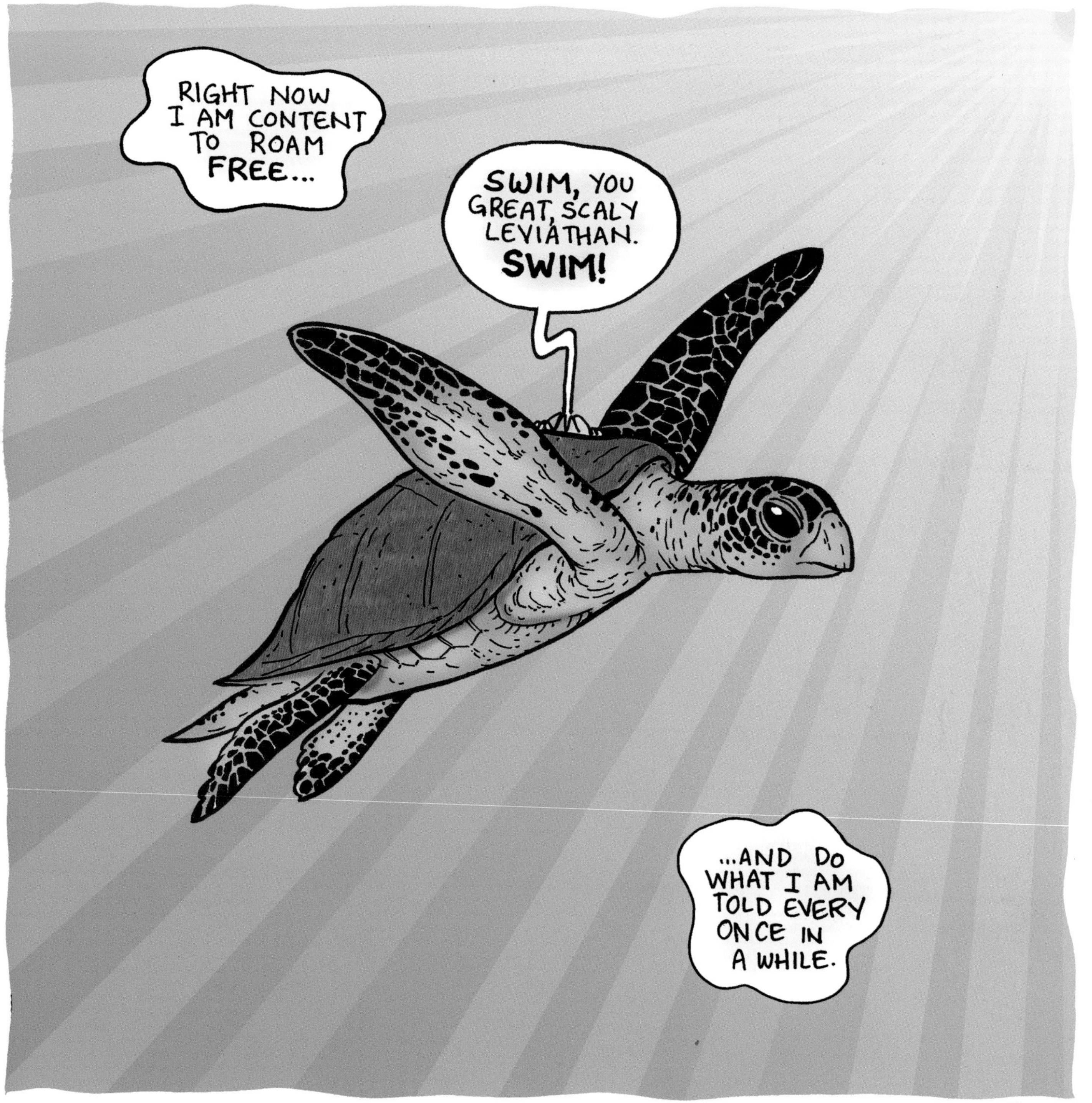
RIGHT NOW I AM CONTENT TO ROAM FREE...
SWIM, YOU GREAT, SCALY LEVIATHAN. SWIM!
...AND DO WHAT I AM TOLD EVERY ONCE IN A WHILE.

THE GALAPAGOS

Story and Illustrations by Matt Dembicki
Colors by Jason E. Axtell

THE GALAPAGOS ISLANDS, which sit on the equator just west of Ecuador, are best known for the species studied by Charles Darwin—the species that led to his theory of evolution by natural selection. Tortoises, marine iguanas, and the blue-footed booby are the native animals that typically come to mind when thinking about this UNESCO World Heritage Site.

There is, however, another dimension to the Galapagos, just off the coast. The Galapagos Marine Reserve protects the inhabitants of the islands' unique underwater ecosystem, which is home to whales, manta rays, coral reefs, and sharks, among others.

The protection bestowed on the reserve often isn't enough to deter certain fishermen. Many of the animals are at risk, as poachers frequently venture into the safe area for a potential lucrative catch. Hammerhead sharks are especially vulnerable: their fins fetch top dollar in certain parts of the world, and it just so happens that these waters draw a lot of hammerheads. This story focuses on the cat-and-mouse game between the park rangers who patrol the islands' rich waters and the fishermen eager to cast their nets and lines to catch the endangered animals that live in them.

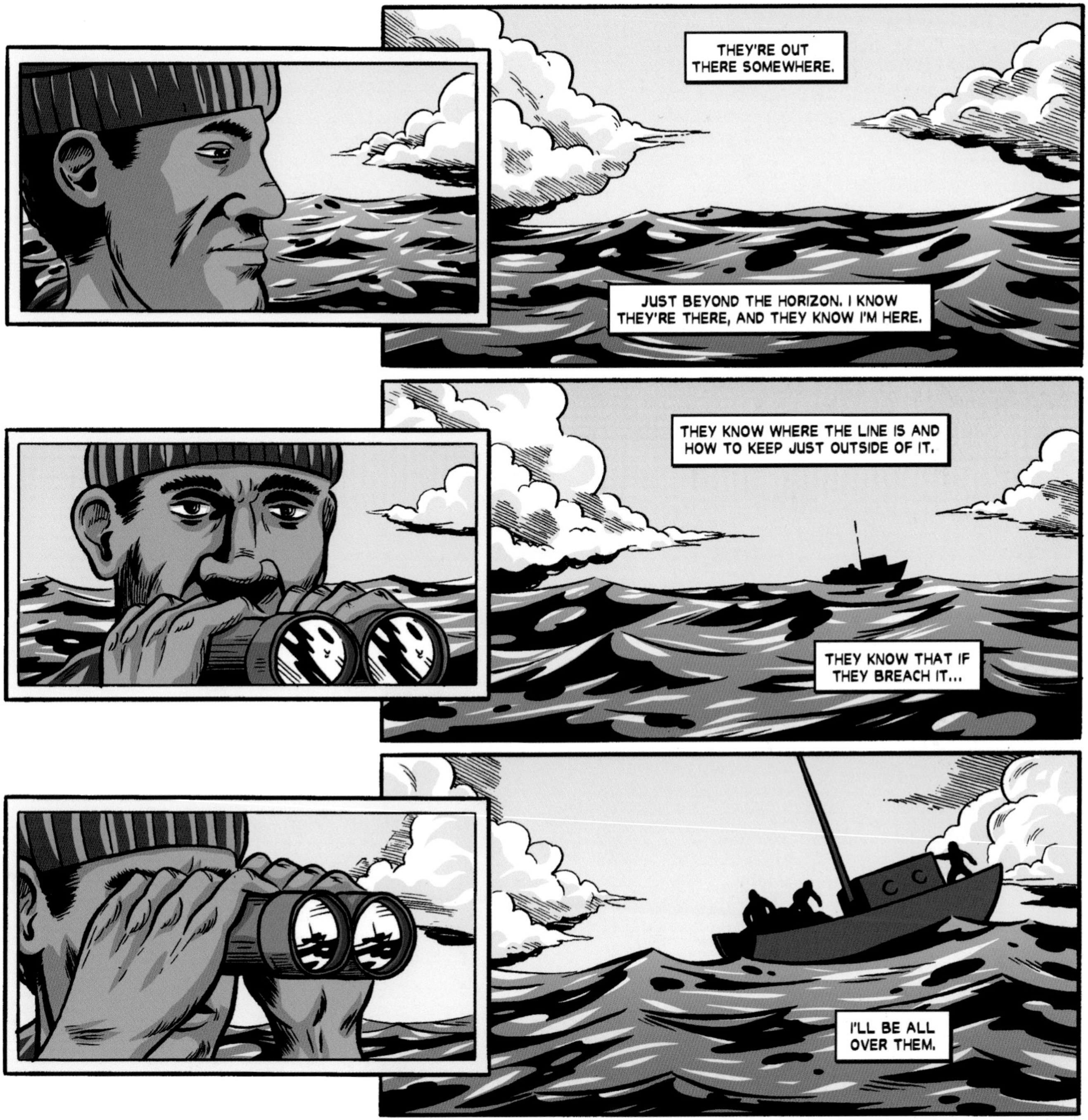
THEY'RE OUT THERE SOMEWHERE.
JUST BEYOND THE HORIZON. I KNOW THEY'RE THERE, AND THEY KNOW I'M HERE.
THEY KNOW WHERE THE LINE IS AND HOW TO KEEP JUST OUTSIDE OF IT.
THEY KNOW THAT IF THEY BREACH IT...
I'LL BE ALL OVER THEM.

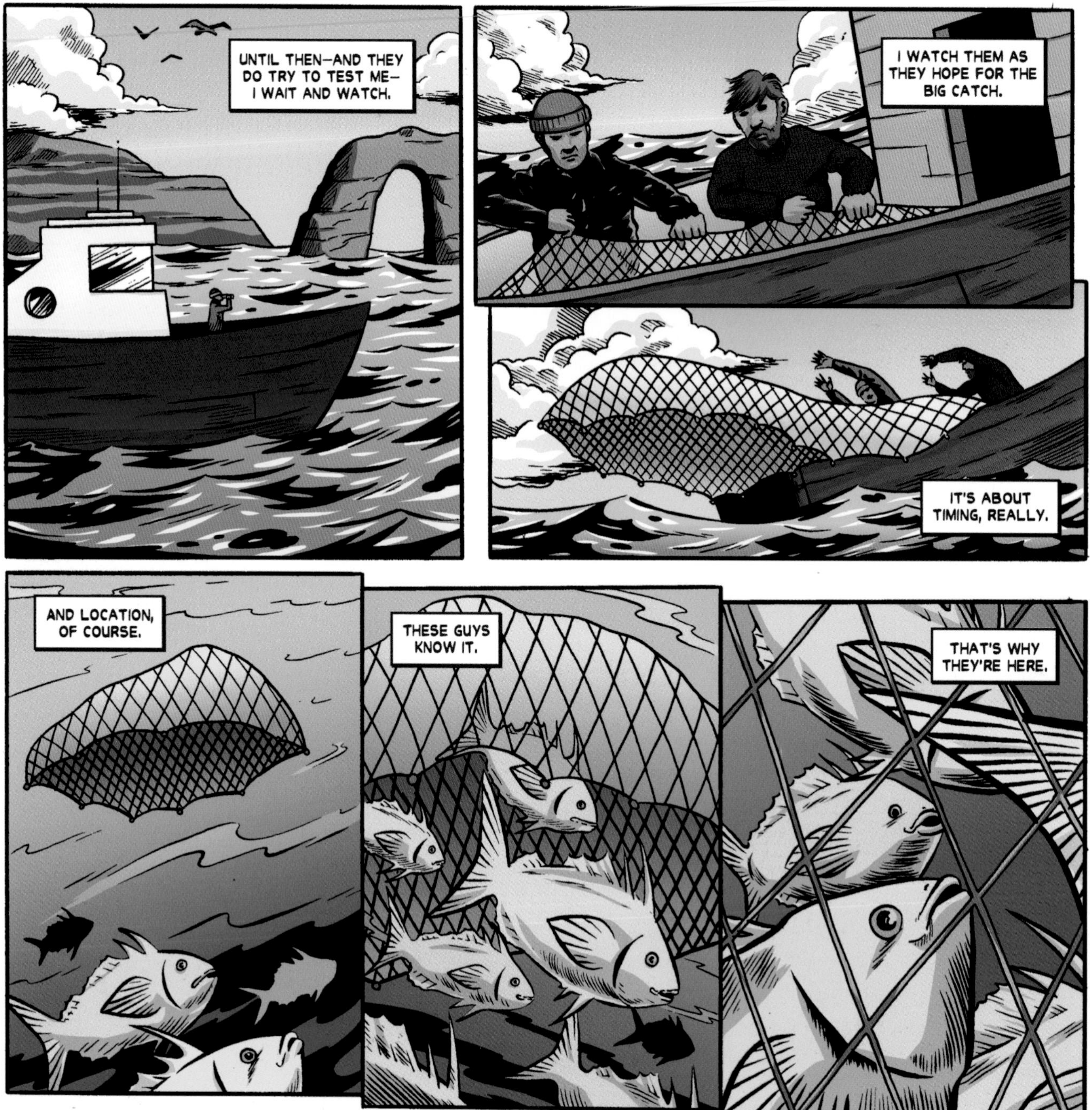
UNTIL THEN—AND THEY DO TRY TO TEST ME—I WAIT AND WATCH.
I WATCH THEM AS THEY HOPE FOR THE BIG CATCH.
IT'S ABOUT TIMING, REALLY.
AND LOCATION, OF COURSE.
THESE GUYS KNOW IT.
THAT'S WHY THEY'RE HERE.

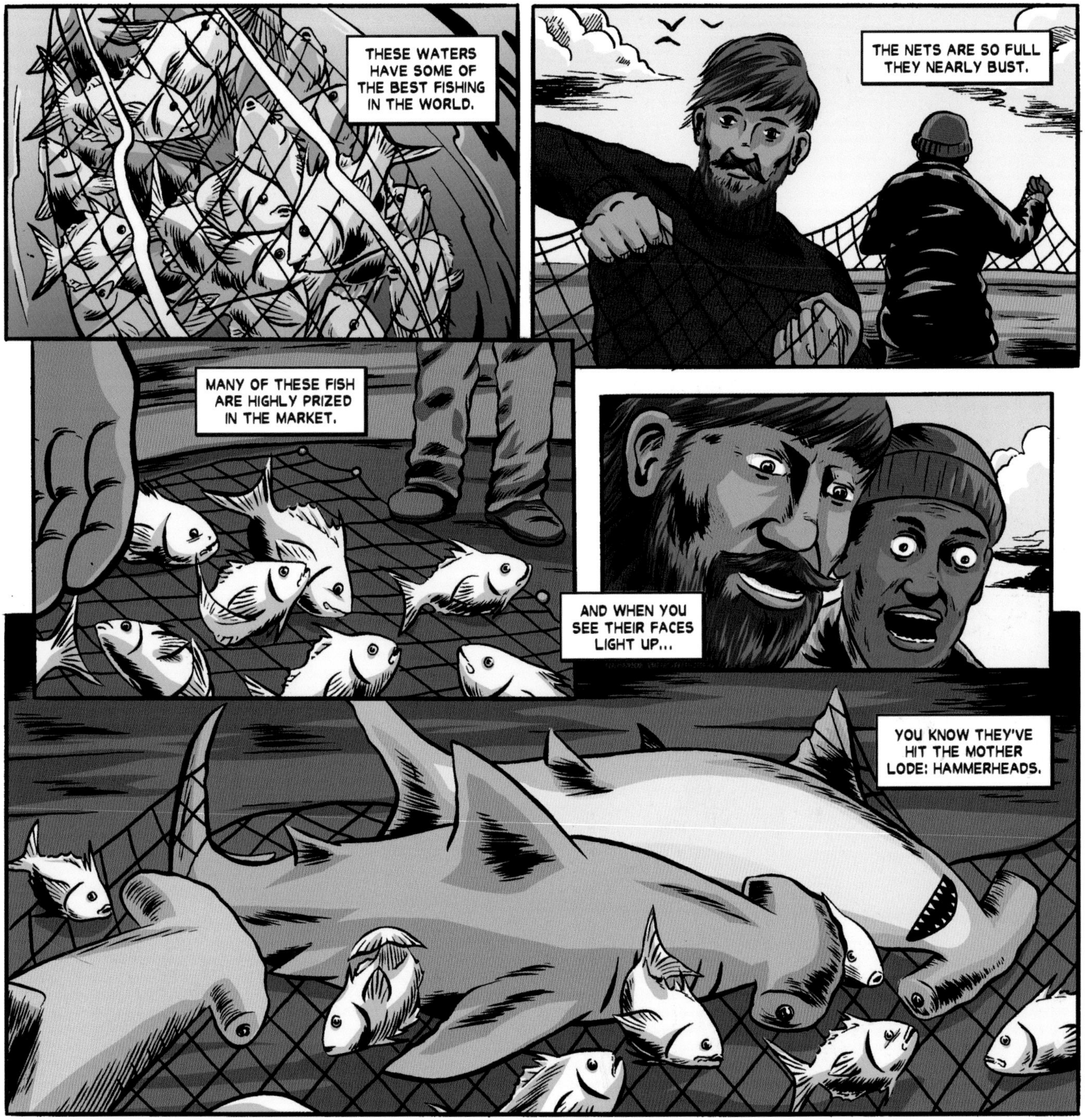
THESE WATERS HAVE SOME OF THE BEST FISHING IN THE WORLD.
THE NETS ARE SO FULL THEY NEARLY BUST.
MANY OF THESE FISH ARE HIGHLY PRIZED IN THE MARKET.
AND WHEN YOU SEE THEIR FACES LIGHT UP...
YOU KNOW THEY'VE HIT THE MOTHER LODE: HAMMERHEADS.

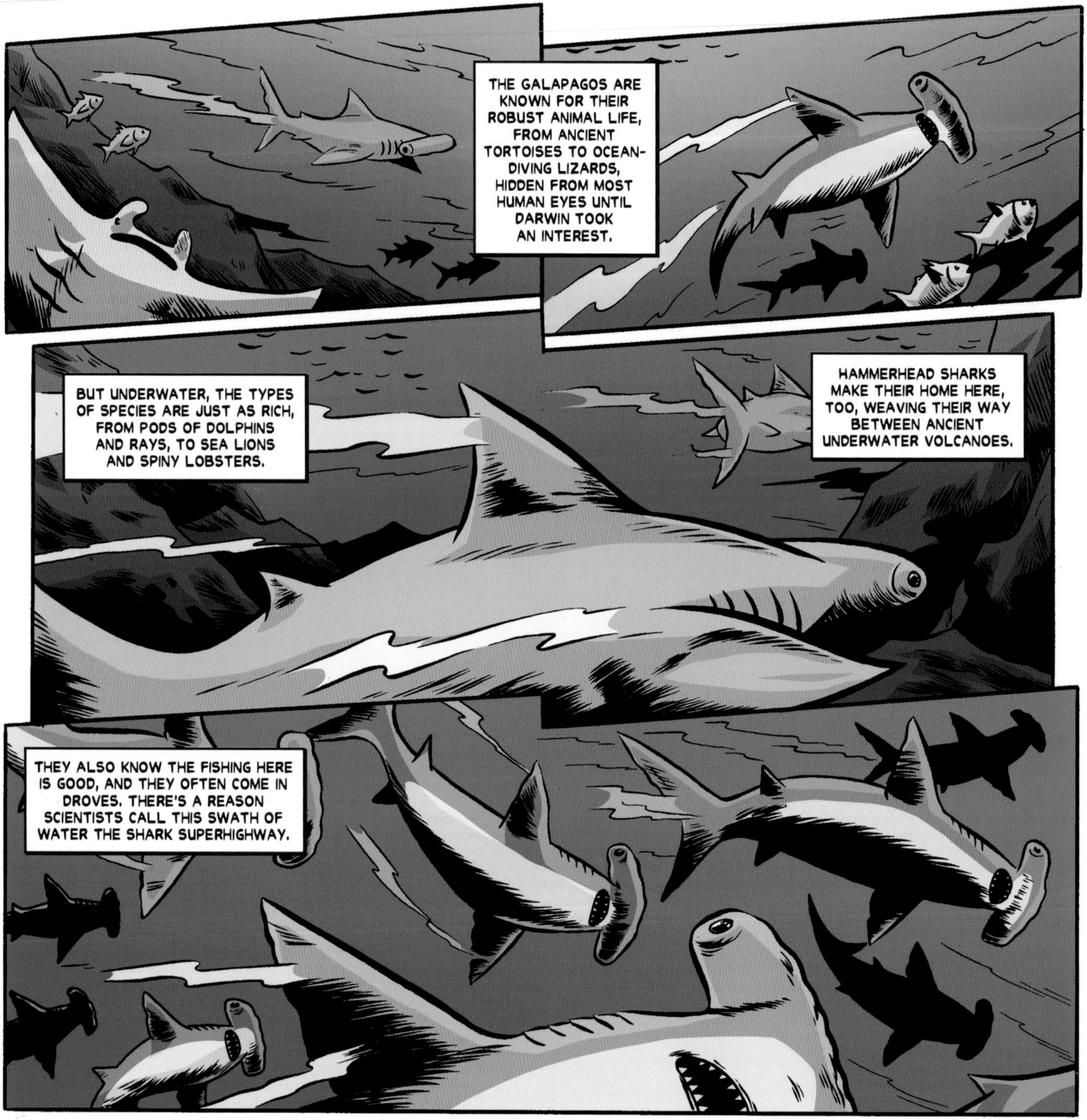
THE GALAPAGOS ARE KNOWN FOR THEIR ROBUST ANIMAL LIFE, FROM ANCIENT TORTOISES TO OCEAN-DIVING LIZARDS, HIDDEN FROM MOST HUMAN EYES UNTIL DARWIN TOOK AN INTEREST.
BUT UNDERWATER, THE TYPES OF SPECIES ARE JUST AS RICH, FROM PODS OF DOLPHINS AND RAYS, TO SEA LIONS AND SPINY LOBSTERS.
HAMMERHEAD SHARKS MAKE THEIR HOME HERE, TOO, WEAVING THEIR WAY BETWEEN ANCIENT UNDERWATER VOLCANOES.
THEY ALSO KNOW THE FISHING HERE IS GOOD, AND THEY OFTEN COME IN DROVES. THERE'S A REASON SCIENTISTS CALL THIS SWATH OF WATER THE SHARK SUPERHIGHWAY.

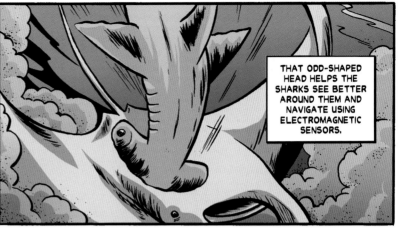

ONE OF THE BENEFITS OF THIS JOB IS GETTING TO SEE THESE MARVELS—ESPECIALLY HOW THEY HUNT.

THAT ODD-SHAPED HEAD HELPS THE SHARKS SEE BETTER AROUND THEM AND NAVIGATE USING ELECTROMAGNETIC SENSORS.

IT'S ALSO USED FOR SIMPLE THINGS, LIKE HOLDING DOWN PREY.

UNFORTUNATELY, THE HAMMERHEADS HAVE THEMSELVES BECOME PREY.

THEIR FINS ARE HIGHLY SOUGHT IN CERTAIN PARTS OF THE WORLD, PARTICULARLY IN CHINA, WHERE THEY ARE A DELICACY.

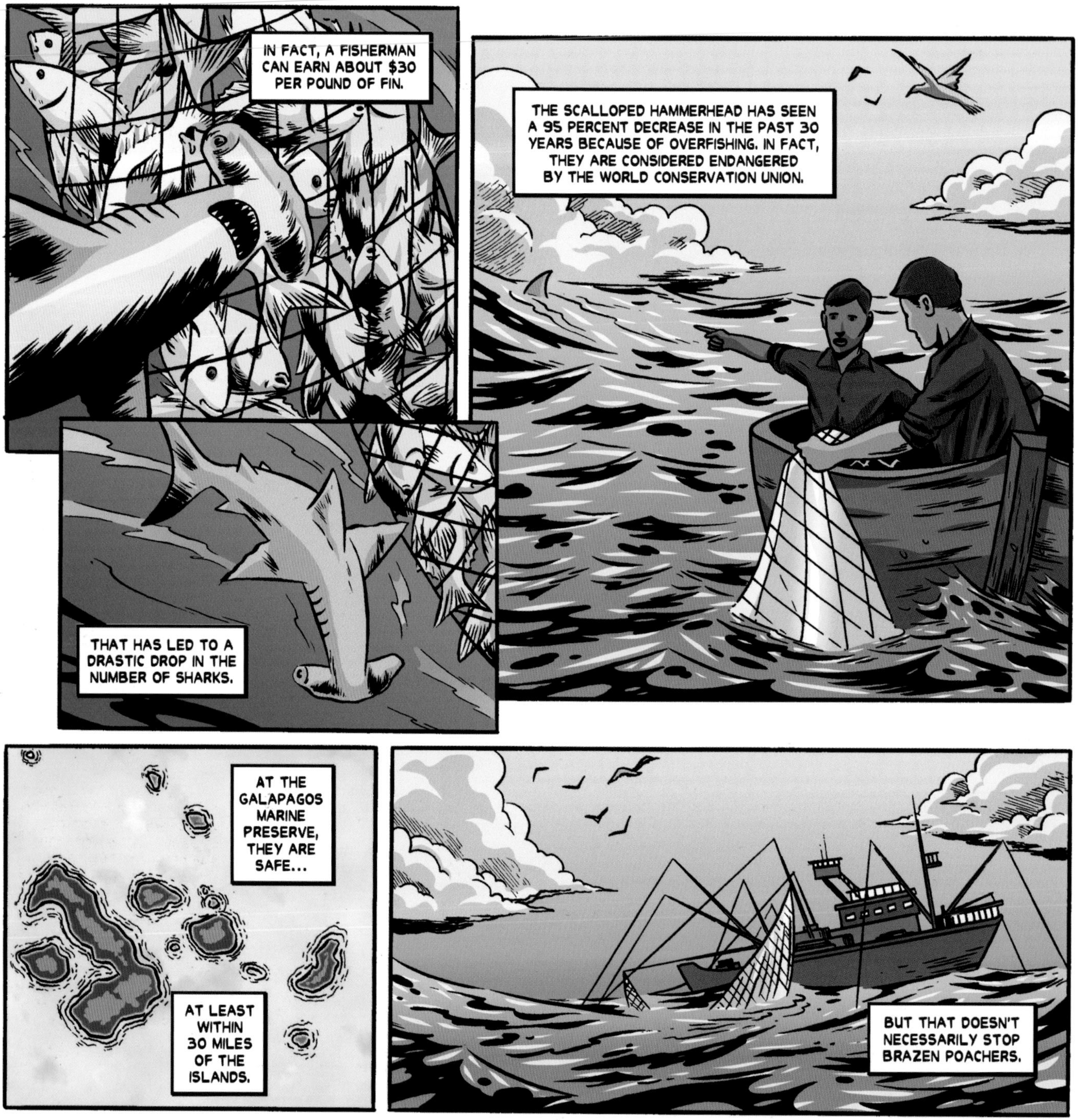
IN FACT, A FISHERMAN CAN EARN ABOUT $30 PER POUND OF FIN.
THAT HAS LED TO A DRASTIC DROP IN THE NUMBER OF SHARKS.
THE SCALLOPED HAMMERHEAD HAS SEEN A 95 PERCENT DECREASE IN THE PAST 30 YEARS BECAUSE OF OVERFISHING. IN FACT, THEY ARE CONSIDERED ENDANGERED BY THE WORLD CONSERVATION UNION.
AT THE GALAPAGOS MARINE PRESERVE, THEY ARE SAFE...
AT LEAST WITHIN 30 MILES OF THE ISLANDS.
BUT THAT DOESN'T NECESSARILY STOP BRAZEN POACHERS.

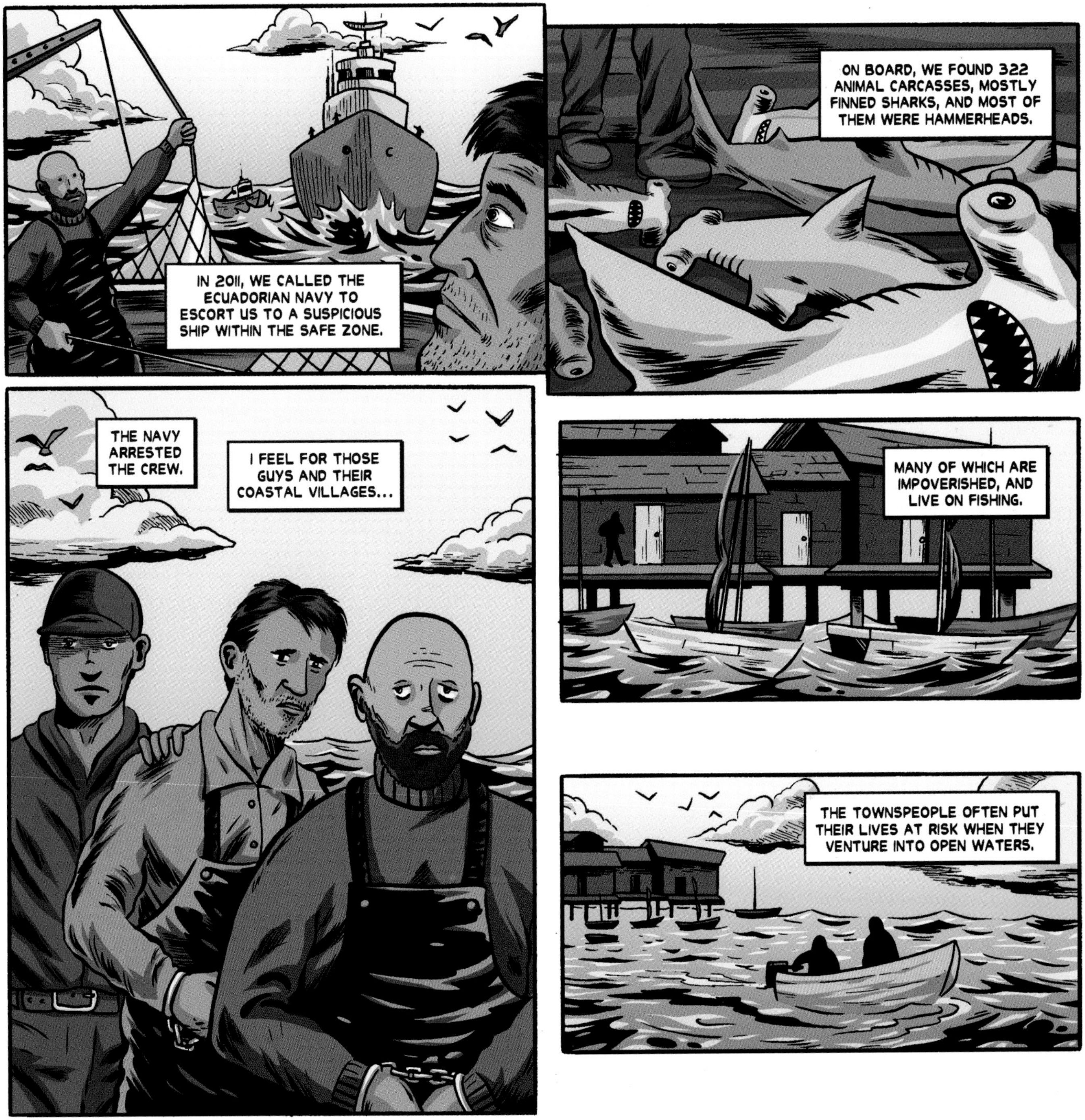
IN 2011, WE CALLED THE ECUADORIAN NAVY TO ESCORT US TO A SUSPICIOUS SHIP WITHIN THE SAFE ZONE.
ON BOARD, WE FOUND 322 ANIMAL CARCASSES, MOSTLY FINNED SHARKS, AND MOST OF THEM WERE HAMMERHEADS.
THE NAVY ARRESTED THE CREW.
I FEEL FOR THOSE GUYS AND THEIR COASTAL VILLAGES...
MANY OF WHICH ARE IMPOVERISHED, AND LIVE ON FISHING.
THE TOWNSPEOPLE OFTEN PUT THEIR LIVES AT RISK WHEN THEY VENTURE INTO OPEN WATERS.

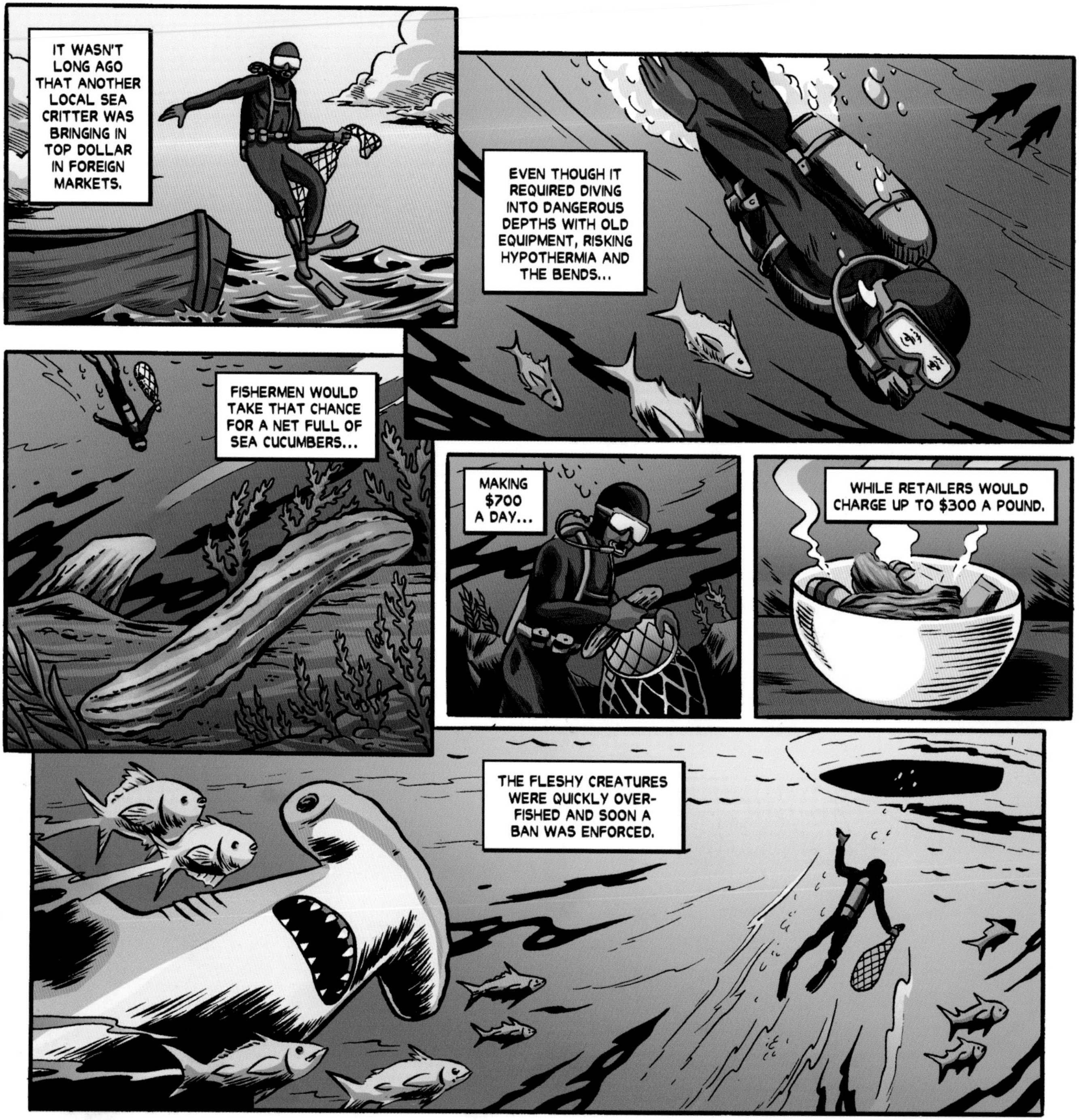
IT WASN'T LONG AGO THAT ANOTHER LOCAL SEA CRITTER WAS BRINGING IN TOP DOLLAR IN FOREIGN MARKETS.
EVEN THOUGH IT REQUIRED DIVING INTO DANGEROUS DEPTHS WITH OLD EQUIPMENT, RISKING HYPOTHERMIA AND THE BENDS...
FISHERMEN WOULD TAKE THAT CHANCE FOR A NET FULL OF SEA CUCUMBERS...
MAKING $700 A DAY...
WHILE RETAILERS WOULD CHARGE UP TO $300 A POUND.
THE FLESHY CREATURES WERE QUICKLY OVER-FISHED AND SOON A BAN WAS ENFORCED.

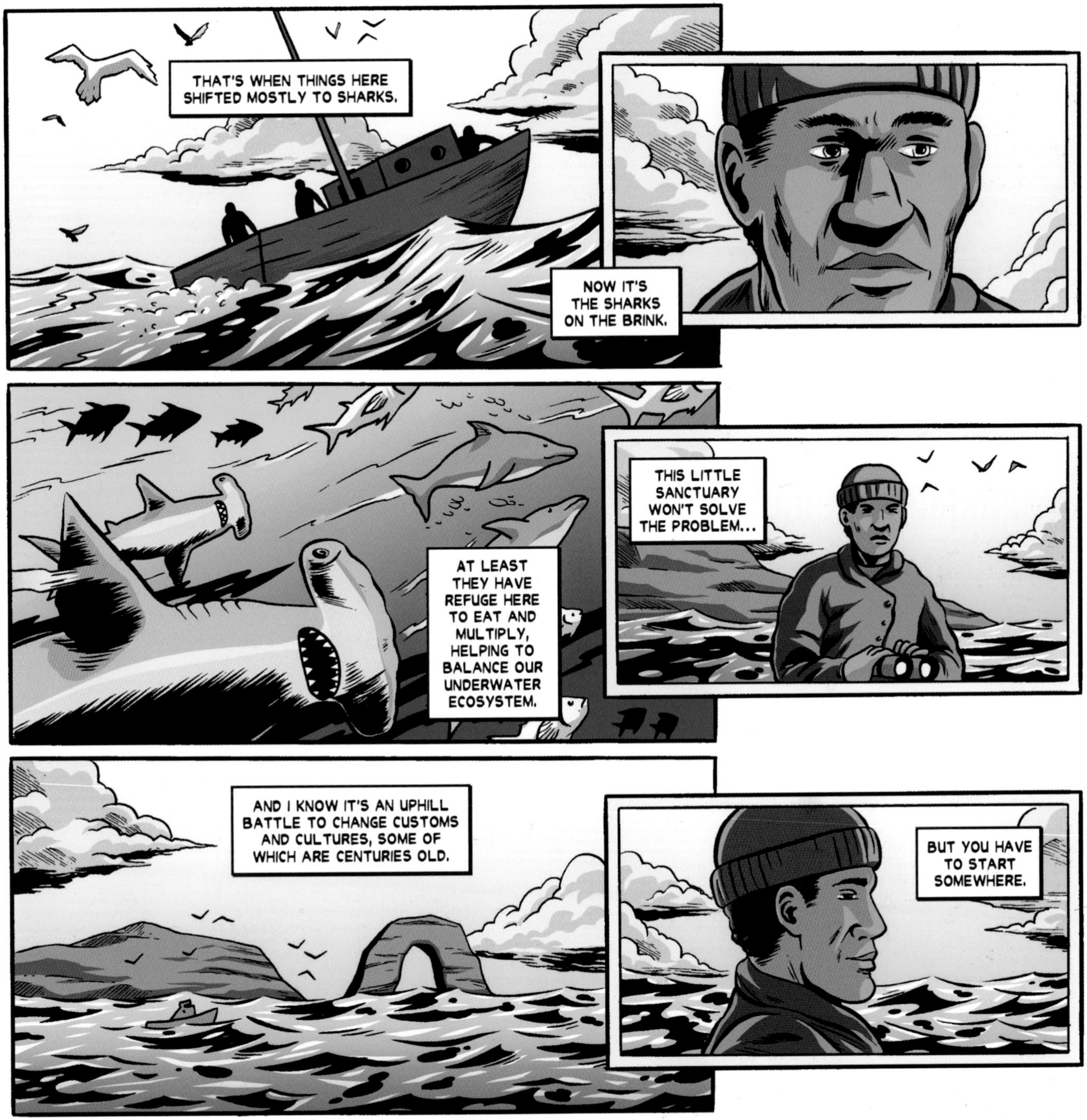
THAT'S WHEN THINGS HERE SHIFTED MOSTLY TO SHARKS.
NOW IT'S THE SHARKS ON THE BRINK.
AT LEAST THEY HAVE REFUGE HERE TO EAT AND MULTIPLY, HELPING TO BALANCE OUR UNDERWATER ECOSYSTEM.
THIS LITTLE SANCTUARY WON'T SOLVE THE PROBLEM...
AND I KNOW IT'S AN UPHILL BATTLE TO CHANGE CUSTOMS AND CULTURES, SOME OF WHICH ARE CENTURIES OLD.
BUT YOU HAVE TO START SOMEWHERE.

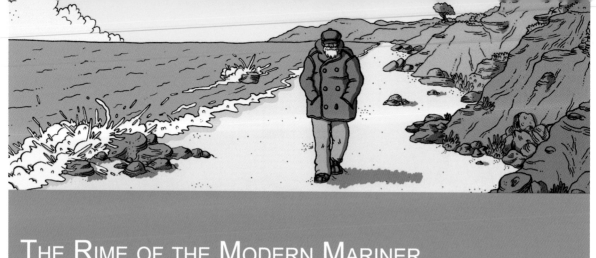

THE RIME OF THE MODERN MARINER

Story and Art by Andy K.

THE OCEAN'S ECOSYSTEM is not limited to creatures that dwell underwater. Consider the albatross—a seabird that will spend most of its life at sea, traversing Olympian distances as a master of the winds. These majestic birds make the Pacific Ocean their home. While they retain freedom among the skies, they barely escaped extinction in the late nineteenth century, when they were hunted doggedly for their feathers. Today, albatrosses continue to face a number of threats, including the devastating effects of longline fishing—a type of fishing that uses lines in which the beautiful birds become trapped and drown.

Inspired by Samuel Taylor Coleridge's "Rime of the Ancient Mariner," this story represents a spiritual allegory of the human condition—encompassing concepts such as faith, isolation, and repentance—in relation to the short-tailed albatross. This piece of graphic fiction focuses on a modern mariner who washes ashore after attempting to take his own life.

Chance finds this sailor revived by a stranger, who imparts wisdom based both on his own experiences and that of the albatross.

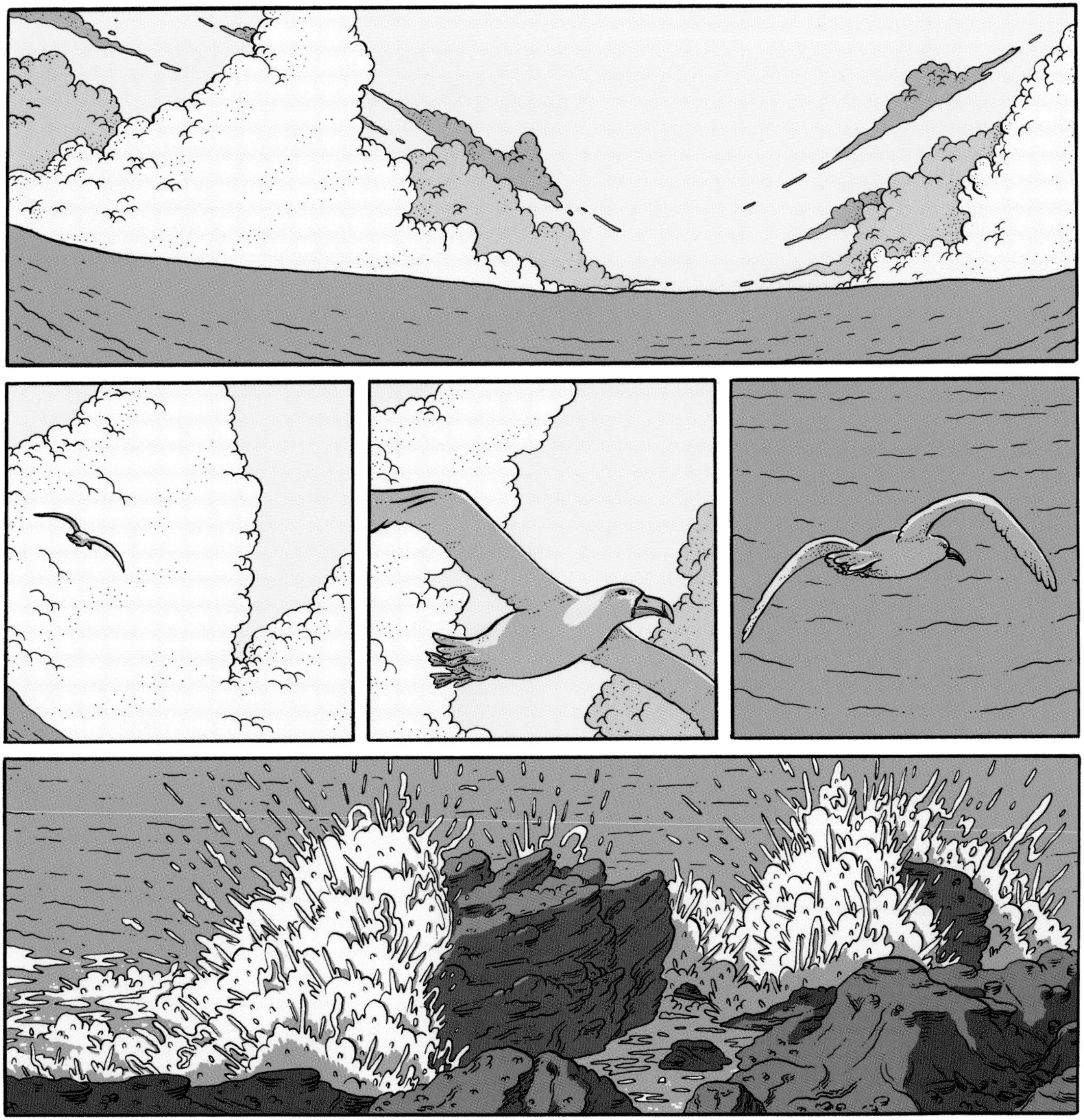

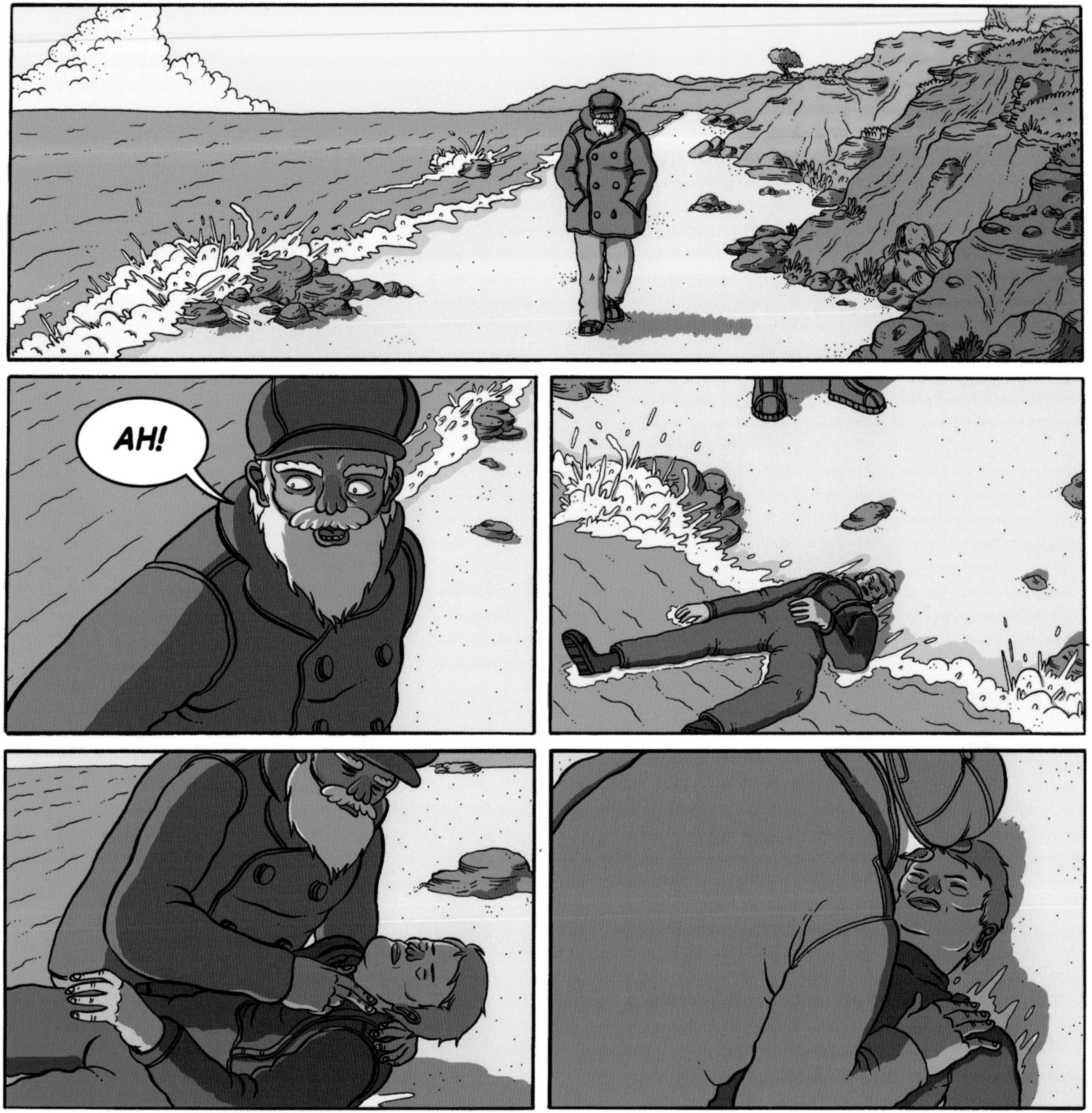
AH!

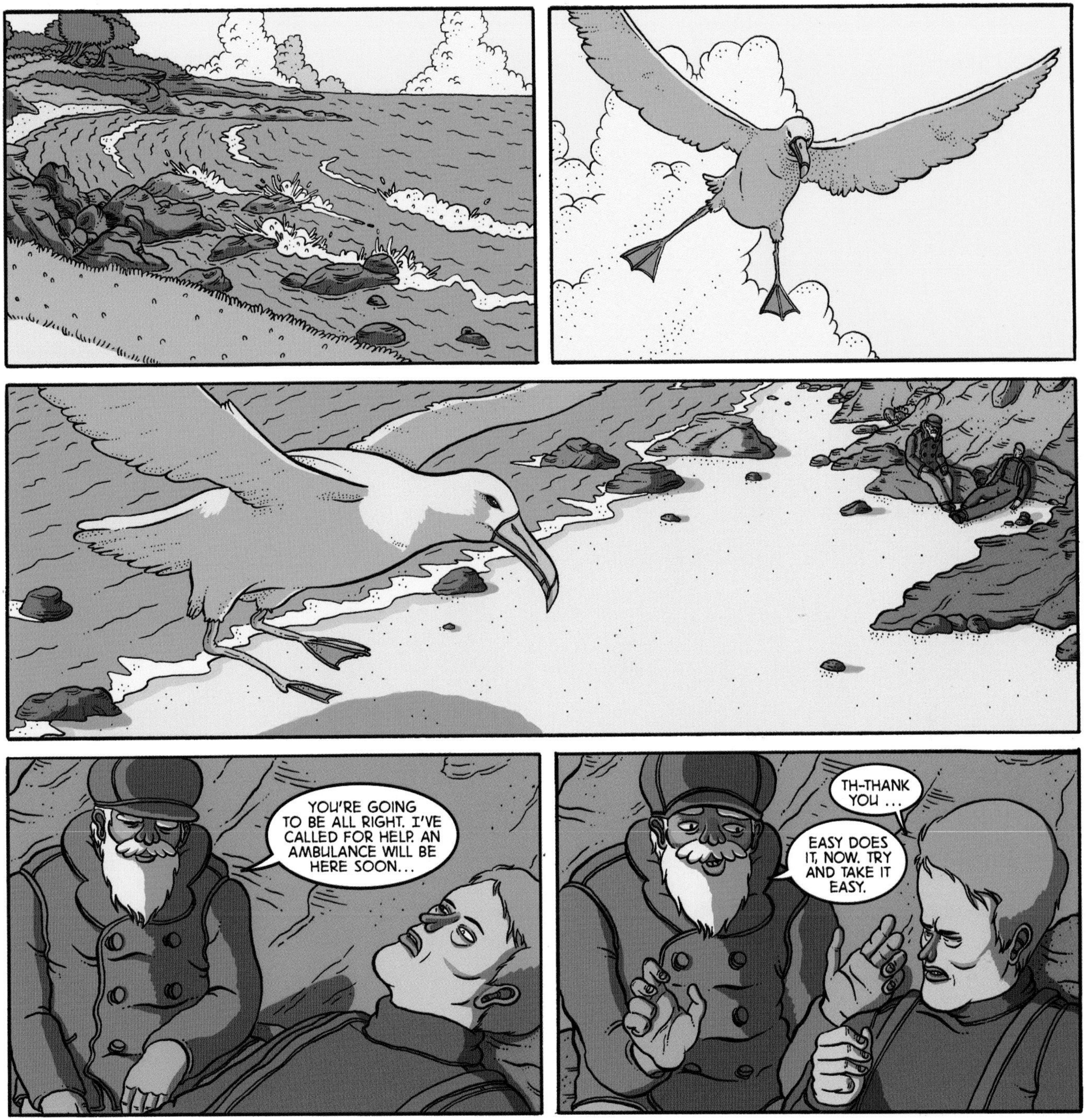
YOU'RE GOING TO BE ALL RIGHT. I'VE CALLED FOR HELP. AN AMBULANCE WILL BE HERE SOON...
TH-THANK YOU ...
EASY DOES IT, NOW. TRY AND TAKE IT EASY.

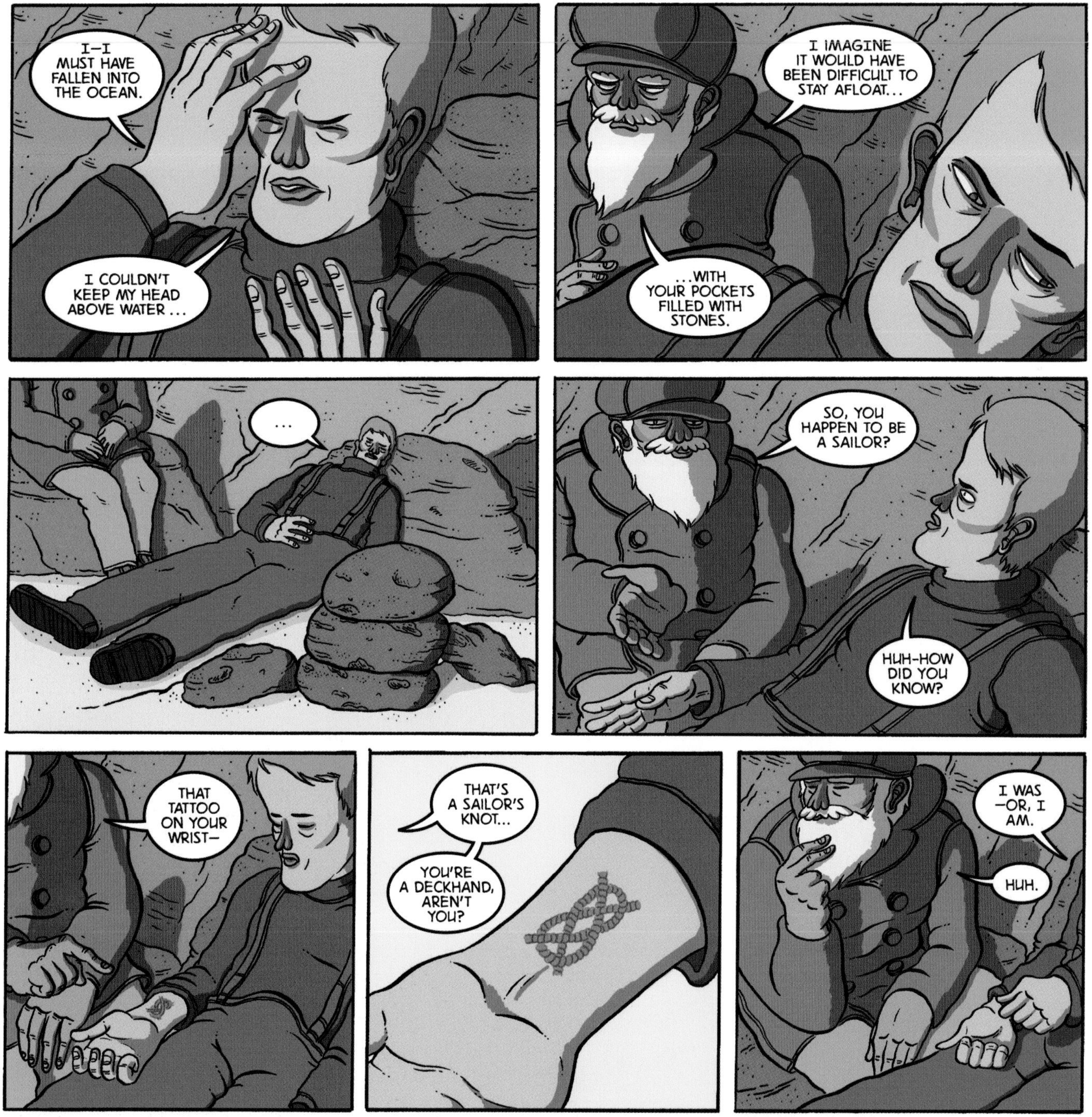
I—I MUST HAVE FALLEN INTO THE OCEAN.
I COULDN'T KEEP MY HEAD ABOVE WATER...
I IMAGINE IT WOULD HAVE BEEN DIFFICULT TO STAY AFLOAT...
...WITH YOUR POCKETS FILLED WITH STONES.
...
SO, YOU HAPPEN TO BE A SAILOR?
HUH-HOW DID YOU KNOW?
THAT TATTOO ON YOUR WRIST—
THAT'S A SAILOR'S KNOT...
YOU'RE A DECKHAND, AREN'T YOU?
I WAS —OR, I AM.
HUH.

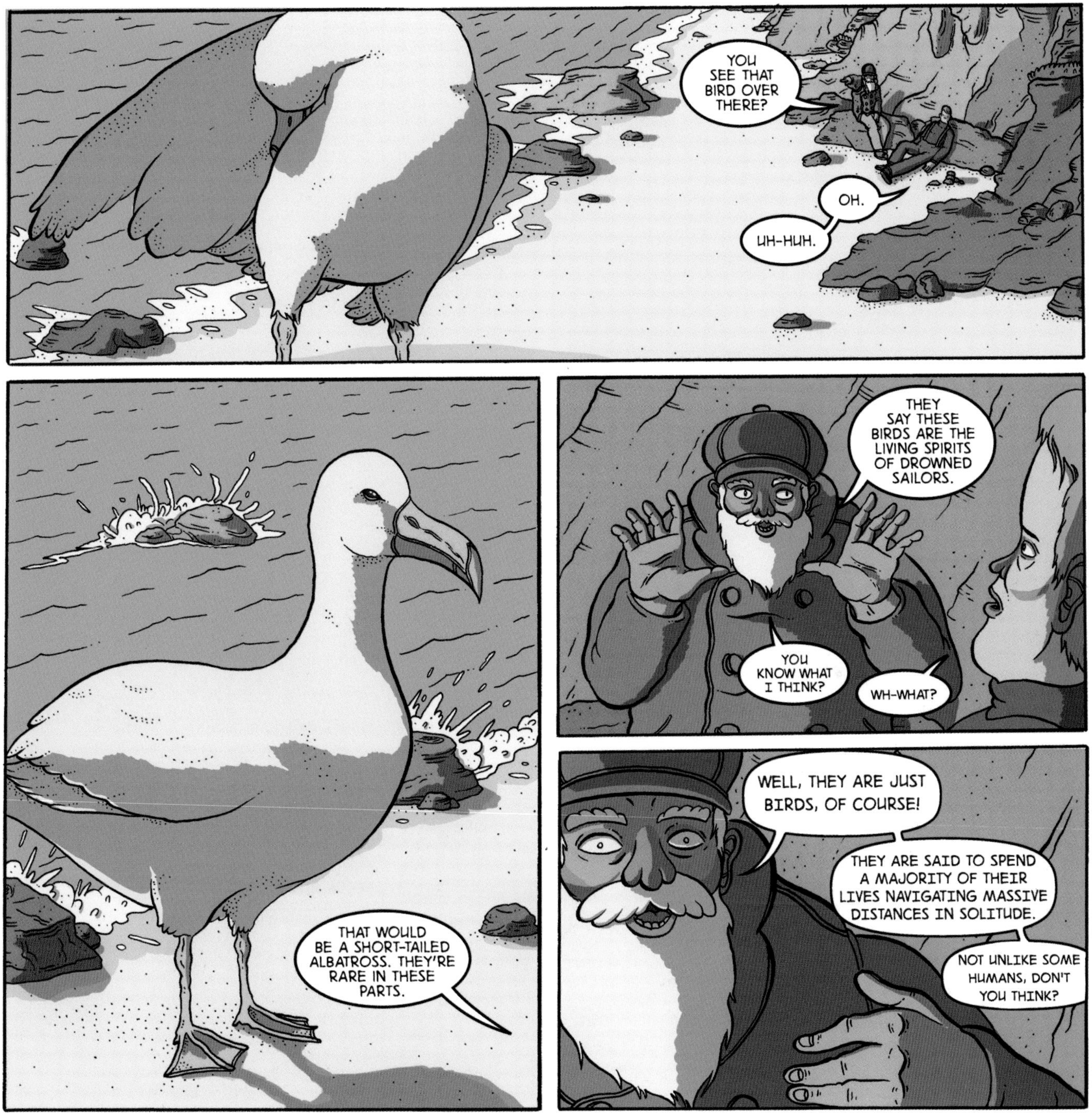
YOU SEE THAT BIRD OVER THERE?
OH.
UH-HUH.
THAT WOULD BE A SHORT-TAILED ALBATROSS. THEY'RE RARE IN THESE PARTS.
THEY SAY THESE BIRDS ARE THE LIVING SPIRITS OF DROWNED SAILORS.
YOU KNOW WHAT I THINK?
WH-WHAT?
WELL, THEY ARE JUST BIRDS, OF COURSE!
THEY ARE SAID TO SPEND A MAJORITY OF THEIR LIVES NAVIGATING MASSIVE DISTANCES IN SOLITUDE.
NOT UNLIKE SOME HUMANS, DON'T YOU THINK?

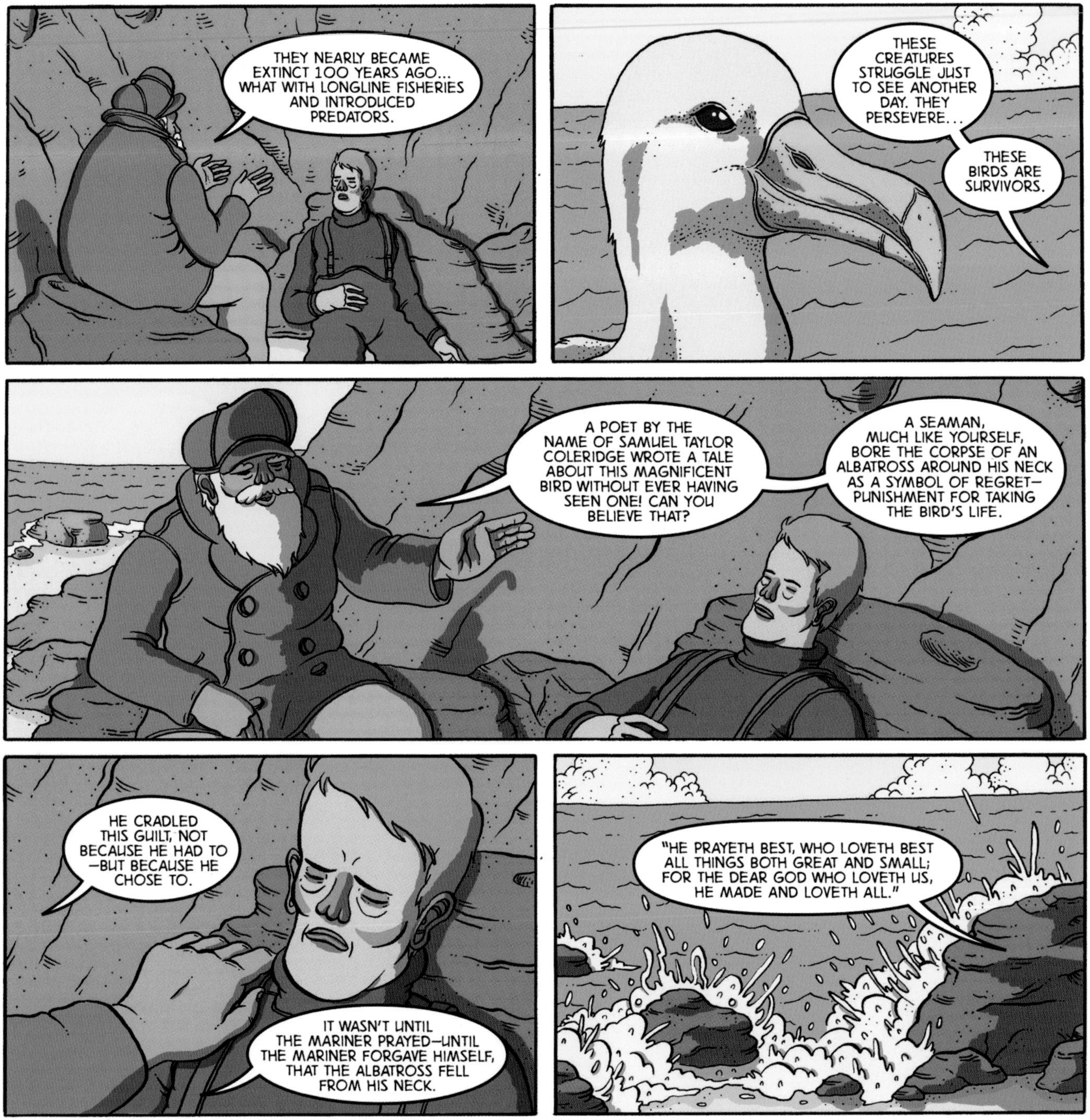
THEY NEARLY BECAME EXTINCT 100 YEARS AGO... WHAT WITH LONGLINE FISHERIES AND INTRODUCED PREDATORS.
THESE CREATURES STRUGGLE JUST TO SEE ANOTHER DAY. THEY PERSEVERE...
THESE BIRDS ARE SURVIVORS.
A POET BY THE NAME OF SAMUEL TAYLOR COLERIDGE WROTE A TALE ABOUT THIS MAGNIFICENT BIRD WITHOUT EVER HAVING SEEN ONE! CAN YOU BELIEVE THAT?
A SEAMAN, MUCH LIKE YOURSELF, BORE THE CORPSE OF AN ALBATROSS AROUND HIS NECK AS A SYMBOL OF REGRET—PUNISHMENT FOR TAKING THE BIRD'S LIFE.
HE CRADLED THIS GUILT, NOT BECAUSE HE HAD TO—BUT BECAUSE HE CHOSE TO.
IT WASN'T UNTIL THE MARINER PRAYED—UNTIL THE MARINER FORGAVE HIMSELF, THAT THE ALBATROSS FELL FROM HIS NECK.
"HE PRAYETH BEST, WHO LOVETH BEST ALL THINGS BOTH GREAT AND SMALL; FOR THE DEAR GOD WHO LOVETH US, HE MADE AND LOVETH ALL."

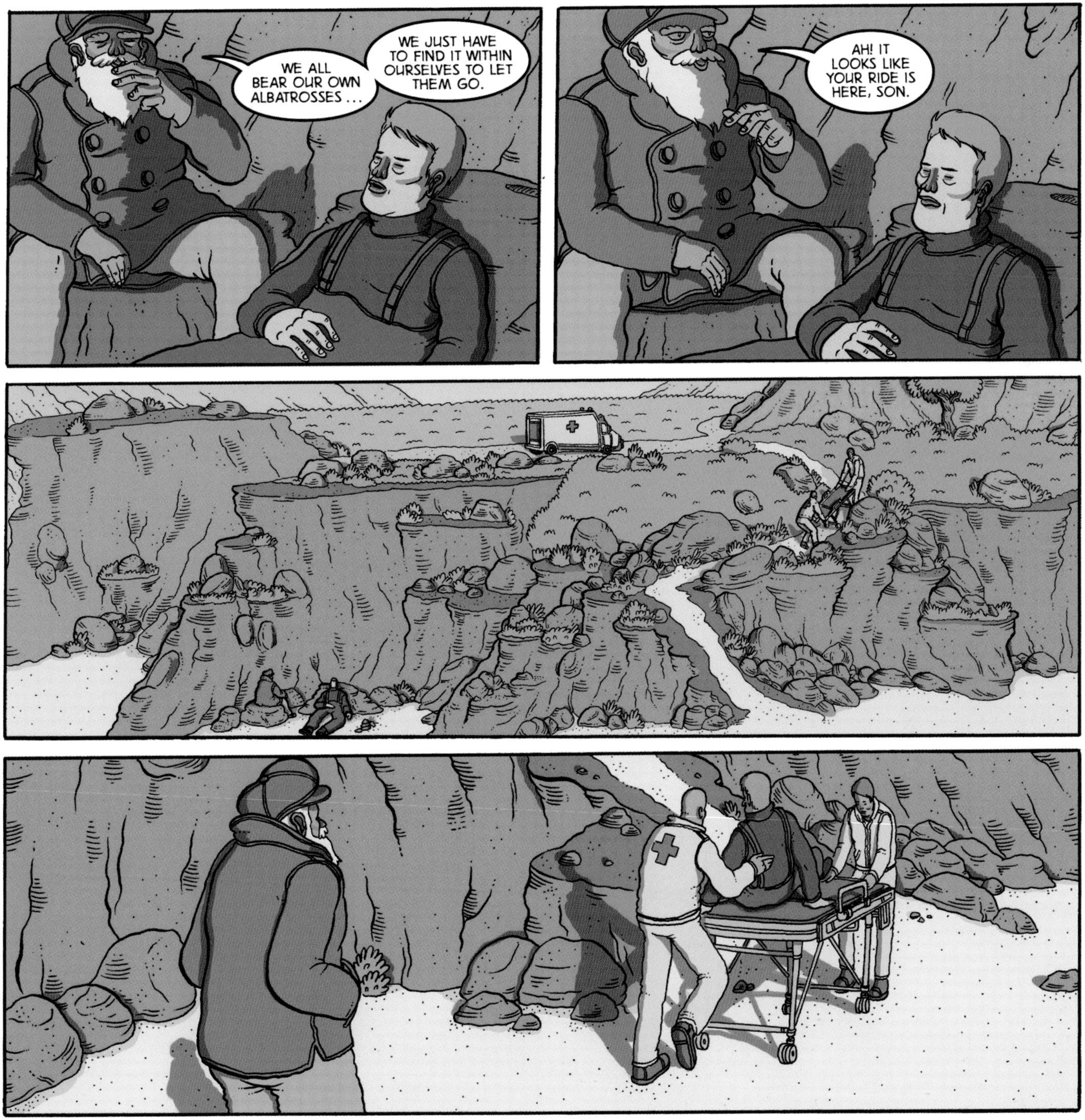
WE ALL BEAR OUR OWN ALBATROSSES . . .
WE JUST HAVE TO FIND IT WITHIN OURSELVES TO LET THEM GO.
AH! IT LOOKS LIKE YOUR RIDE IS HERE, SON.

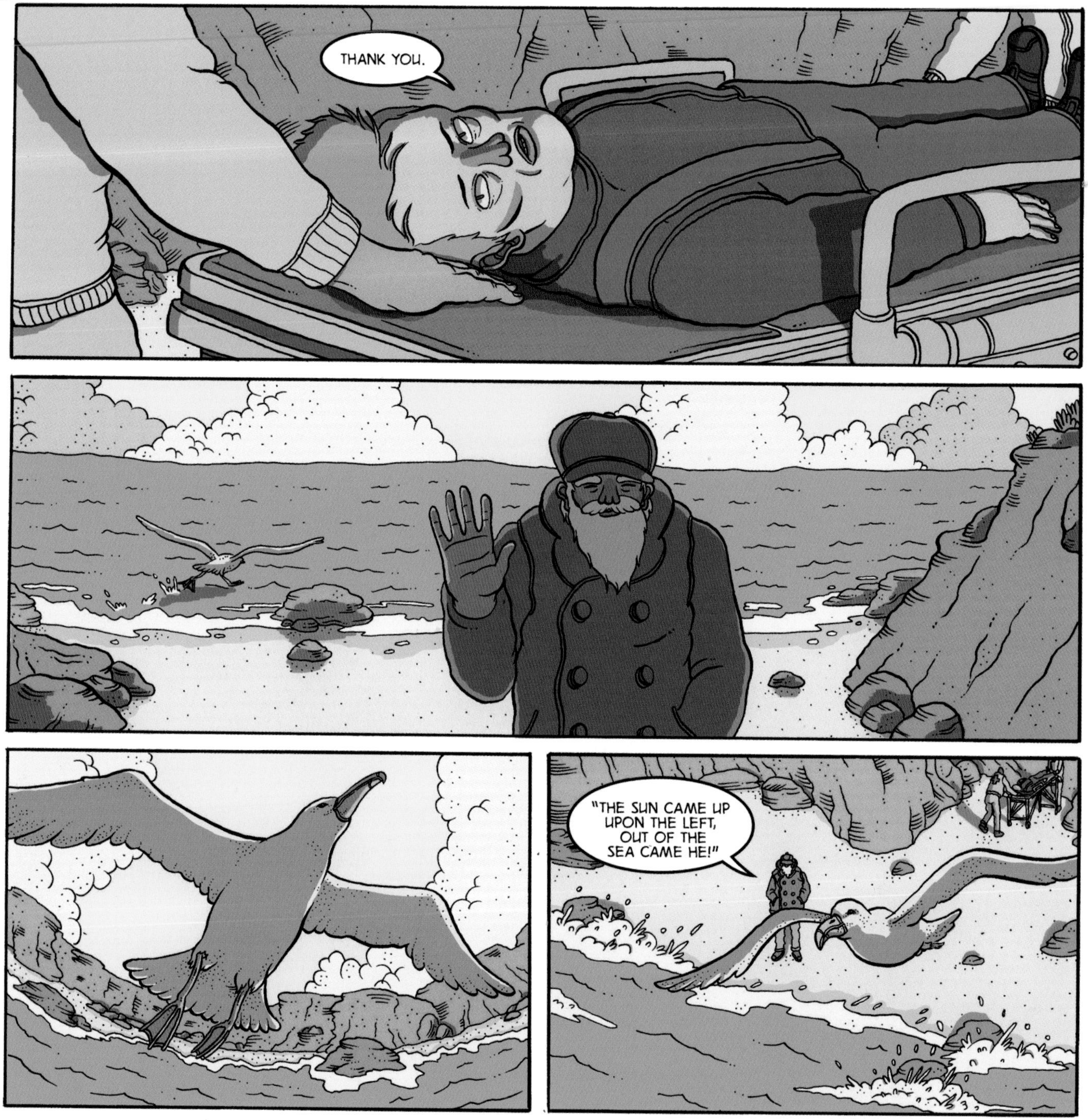
THANK YOU.
"THE SUN CAME UP UPON THE LEFT, OUT OF THE SEA CAME HE!"

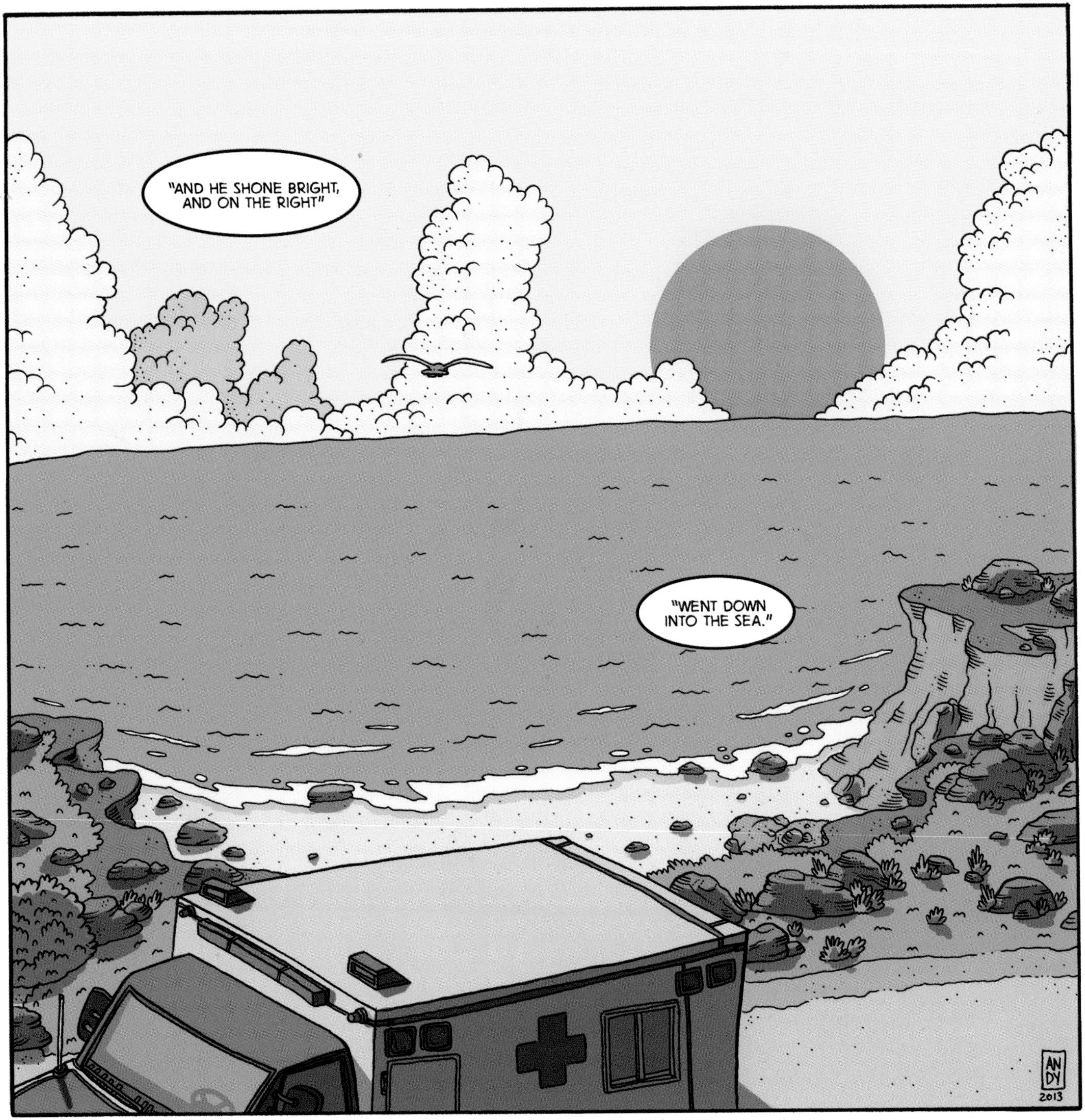
"AND HE SHONE BRIGHT, AND ON THE RIGHT"
"WENT DOWN INTO THE SEA."
ANDY 2013

THE SHAPE OF THE FUTURE

Story by Michael Cowgill
Art by Tom Williams

MASSIVE SIZE... huge, wing-shaped pectoral fins... cephalic—or head—fins that stick out like horns on each side of its mouth... It is little wonder that the manta ray once inspired fear in people, who labeled them "giant devil rays" and "great sea devils."

In truth, manta rays are docile, migratory creatures that today actually attract divers to swim with them in areas such as Micronesia and the Maldives. Although they sometimes eat small fish, manta rays mainly feed on tiny ocean animals called plankton. Their cephalic fins swish food-rich water into the spongy "rakers," or filters, in their gills.

Unfortunately, manta rays also attract poachers, who have a long history of harvesting the rays' skin and liver, and more recently their gill rakers, to make traditional (and unproven) medicines. Overfishing is also a severe threat to manta rays' survival, and each year countless rays become entangled—and die—in fishing lines and nets.

Artists have portrayed manta rays in one shape or another in comic books such as *Aquaman* and movies such as *The Incredibles*, but as you'll see, the stuff of imagination has begun to take shape in the real world.

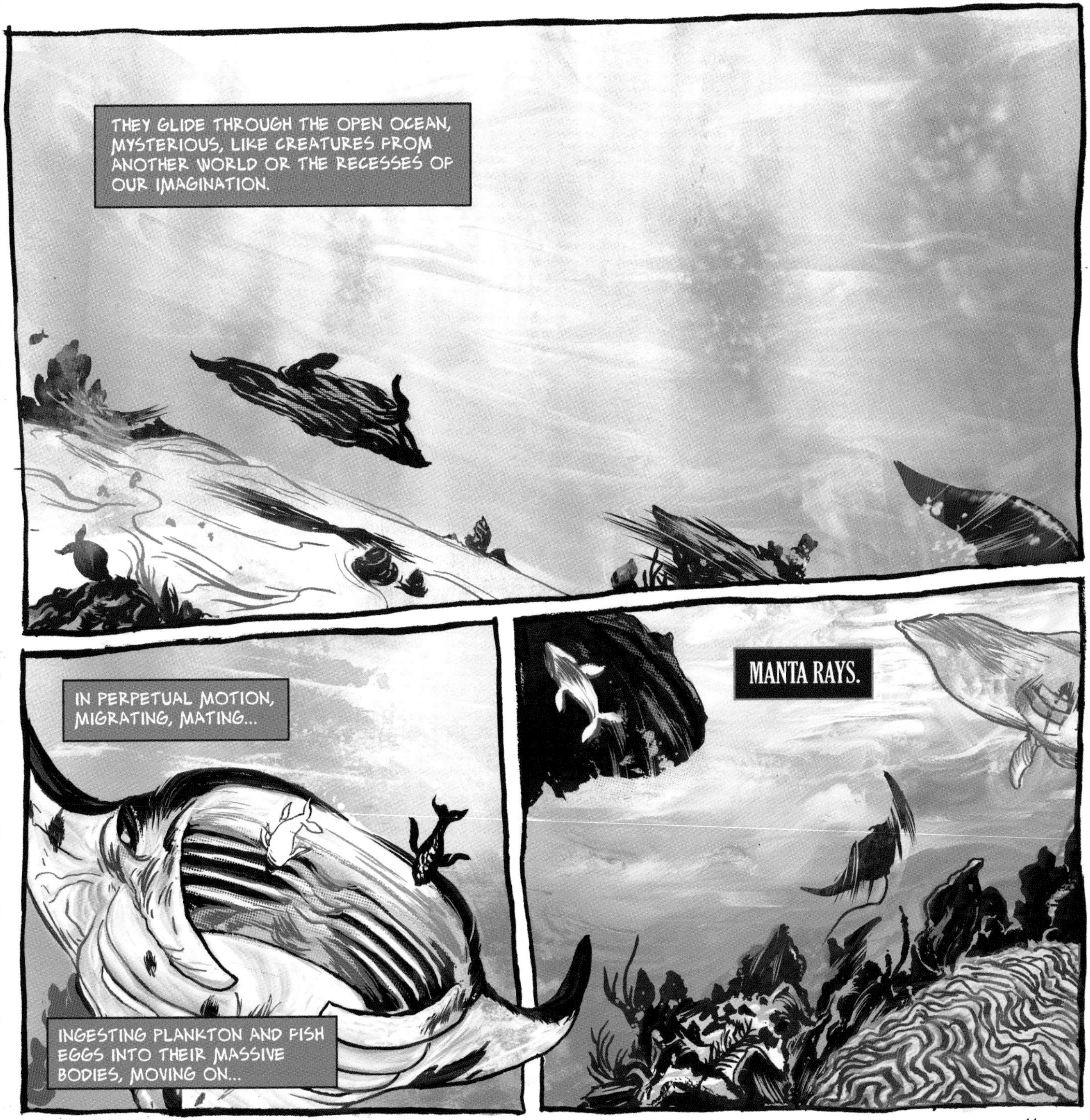
THEY GLIDE THROUGH THE OPEN OCEAN, MYSTERIOUS, LIKE CREATURES FROM ANOTHER WORLD OR THE RECESSES OF OUR IMAGINATION.
IN PERPETUAL MOTION, MIGRATING, MATING...
INGESTING PLANKTON AND FISH EGGS INTO THEIR MASSIVE BODIES, MOVING ON...
MANTA RAYS.

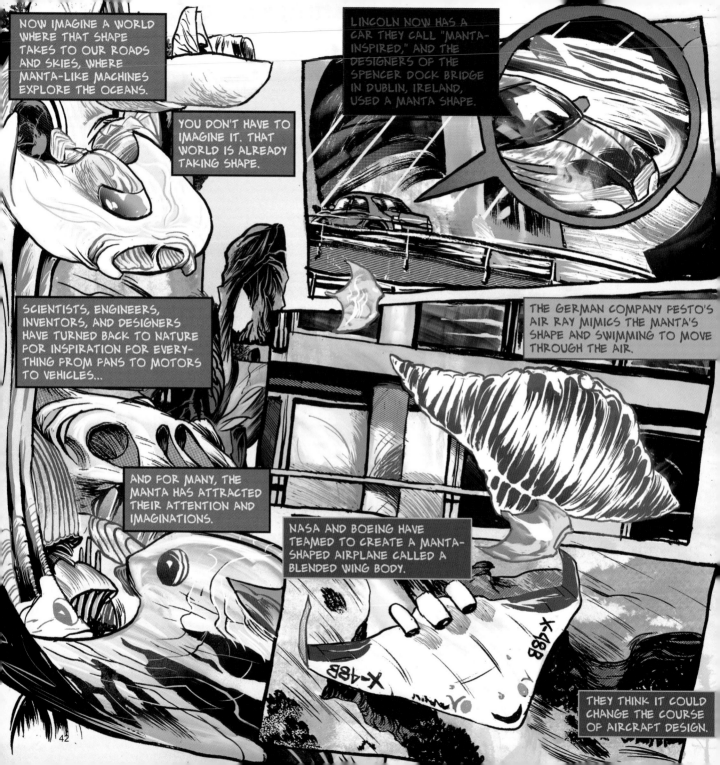

NOW IMAGINE A WORLD WHERE THAT SHAPE TAKES TO OUR ROADS AND SKIES, WHERE MANTA-LIKE MACHINES EXPLORE THE OCEANS.

YOU DON'T HAVE TO IMAGINE IT. THAT WORLD IS ALREADY TAKING SHAPE.

LINCOLN NOW HAS A CAR THEY CALL "MANTA-INSPIRED," AND THE DESIGNERS OF THE SPENCER DOCK BRIDGE IN DUBLIN, IRELAND, USED A MANTA SHAPE.

THE GERMAN COMPANY FESTO'S AIR RAY MIMICS THE MANTA'S SHAPE AND SWIMMING TO MOVE THROUGH THE AIR.

SCIENTISTS, ENGINEERS, INVENTORS, AND DESIGNERS HAVE TURNED BACK TO NATURE FOR INSPIRATION FOR EVERYTHING FROM FANS TO MOTORS TO VEHICLES...

AND FOR MANY, THE MANTA HAS ATTRACTED THEIR ATTENTION AND IMAGINATIONS.

NASA AND BOEING HAVE TEAMED TO CREATE A MANTA-SHAPED AIRPLANE CALLED A BLENDED WING BODY.

THEY THINK IT COULD CHANGE THE COURSE OF AIRCRAFT DESIGN.

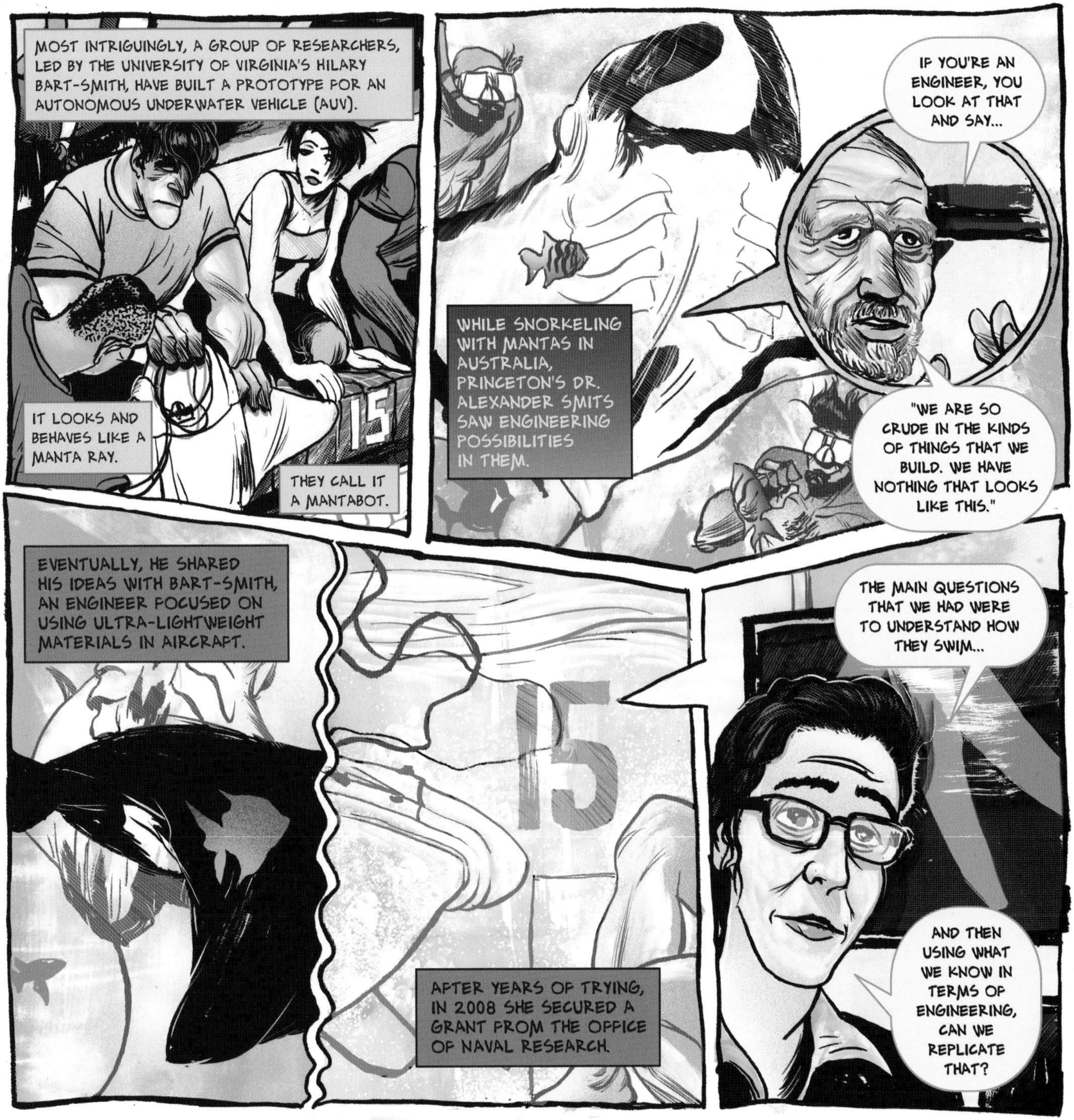
MOST INTRIGUINGLY, A GROUP OF RESEARCHERS, LED BY THE UNIVERSITY OF VIRGINIA'S HILARY BART-SMITH, HAVE BUILT A PROTOTYPE FOR AN AUTONOMOUS UNDERWATER VEHICLE (AUV).
IT LOOKS AND BEHAVES LIKE A MANTA RAY.
15
THEY CALL IT A MANTABOT.
WHILE SNORKELING WITH MANTAS IN AUSTRALIA, PRINCETON'S DR. ALEXANDER SMITS SAW ENGINEERING POSSIBILITIES IN THEM.
IF YOU'RE AN ENGINEER, YOU LOOK AT THAT AND SAY...
"WE ARE SO CRUDE IN THE KINDS OF THINGS THAT WE BUILD. WE HAVE NOTHING THAT LOOKS LIKE THIS."
EVENTUALLY, HE SHARED HIS IDEAS WITH BART-SMITH, AN ENGINEER FOCUSED ON USING ULTRA-LIGHTWEIGHT MATERIALS IN AIRCRAFT.
15
AFTER YEARS OF TRYING, IN 2008 SHE SECURED A GRANT FROM THE OFFICE OF NAVAL RESEARCH.
THE MAIN QUESTIONS THAT WE HAD WERE TO UNDERSTAND HOW THEY SWIM...
AND THEN USING WHAT WE KNOW IN TERMS OF ENGINEERING, CAN WE REPLICATE THAT?

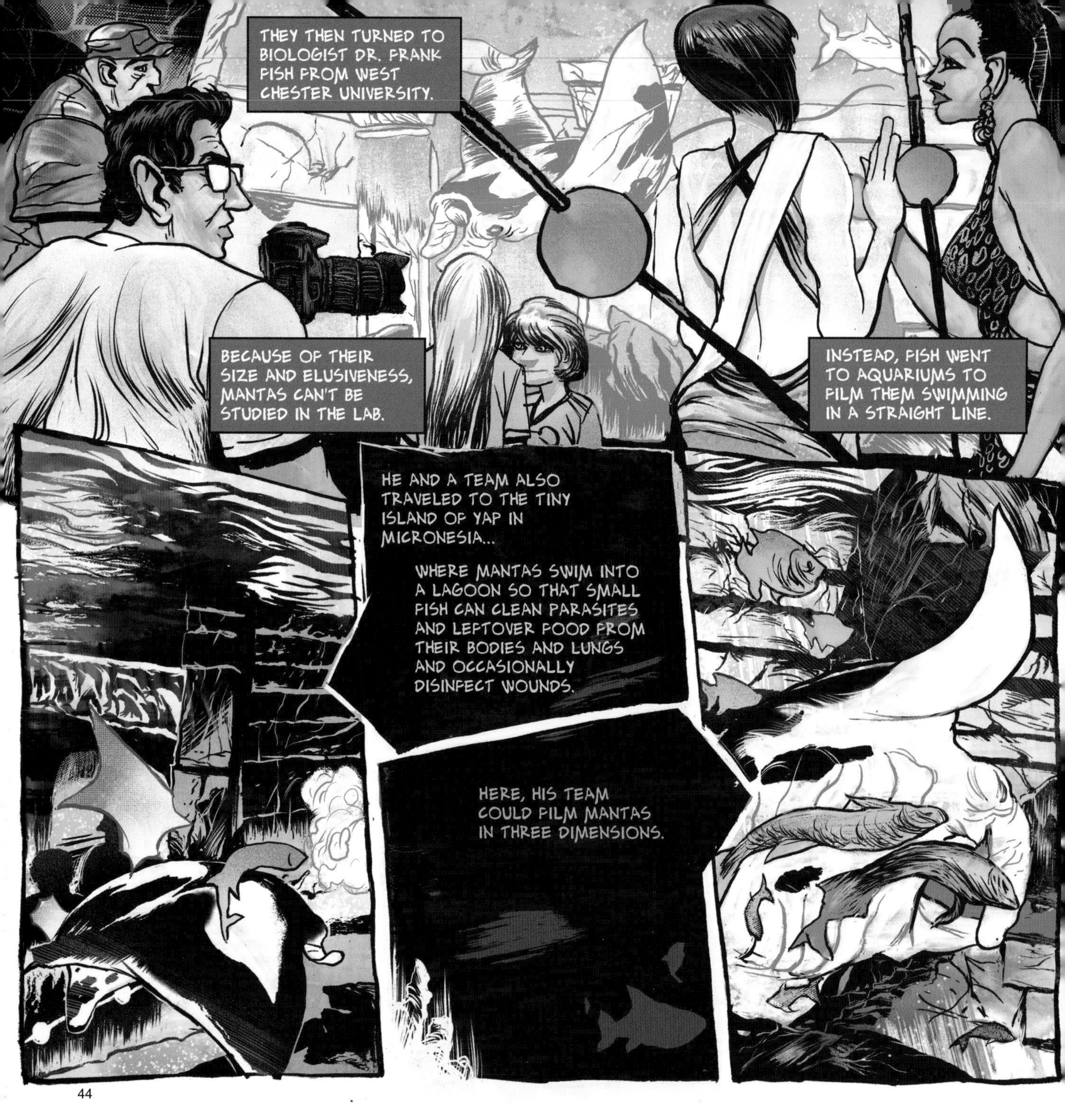

THEY THEN TURNED TO BIOLOGIST DR. FRANK FISH FROM WEST CHESTER UNIVERSITY.
BECAUSE OF THEIR SIZE AND ELUSIVENESS, MANTAS CAN'T BE STUDIED IN THE LAB.
INSTEAD, FISH WENT TO AQUARIUMS TO FILM THEM SWIMMING IN A STRAIGHT LINE.
HE AND A TEAM ALSO TRAVELED TO THE TINY ISLAND OF YAP IN MICRONESIA...
WHERE MANTAS SWIM INTO A LAGOON SO THAT SMALL FISH CAN CLEAN PARASITES AND LEFTOVER FOOD FROM THEIR BODIES AND LUNGS AND OCCASIONALLY DISINFECT WOUNDS.
HERE, HIS TEAM COULD FILM MANTAS IN THREE DIMENSIONS.

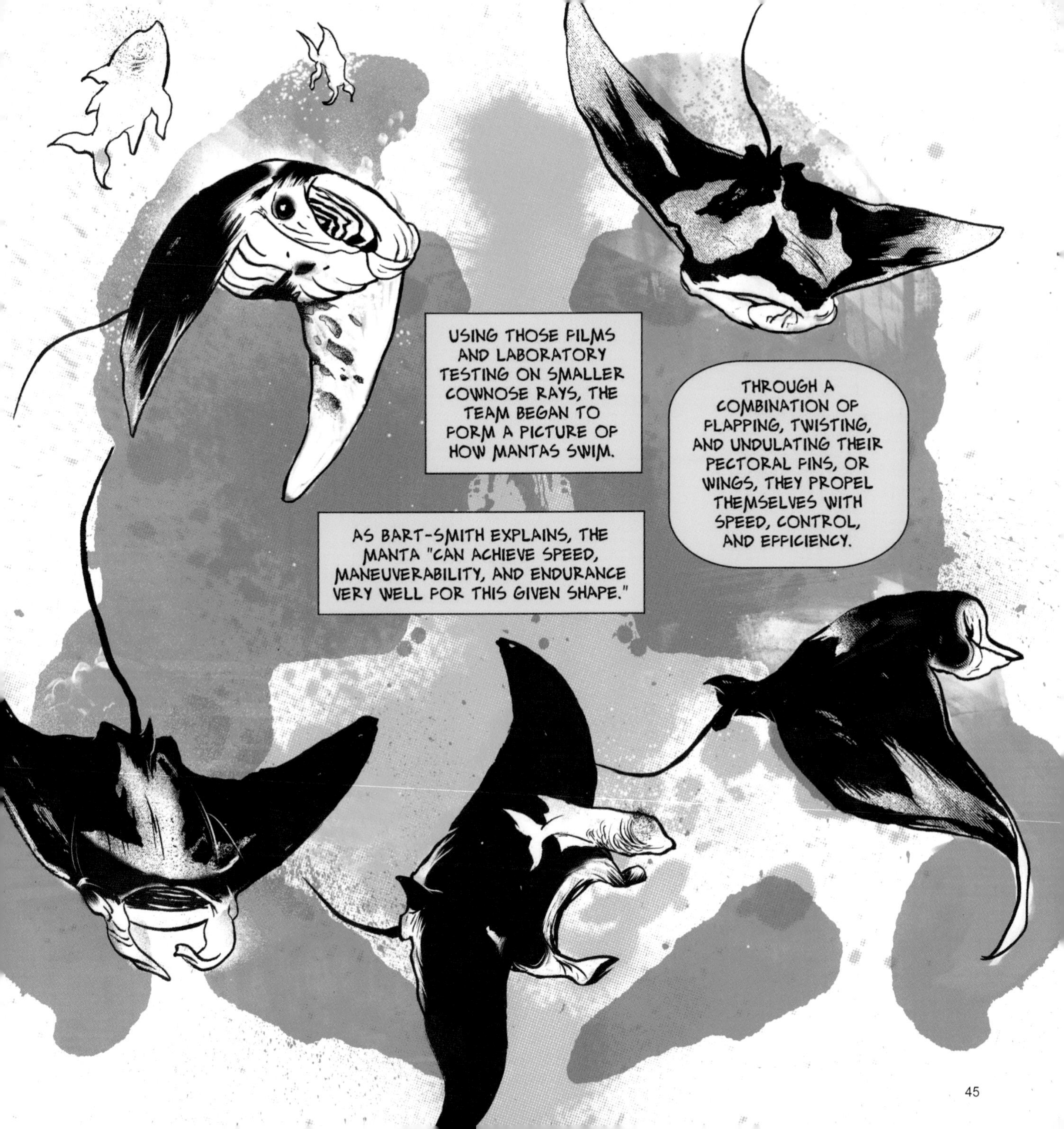
USING THOSE FILMS AND LABORATORY TESTING ON SMALLER COWNOSE RAYS, THE TEAM BEGAN TO FORM A PICTURE OF HOW MANTAS SWIM.
THROUGH A COMBINATION OF FLAPPING, TWISTING, AND UNDULATING THEIR PECTORAL FINS, OR WINGS, THEY PROPEL THEMSELVES WITH SPEED, CONTROL, AND EFFICIENCY.
AS BART-SMITH EXPLAINS, THE MANTA "CAN ACHIEVE SPEED, MANEUVERABILITY, AND ENDURANCE VERY WELL FOR THIS GIVEN SHAPE."

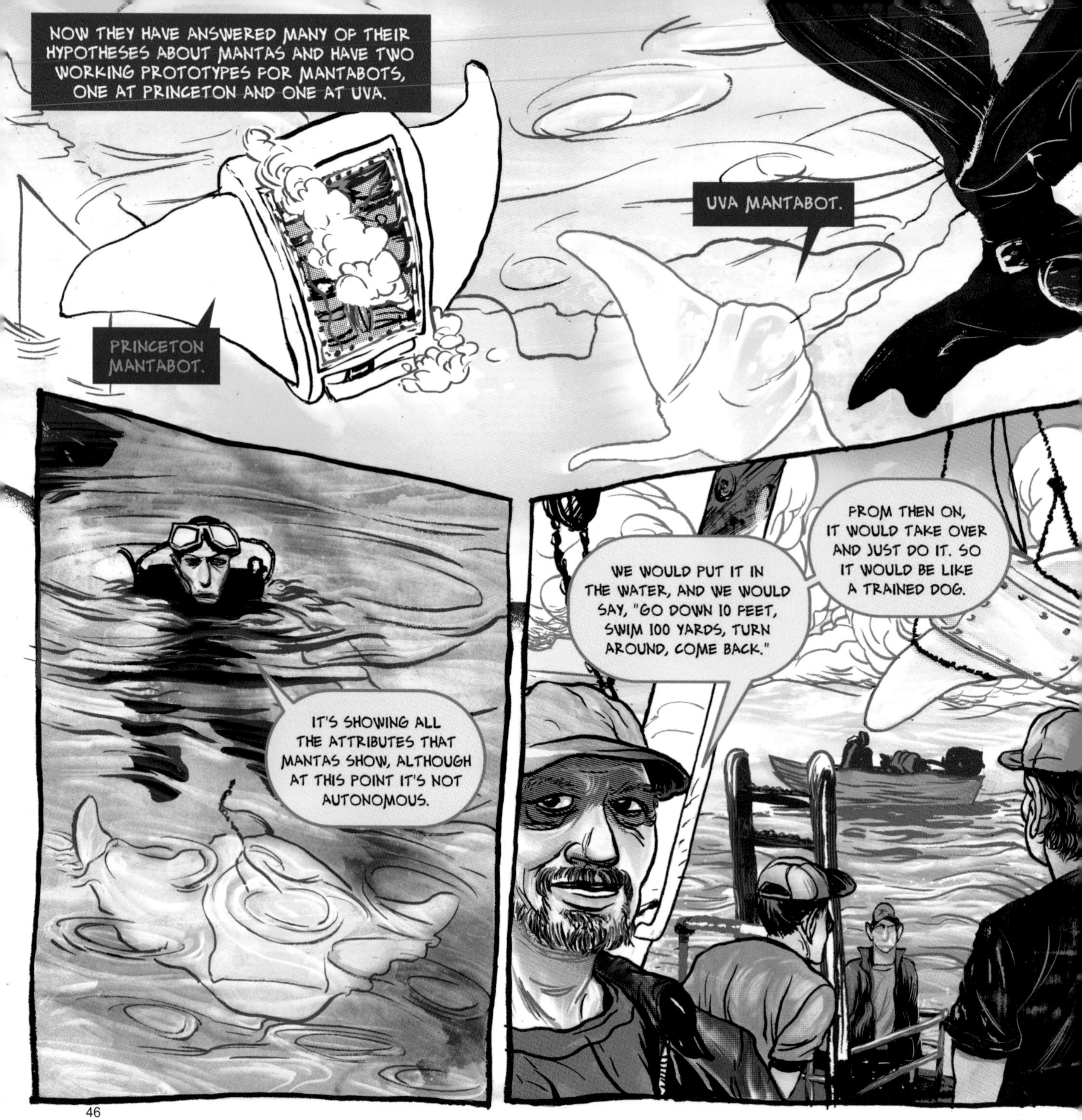
NOW THEY HAVE ANSWERED MANY OF THEIR HYPOTHESES ABOUT MANTAS AND HAVE TWO WORKING PROTOTYPES FOR MANTABOTS, ONE AT PRINCETON AND ONE AT UVA.
UVA MANTABOT.
PRINCETON MANTABOT.
IT'S SHOWING ALL THE ATTRIBUTES THAT MANTAS SHOW, ALTHOUGH AT THIS POINT IT'S NOT AUTONOMOUS.
WE WOULD PUT IT IN THE WATER, AND WE WOULD SAY, "GO DOWN 10 FEET, SWIM 100 YARDS, TURN AROUND, COME BACK."
FROM THEN ON, IT WOULD TAKE OVER AND JUST DO IT. SO IT WOULD BE LIKE A TRAINED DOG.

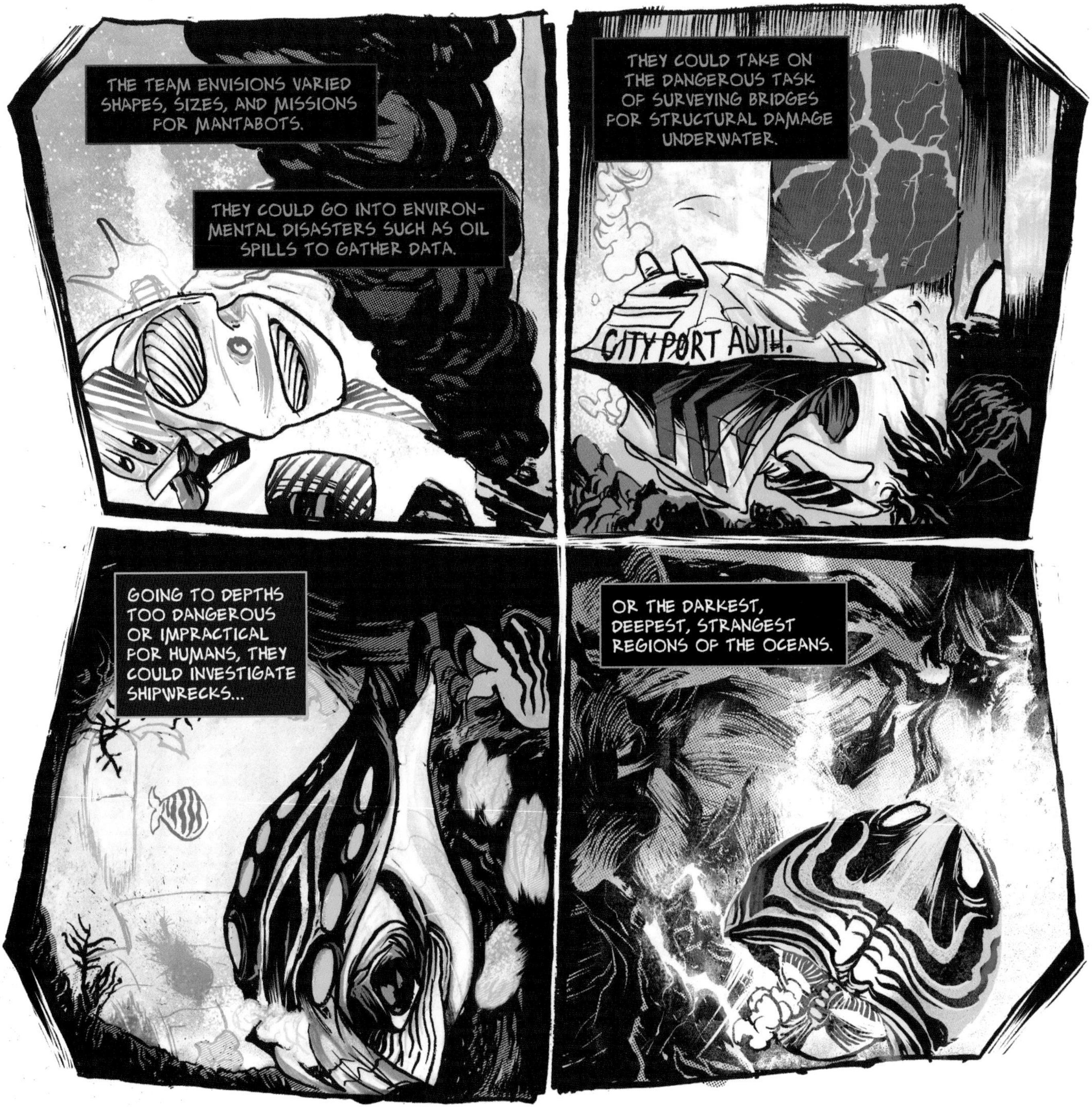

THE TEAM ENVISIONS VARIED SHAPES, SIZES, AND MISSIONS FOR MANTABOTS.
THEY COULD GO INTO ENVIRONMENTAL DISASTERS SUCH AS OIL SPILLS TO GATHER DATA.
THEY COULD TAKE ON THE DANGEROUS TASK OF SURVEYING BRIDGES FOR STRUCTURAL DAMAGE UNDERWATER.
CITY PORT AUTH.
GOING TO DEPTHS TOO DANGEROUS OR IMPRACTICAL FOR HUMANS, THEY COULD INVESTIGATE SHIPWRECKS...
OR THE DARKEST, DEEPEST, STRANGEST REGIONS OF THE OCEANS.

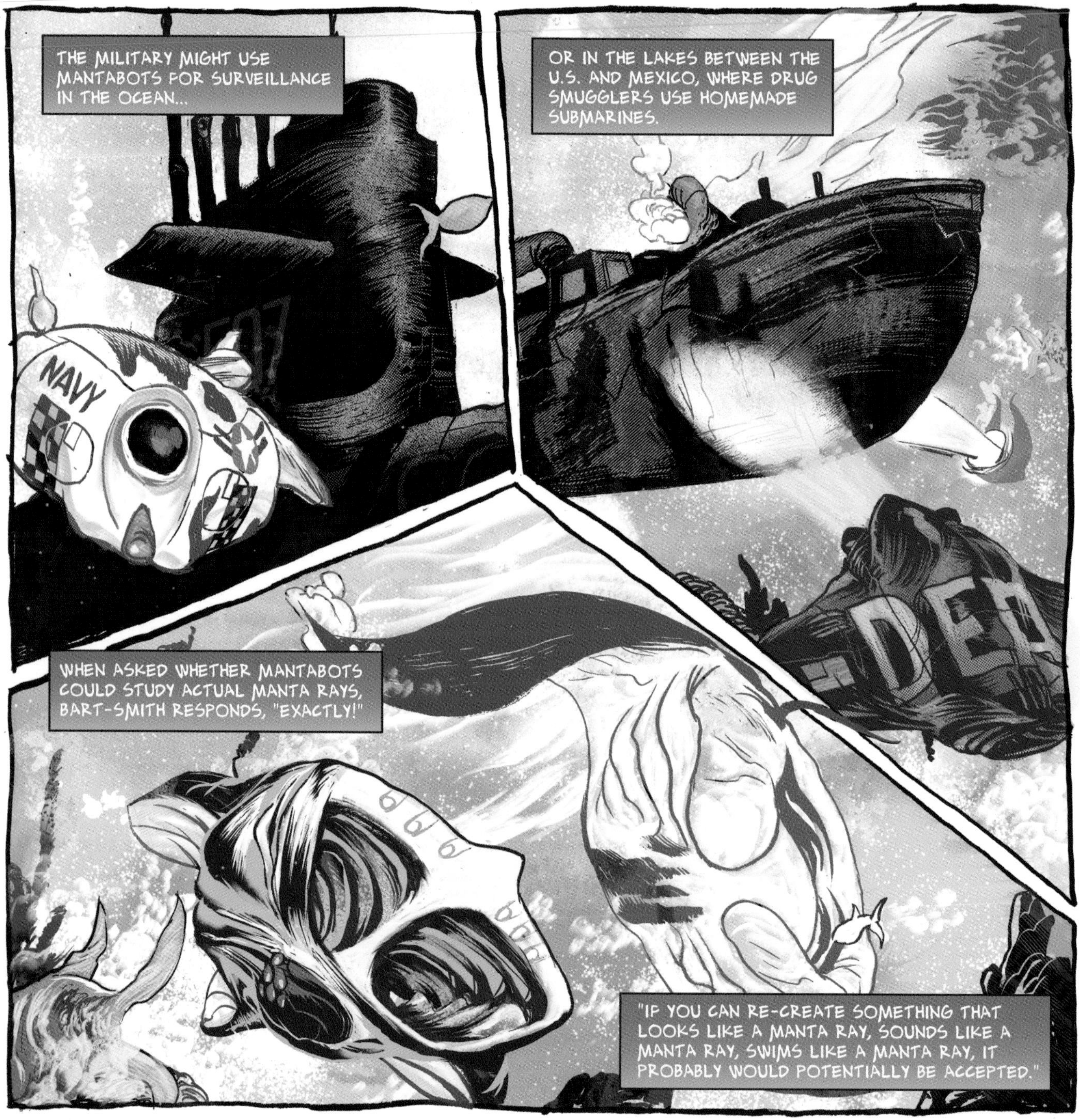
THE MILITARY MIGHT USE MANTABOTS FOR SURVEILLANCE IN THE OCEAN...
NAVY
OR IN THE LAKES BETWEEN THE U.S. AND MEXICO, WHERE DRUG SMUGGLERS USE HOMEMADE SUBMARINES.
DEA
WHEN ASKED WHETHER MANTABOTS COULD STUDY ACTUAL MANTA RAYS, BART-SMITH RESPONDS, "EXACTLY!"
"IF YOU CAN RE-CREATE SOMETHING THAT LOOKS LIKE A MANTA RAY, SOUNDS LIKE A MANTA RAY, SWIMS LIKE A MANTA RAY, IT PROBABLY WOULD POTENTIALLY BE ACCEPTED."

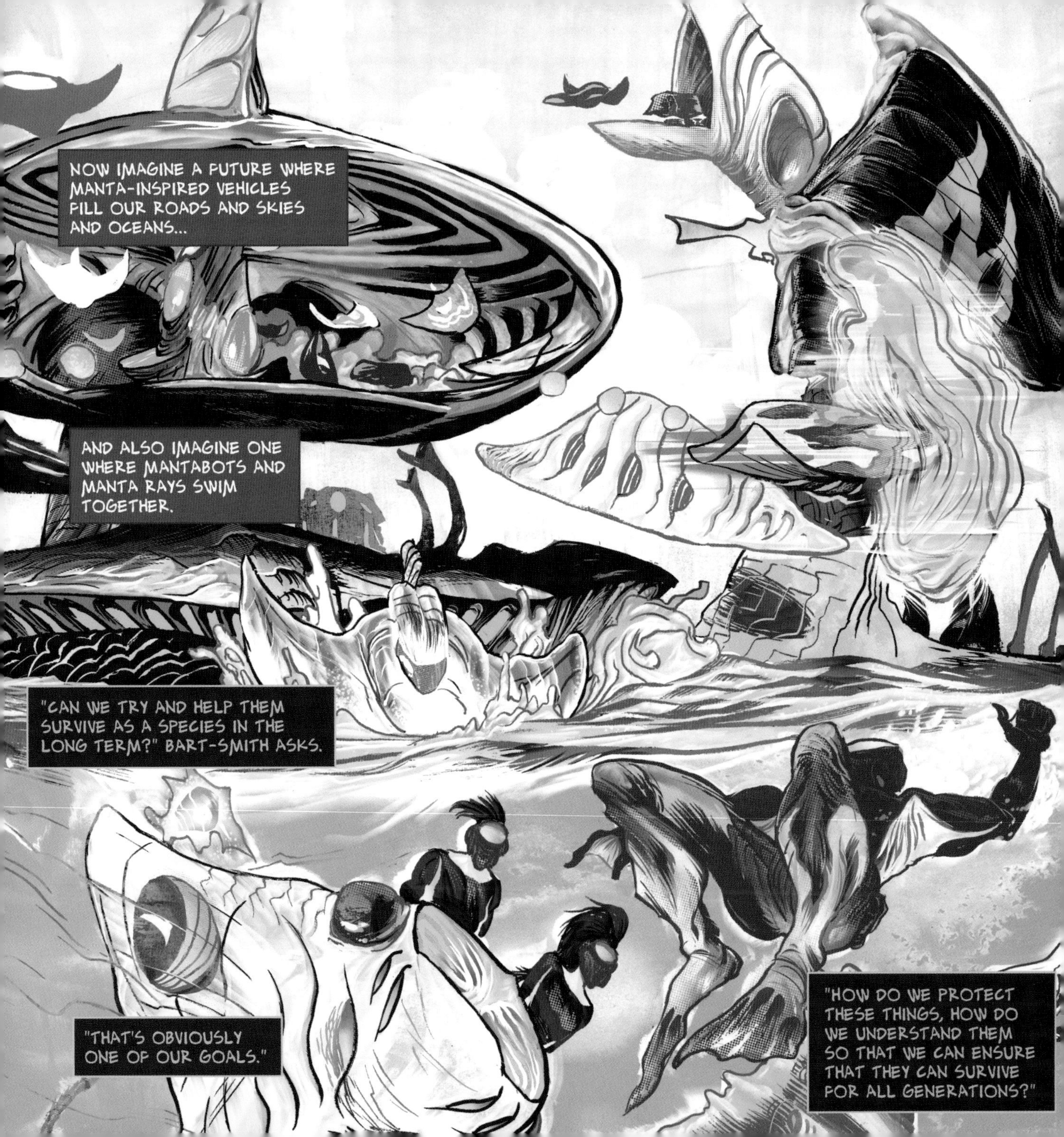
NOW IMAGINE A FUTURE WHERE MANTA-INSPIRED VEHICLES FILL OUR ROADS AND SKIES AND OCEANS...
AND ALSO IMAGINE ONE WHERE MANTABOTS AND MANTA RAYS SWIM TOGETHER.
"CAN WE TRY AND HELP THEM SURVIVE AS A SPECIES IN THE LONG TERM?" BART-SMITH ASKS.
"THAT'S OBVIOUSLY ONE OF OUR GOALS."
"HOW DO WE PROTECT THESE THINGS, HOW DO WE UNDERSTAND THEM SO THAT WE CAN ENSURE THAT THEY CAN SURVIVE FOR ALL GENERATIONS?"

Hawaiian Blues

Story and Art by Dove McHargue
Lettering by David Allan Duncan

AT NEARLY 100 FEET (30.5m), the blue whale is the largest animal to live on Earth—ever. But despite its size, this giant mammal was almost hunted into extinction for its oil in the 1900s. More than 360,000 blue whales were slaughtered during the first sixty years of the 20th century. Even with international whaling protection, blue whales have only made a small comeback, with an estimated 10,000 to 25,000 gliding through our oceans.

While the danger of being hunted has receded, whales may still be attacked by sharks and killer whales. In addition, impacts with large ships kill and injure countless whales each year.

Still, these massive animals are iconic, not only for their length and weight (their hearts alone can weigh as much as a car), but also for characteristics that we as humans can relate to. The whale mother and calf have a tight bond, with the baby staying close to her for up to a year, until it weans and begins to eat krill. That connection between a parent and its young is conveyed in our story about a young boy whose imagination is captured by a new toy.

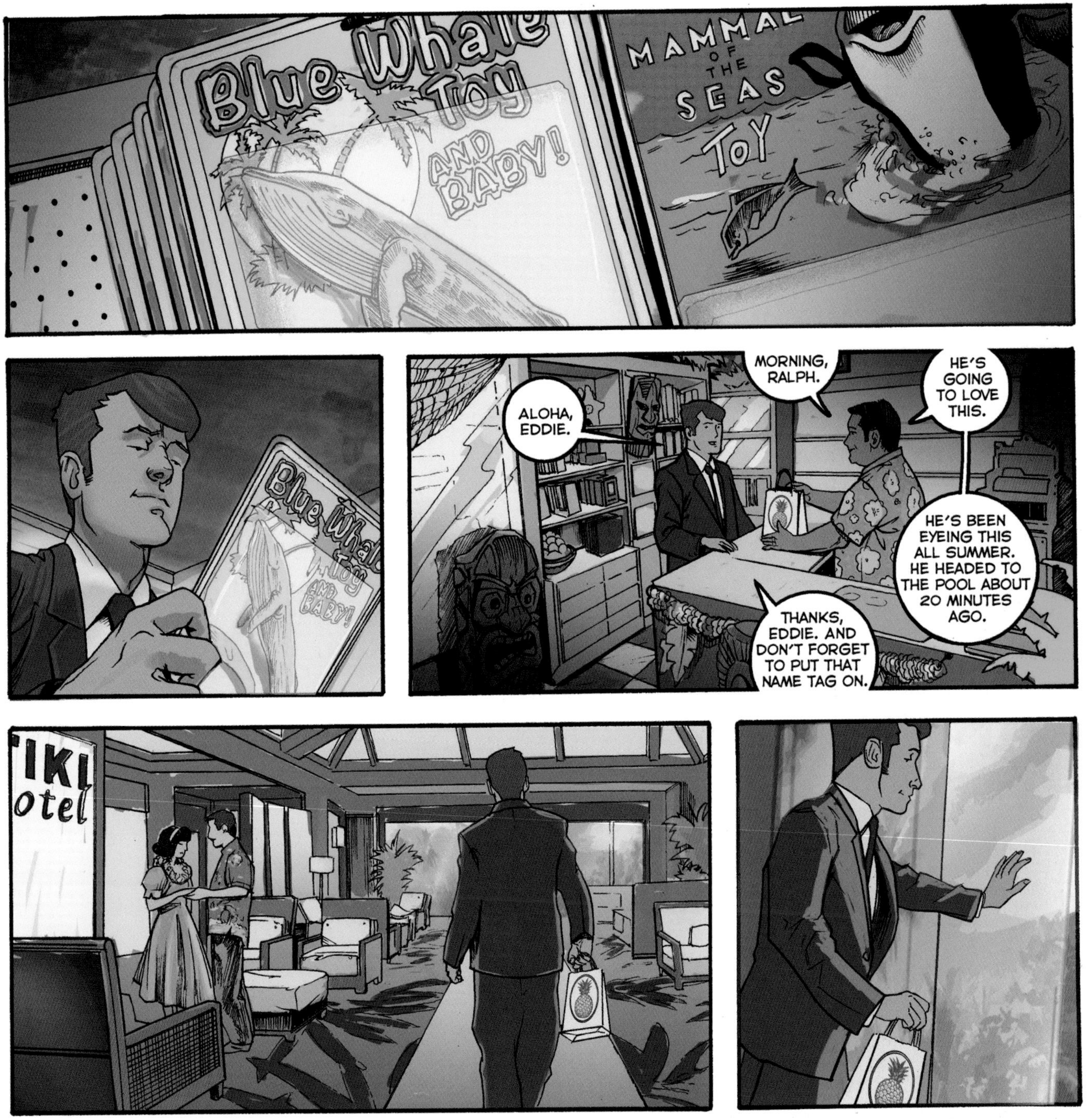
Blue Whale Toy
AND BABY!
MAMMAL OF THE SEAS TOY
ALOHA, EDDIE.
MORNING, RALPH.
HE'S GOING TO LOVE THIS.
HE'S BEEN EYEING THIS ALL SUMMER. HE HEADED TO THE POOL ABOUT 20 MINUTES AGO.
THANKS, EDDIE. AND DON'T FORGET TO PUT THAT NAME TAG ON.
TIKI
otel

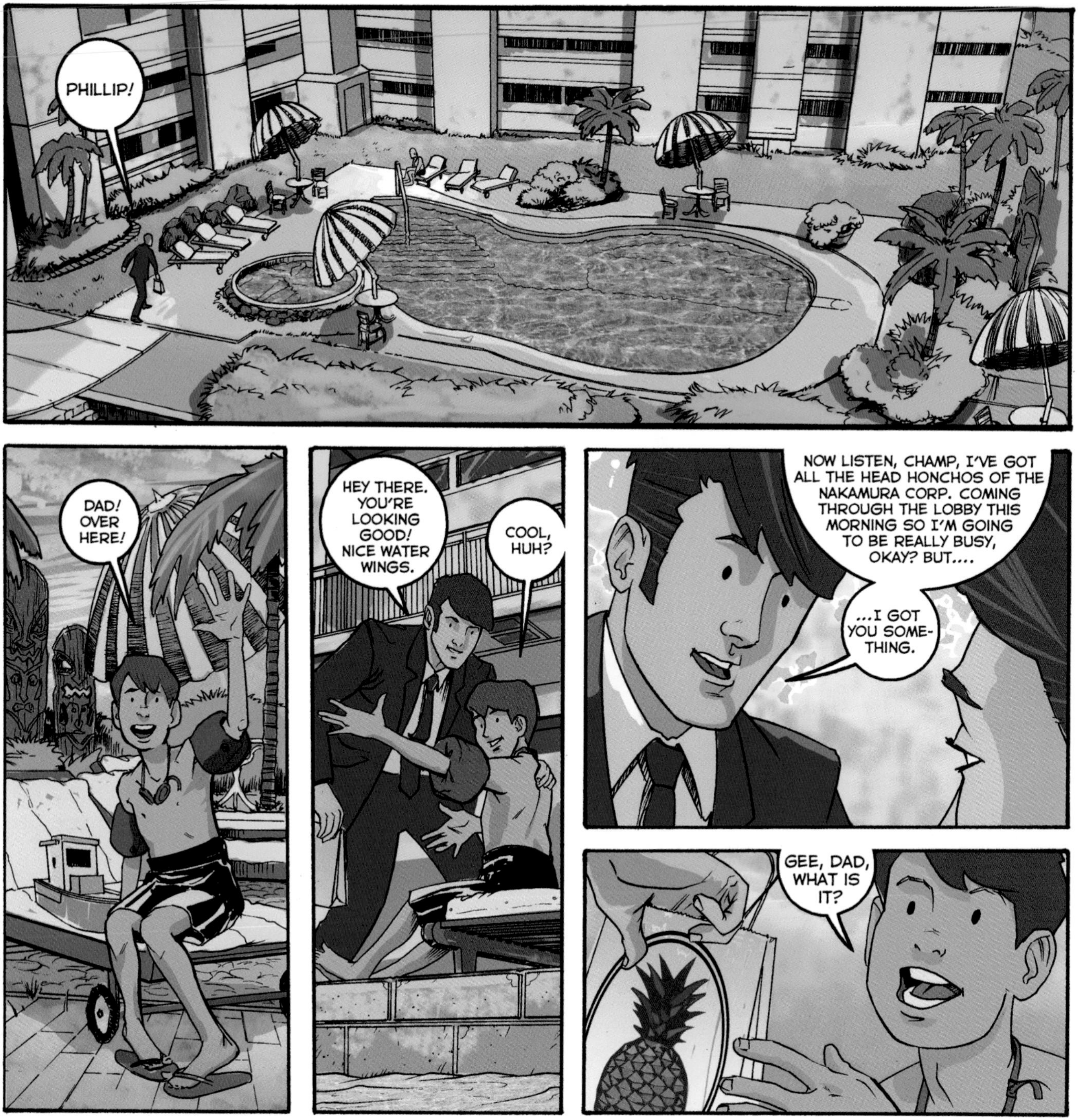
PHILLIP!
DAD! OVER HERE!
HEY THERE. YOU'RE LOOKING GOOD! NICE WATER WINGS.
COOL, HUH?
NOW LISTEN, CHAMP, I'VE GOT ALL THE HEAD HONCHOS OF THE NAKAMURA CORP. COMING THROUGH THE LOBBY THIS MORNING SO I'M GOING TO BE REALLY BUSY, OKAY? BUT....
...I GOT YOU SOME-THING.
GEE, DAD, WHAT IS IT?

WOWEE! THE BLUE WHALE FROM THE GIFT SHOP! THANKS, DAD!

YOU'RE THE BEST!

YOU'RE WELCOME, CHAMP. I'M GLAD YOU LIKE IT.

YOUR SITTER WILL BE HERE IN A COUPLE OF MINUTES ...

SO BE EXTRA CAREFUL. AND...

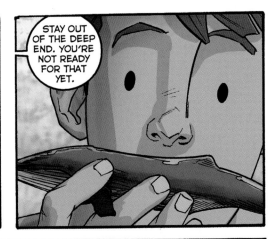

STAY OUT OF THE DEEP END. YOU'RE NOT READY FOR THAT YET.

LOVE YOU, SON.

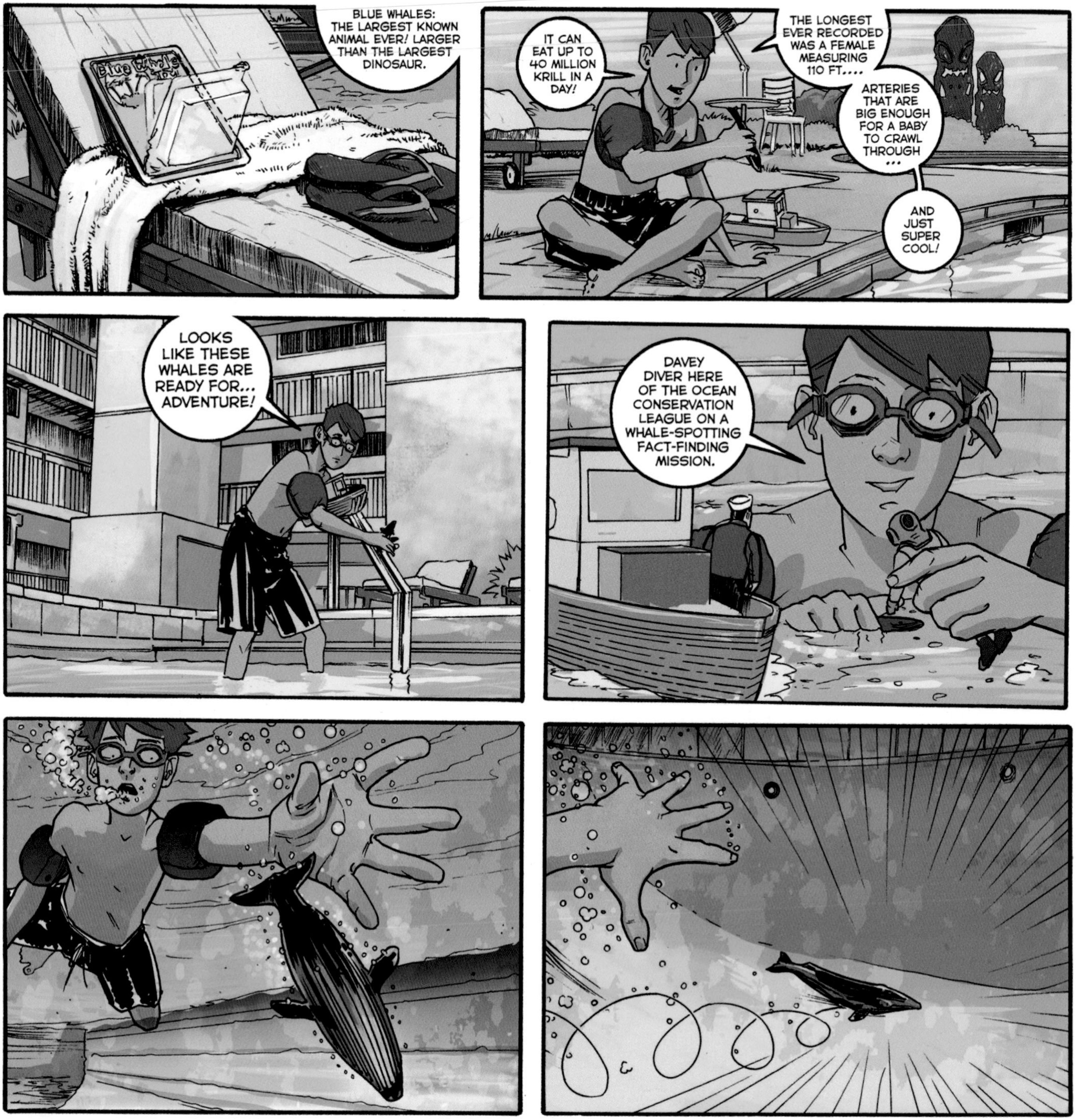

BLUE WHALES: THE LARGEST KNOWN ANIMAL EVER! LARGER THAN THE LARGEST DINOSAUR.
Blue Whale Toy
IT CAN EAT UP TO 40 MILLION KRILL IN A DAY!
THE LONGEST EVER RECORDED WAS A FEMALE MEASURING 110 FT....
ARTERIES THAT ARE BIG ENOUGH FOR A BABY TO CRAWL THROUGH...
AND JUST SUPER COOL!
LOOKS LIKE THESE WHALES ARE READY FOR... ADVENTURE!
DAVEY DIVER HERE OF THE OCEAN CONSERVATION LEAGUE ON A WHALE-SPOTTING FACT-FINDING MISSION.

NO!
NO, NO, NO, NO...
... A SKIMMER!
WE CAN DO THIS, ...RIGHT?

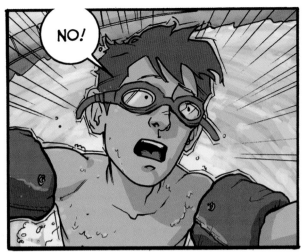

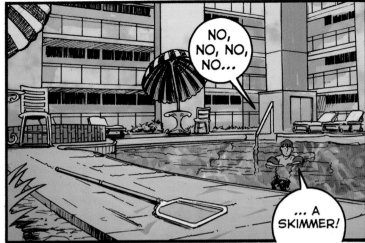

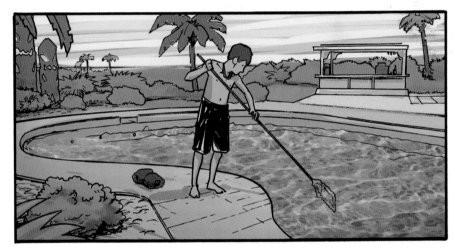

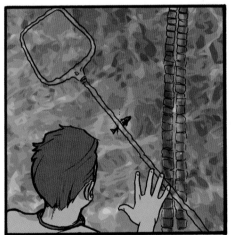

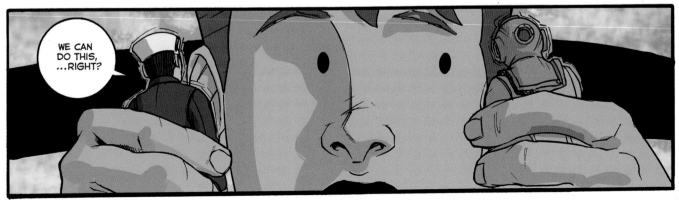

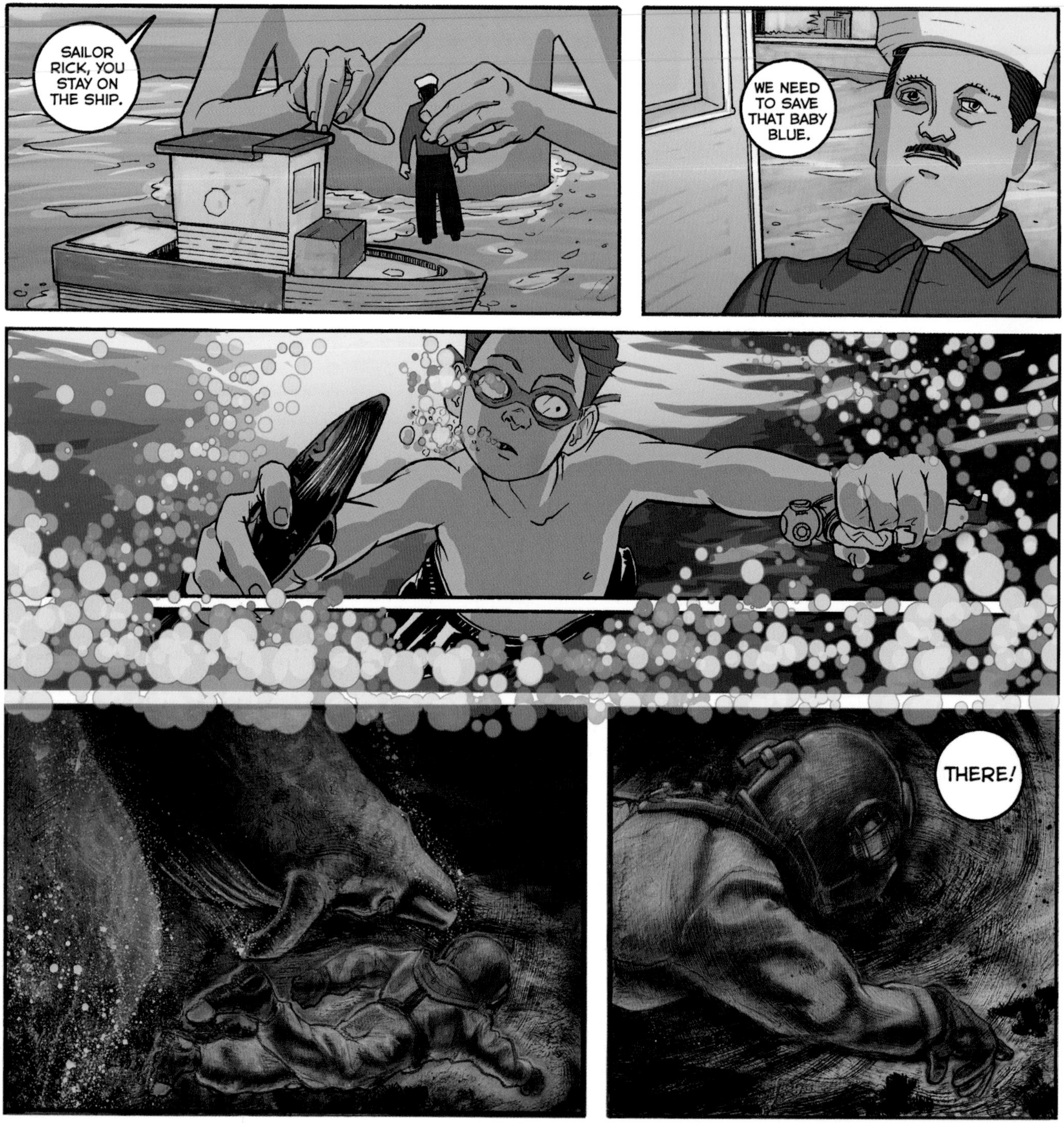
SAILOR RICK, YOU STAY ON THE SHIP.
WE NEED TO SAVE THAT BABY BLUE.
THERE!

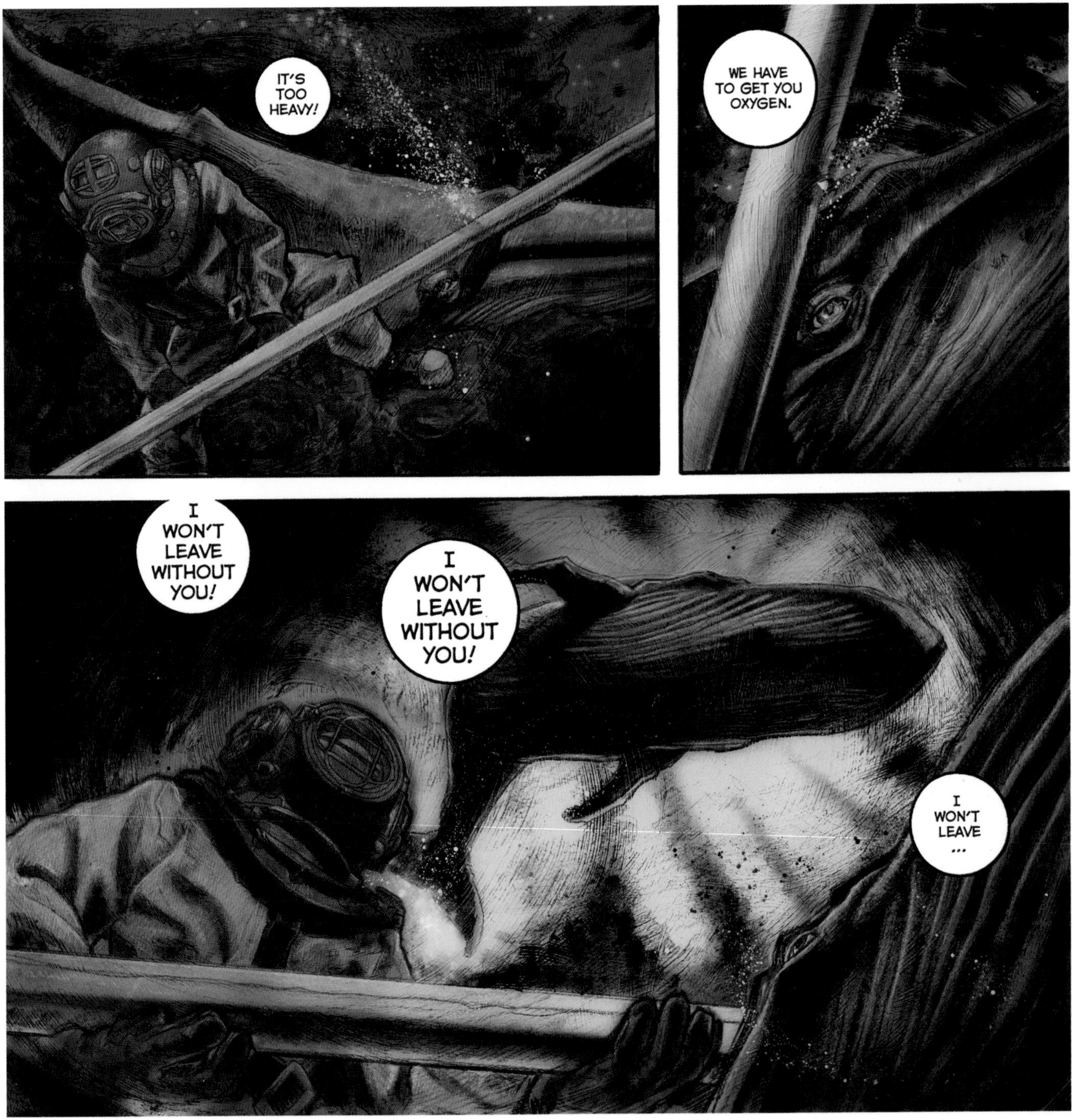
IT'S TOO HEAVY!
WE HAVE TO GET YOU OXYGEN.
I WON'T LEAVE WITHOUT YOU!
I WON'T LEAVE WITHOUT YOU!
I WON'T LEAVE ...

...NOT LEAVING WITHOUT YOU!!
AHHH--HHHHHH!

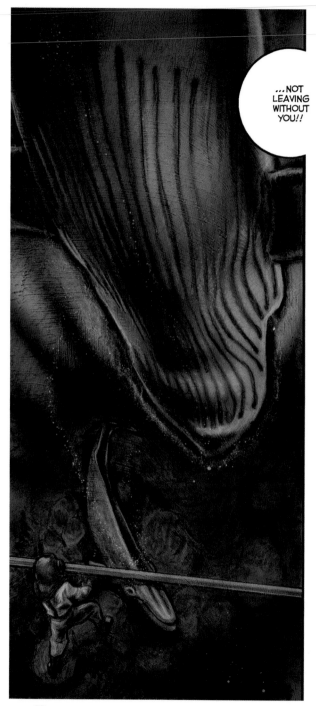

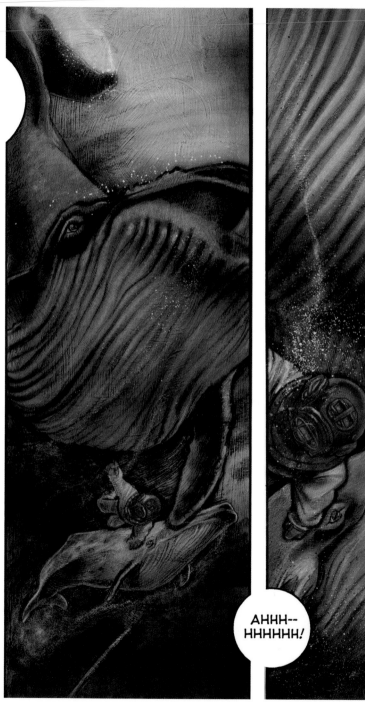

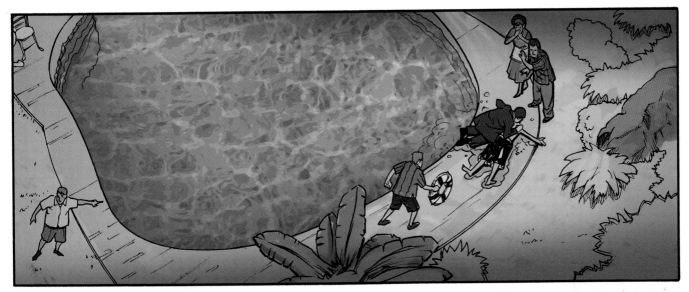

...LEAVE WITHOUT YOU.

DAD ...

...WE DID IT.

59

Seeking Shelter from the Storm

Story and Art by Tammy Stellanova

The Mediterranean monk seal is the most endangered of all pinnipeds. Once plentiful in the eastern Atlantic Ocean and the Mediterranean Sea, the seal's population is now critically low, with only about 450 to 600 left. In the past, seals were hunted extensively for their meat, pelts, and oil, but now this species' survival is jeopardized by many other factors, most involving human activity.

Monk seals are a shy species, and the crowded beaches of the Mediterranean no longer provide suitable places for resting and giving birth to pups. Instead, they must seek out isolated sea caves for these purposes. Unfortunately, only a small number of these caves are appropriate for raising a pup, with locations that keep the pups safe from high tides and storms that can easily carry them away.

Pollution caused by industry, agriculture, and recreation can also drive seals away from what may be an otherwise ideal spot. Food scarcity is another problem, as monk seals compete with Mediterranean fisheries for their food. This tug-of-war on the open seas sometimes results in conflicts between fishermen and seals—conflicts that the seals typically lose.

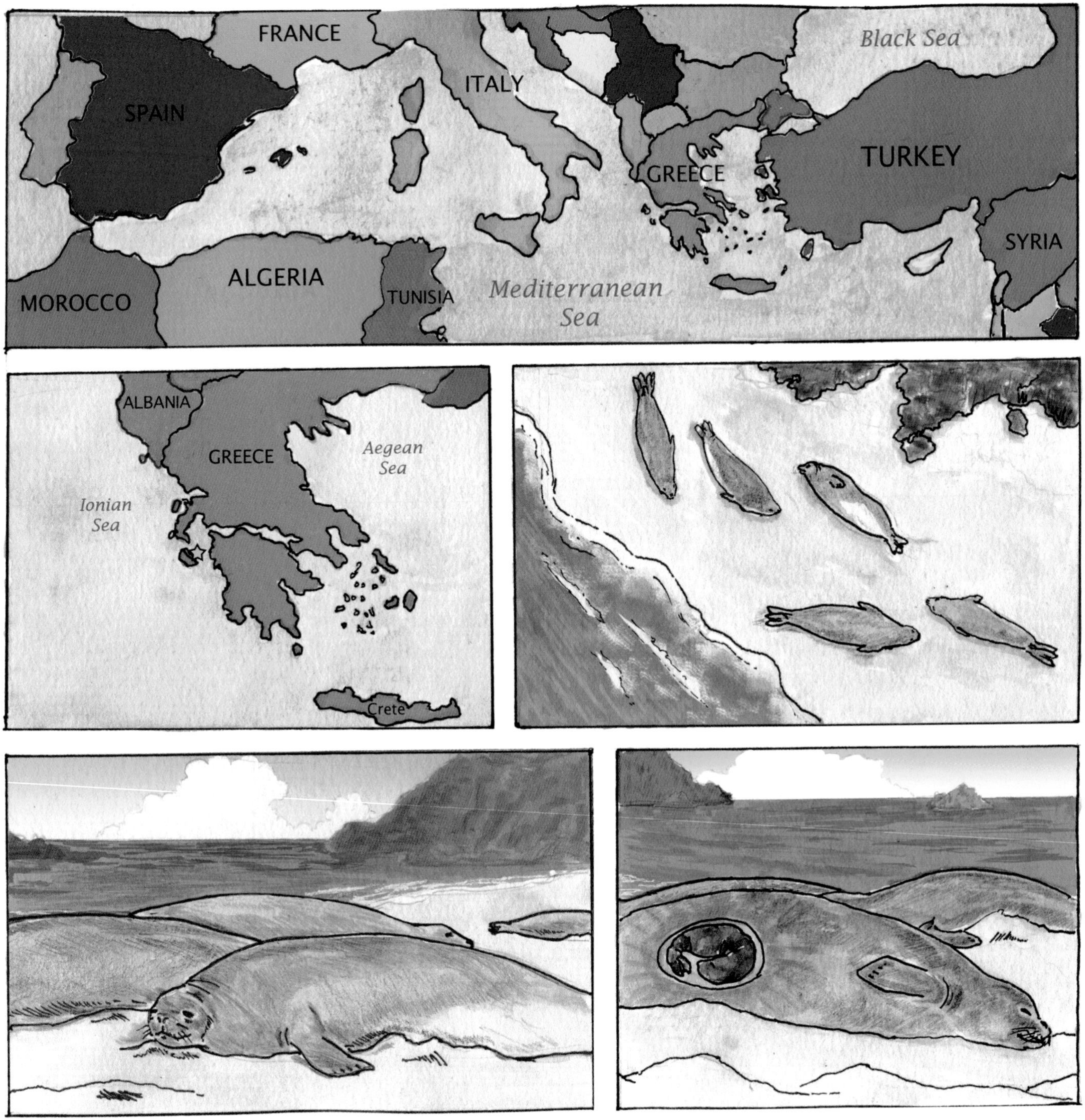
FRANCE
Black Sea
ITALY
SPAIN
TURKEY
GREECE
SYRIA
ALGERIA
MOROCCO
TUNISIA
Mediterranean Sea
ALBANIA
GREECE
Aegean Sea
Ionian Sea
Crete

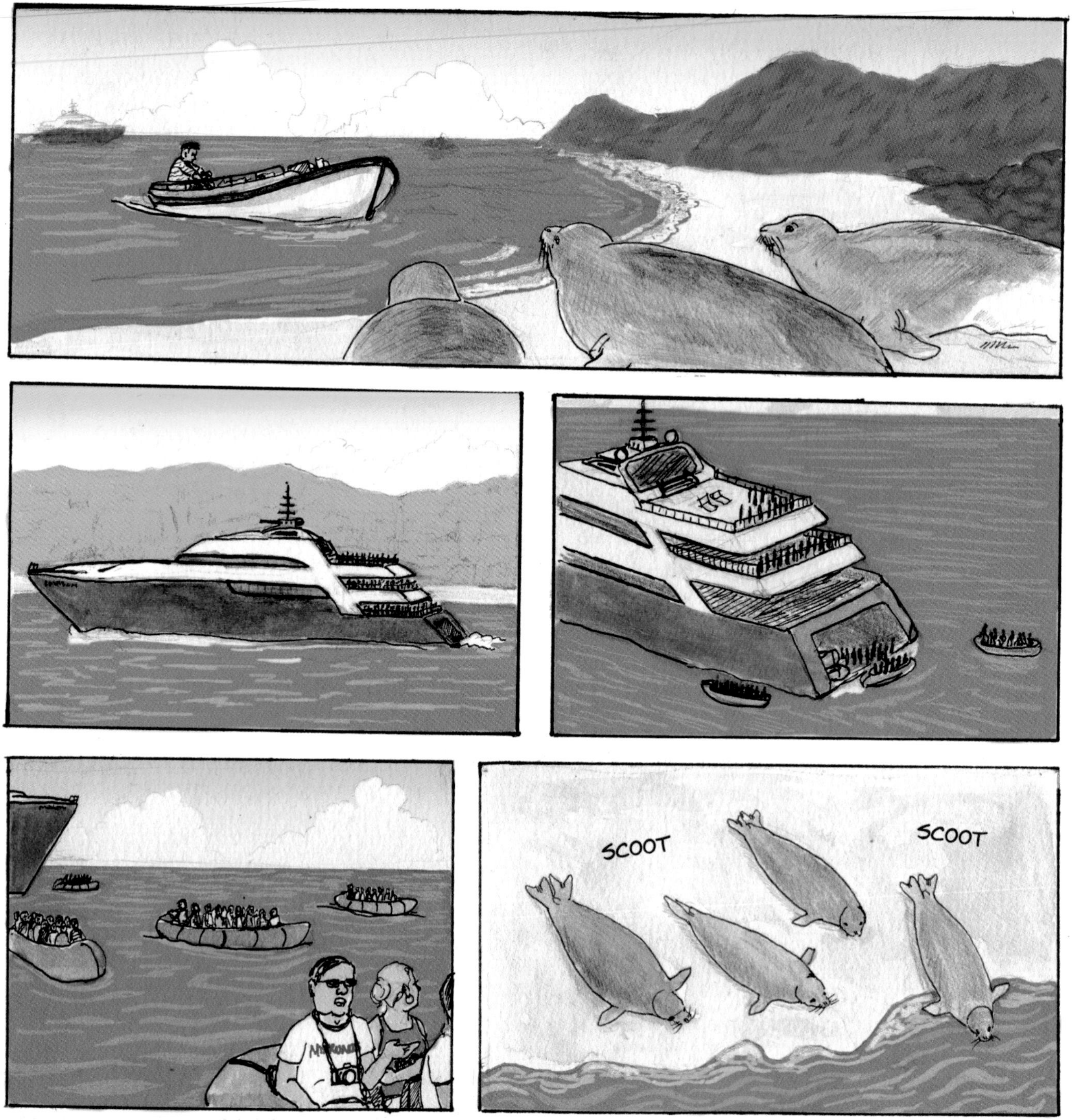
SCOOT
SCOOT

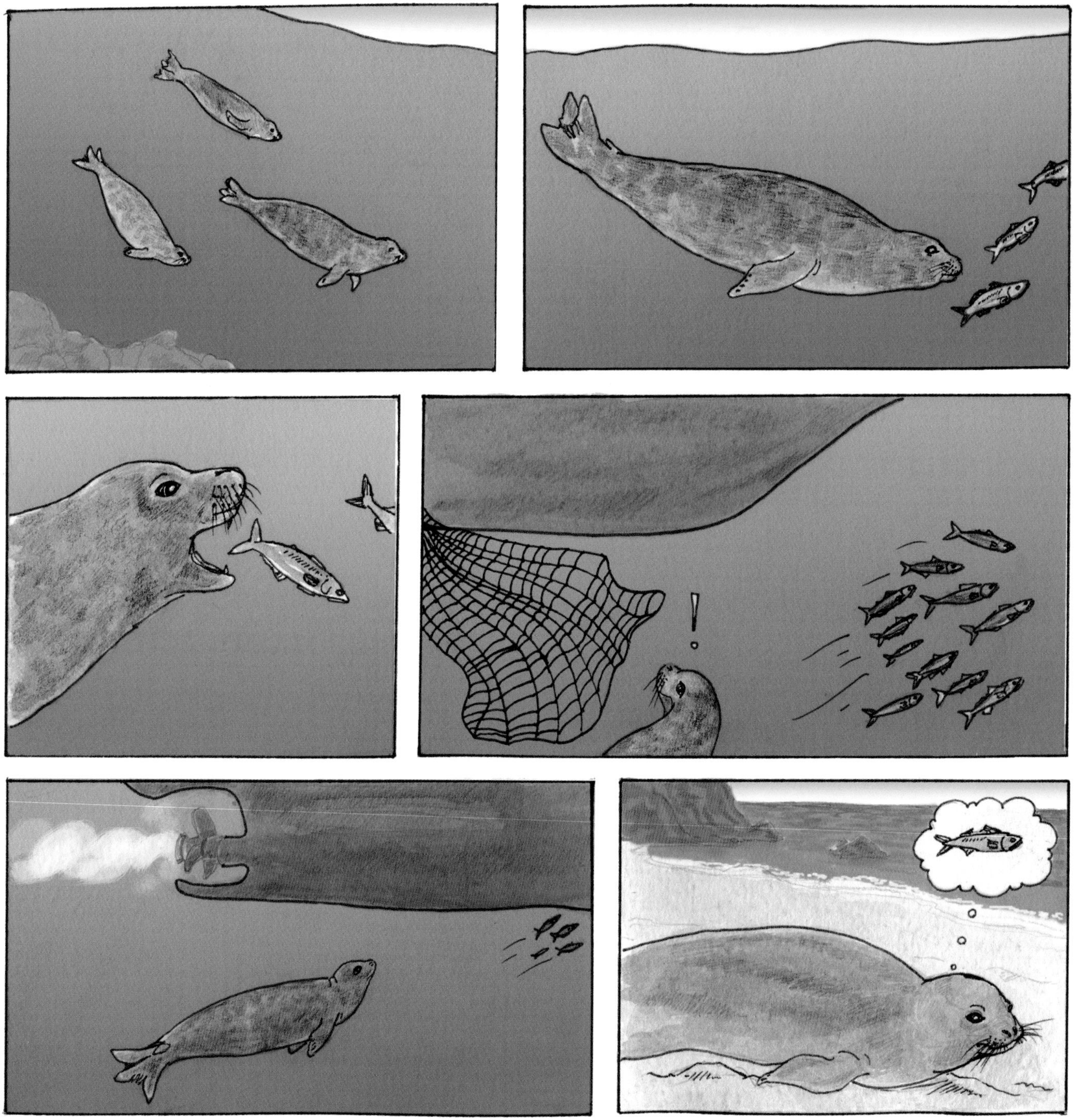
!

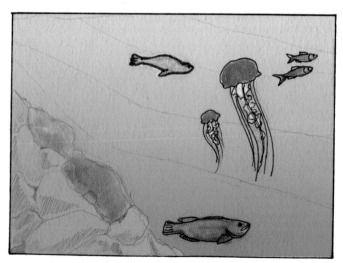

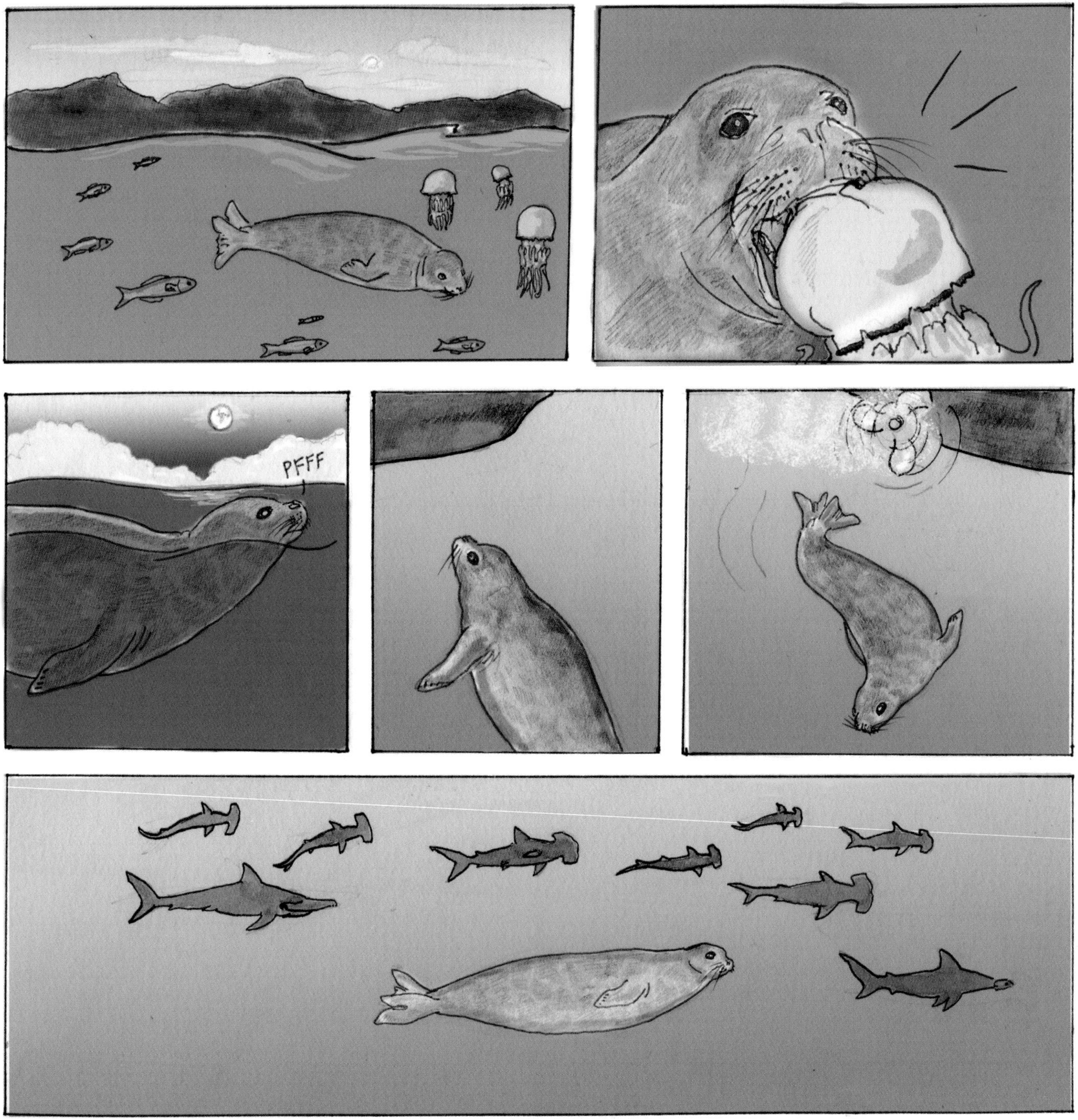
PFFF

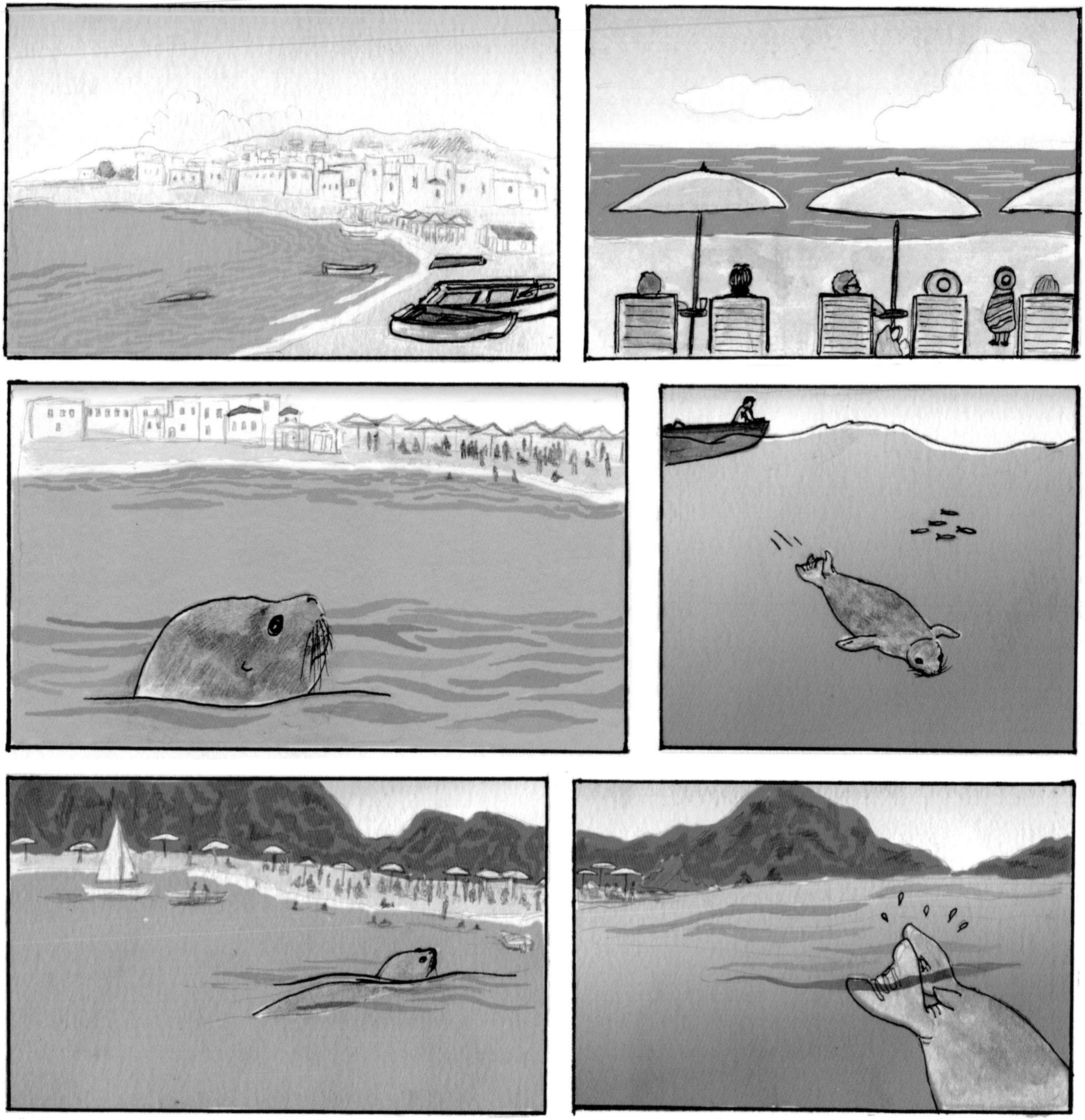

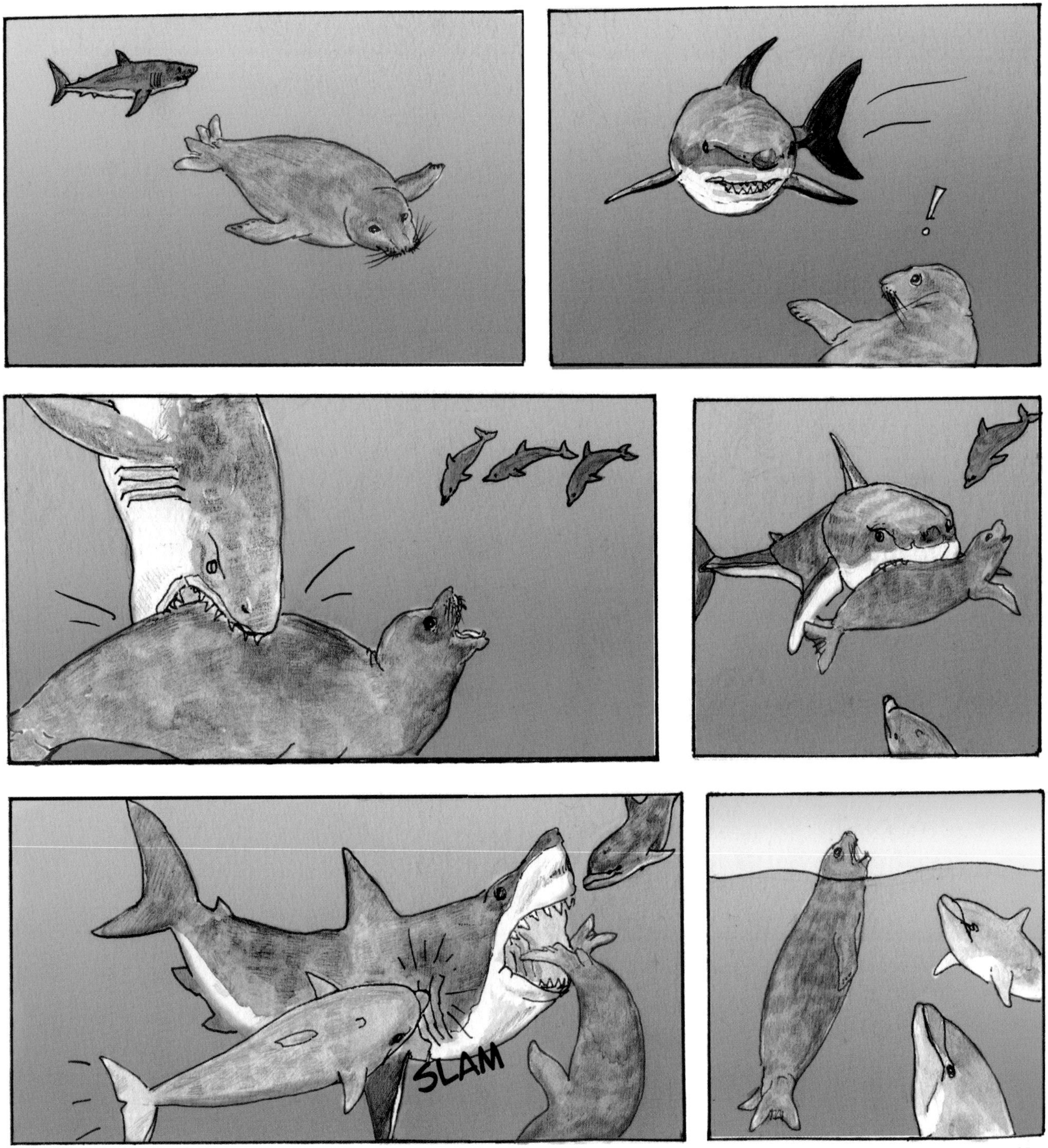
!
SLAM

SMACK!

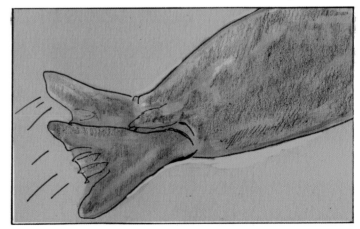

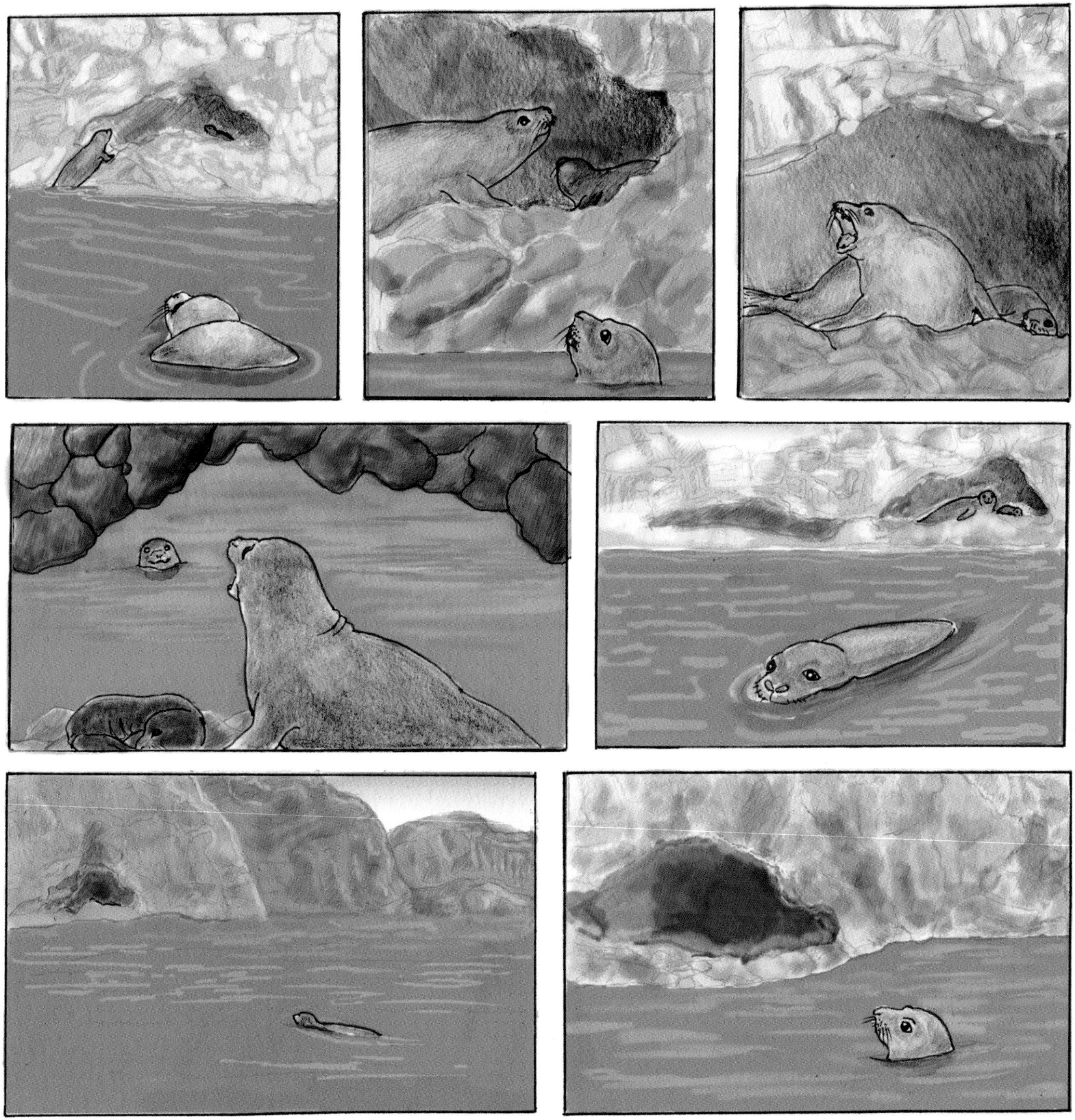

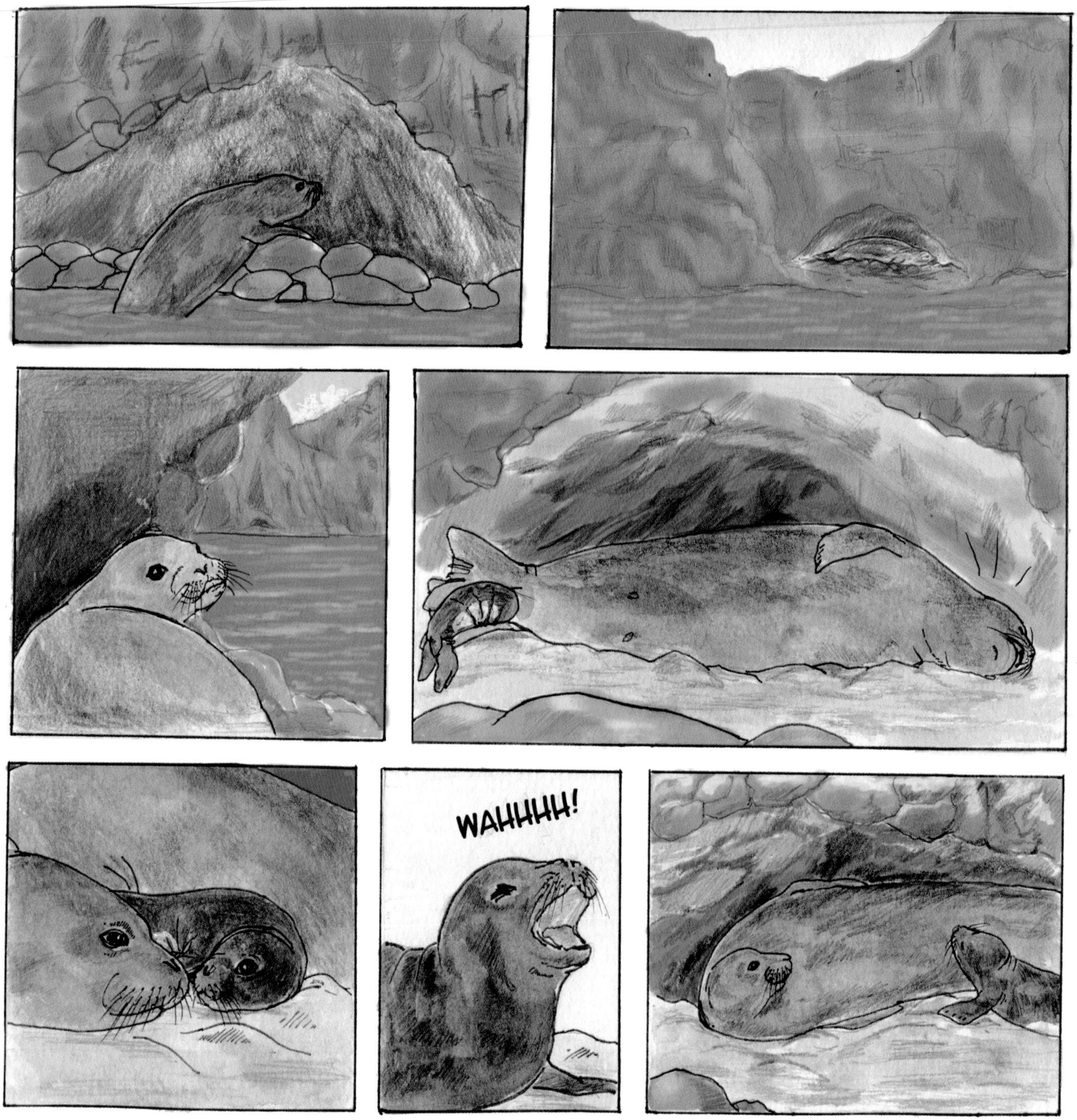
WAHHHH!

VS 2013

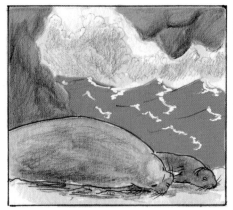

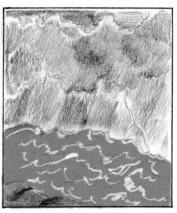

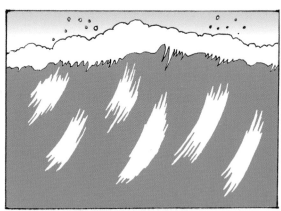

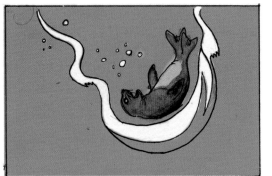

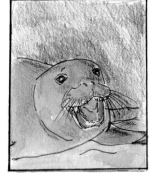

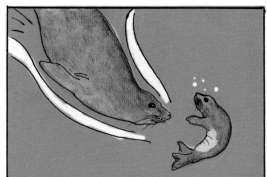

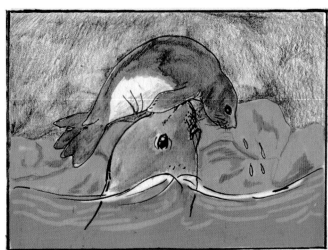

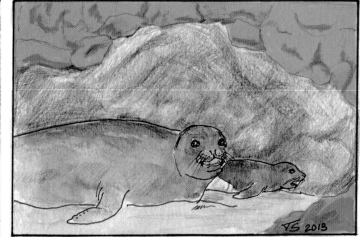

BUTANDING

Story and Art by Pierce Hargan

IN THE PHILIPPINES, the whale shark—the world's largest fish, sometimes measuring more than 40 feet (12 m) long—is called "butanding." It is such a central part of the country's culture and identity that it is pictured on the Philippine 100-peso bill.

A slow-moving, generally nonaggressive fish, these massive creatures, covered in yellow spots and stripes, have historically been hunted for their meat and fins. In 1998, the Philippines banned all fishing, selling, importing, and exporting of whale sharks for commercial purposes, yet they continue to be hunted—sometimes brutally—both there and in other parts of Asia.

That's the background for this story, which is about a lost fisherman's encounter with a school of whale sharks. After falling overboard, he finds himself caught in an old folktale, and face-to-face with a mysterious figure named Ophelia. A simple accident becomes a recipe for danger, mythology, and mercy.

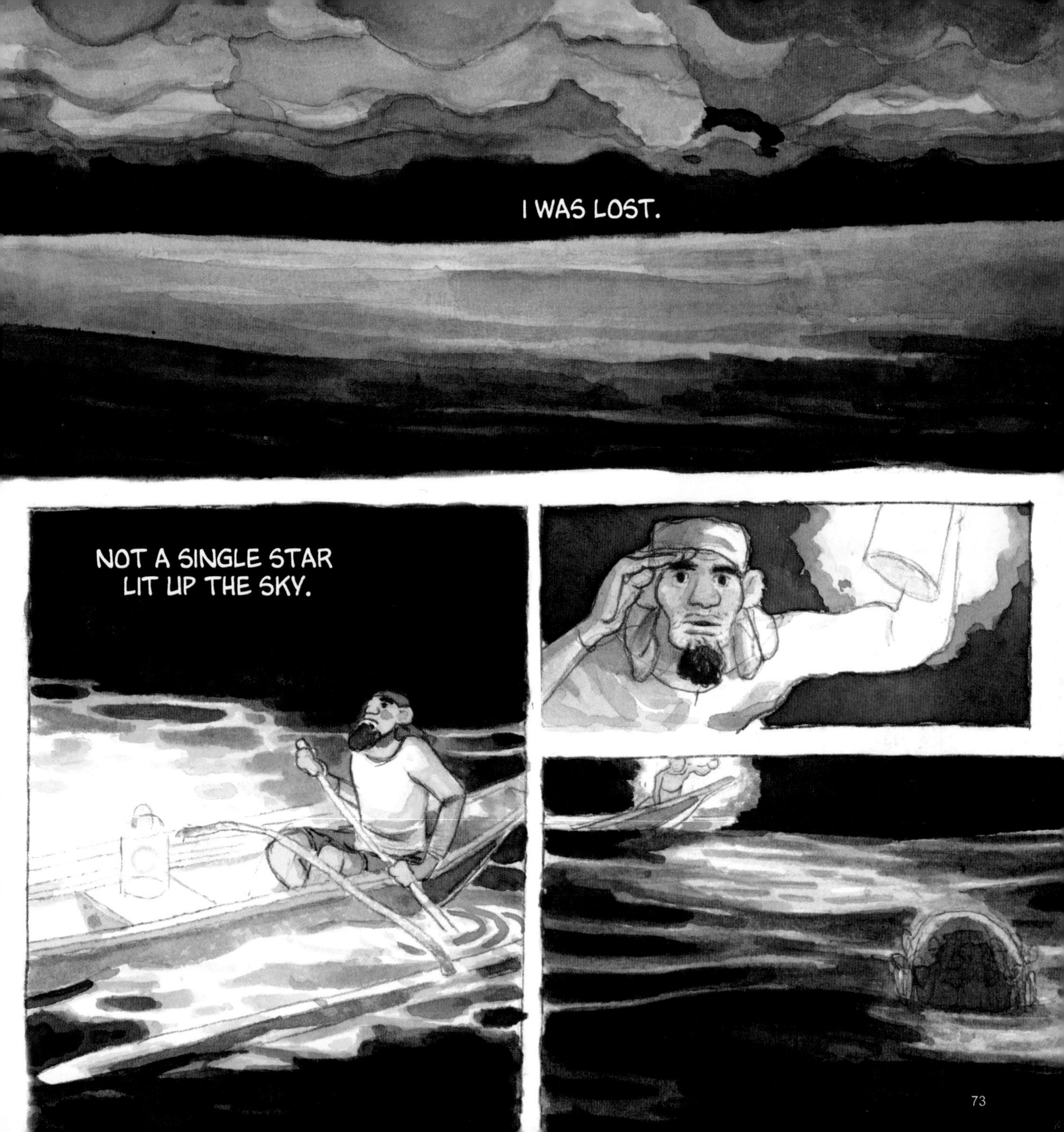
I WAS LOST.
NOT A SINGLE STAR LIT UP THE SKY.

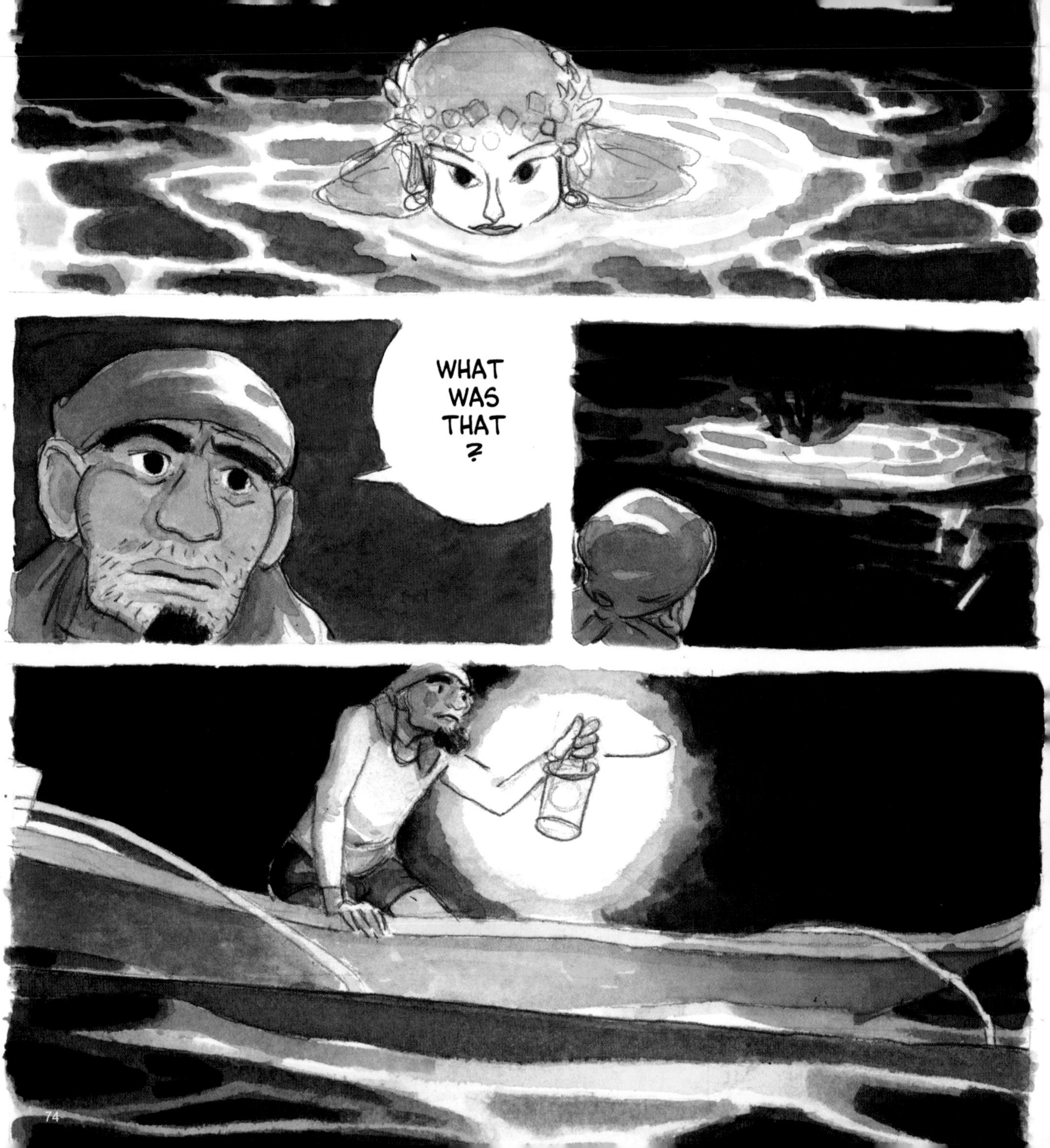
WHAT WAS THAT?

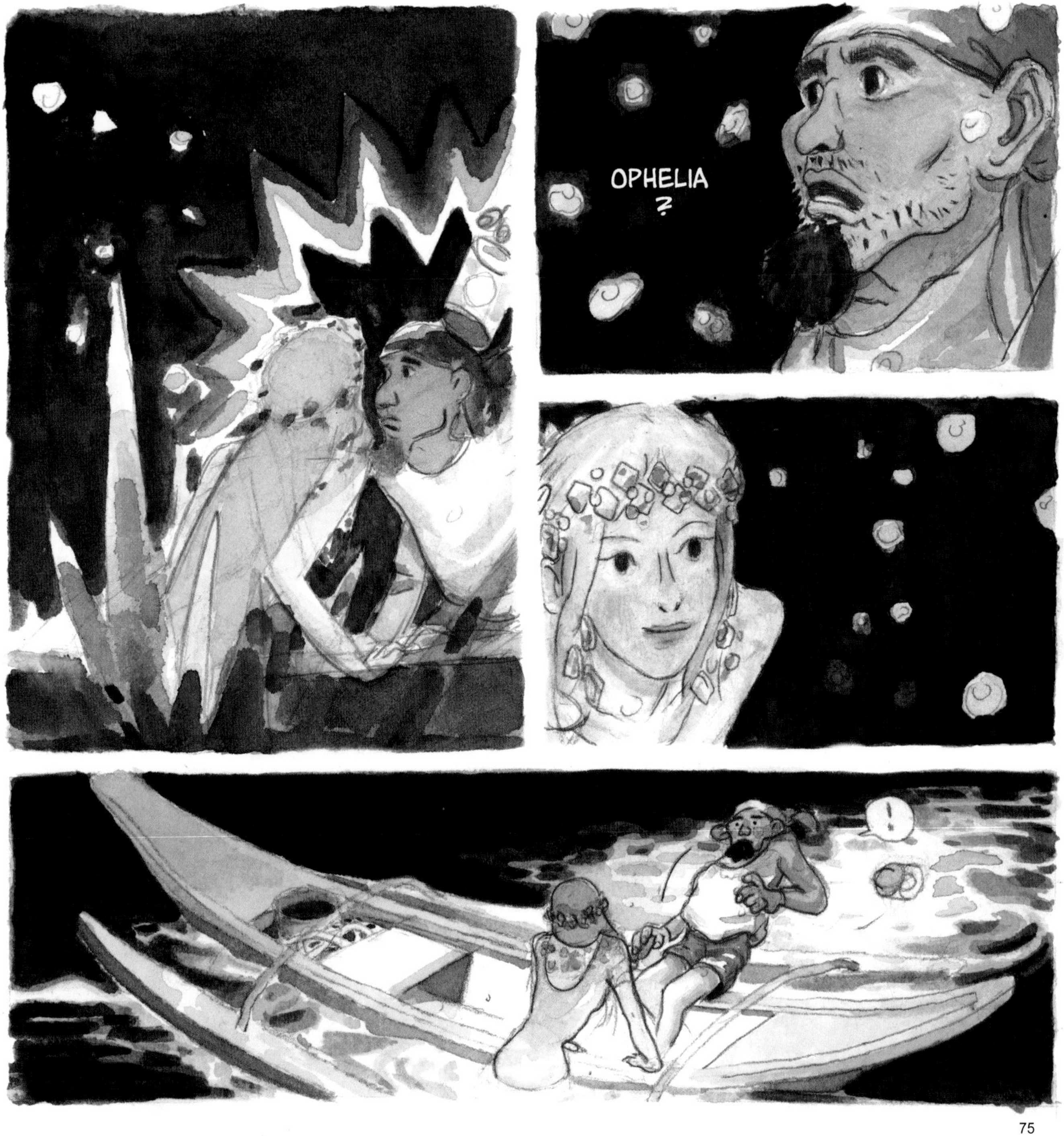
OPHELIA
?
!

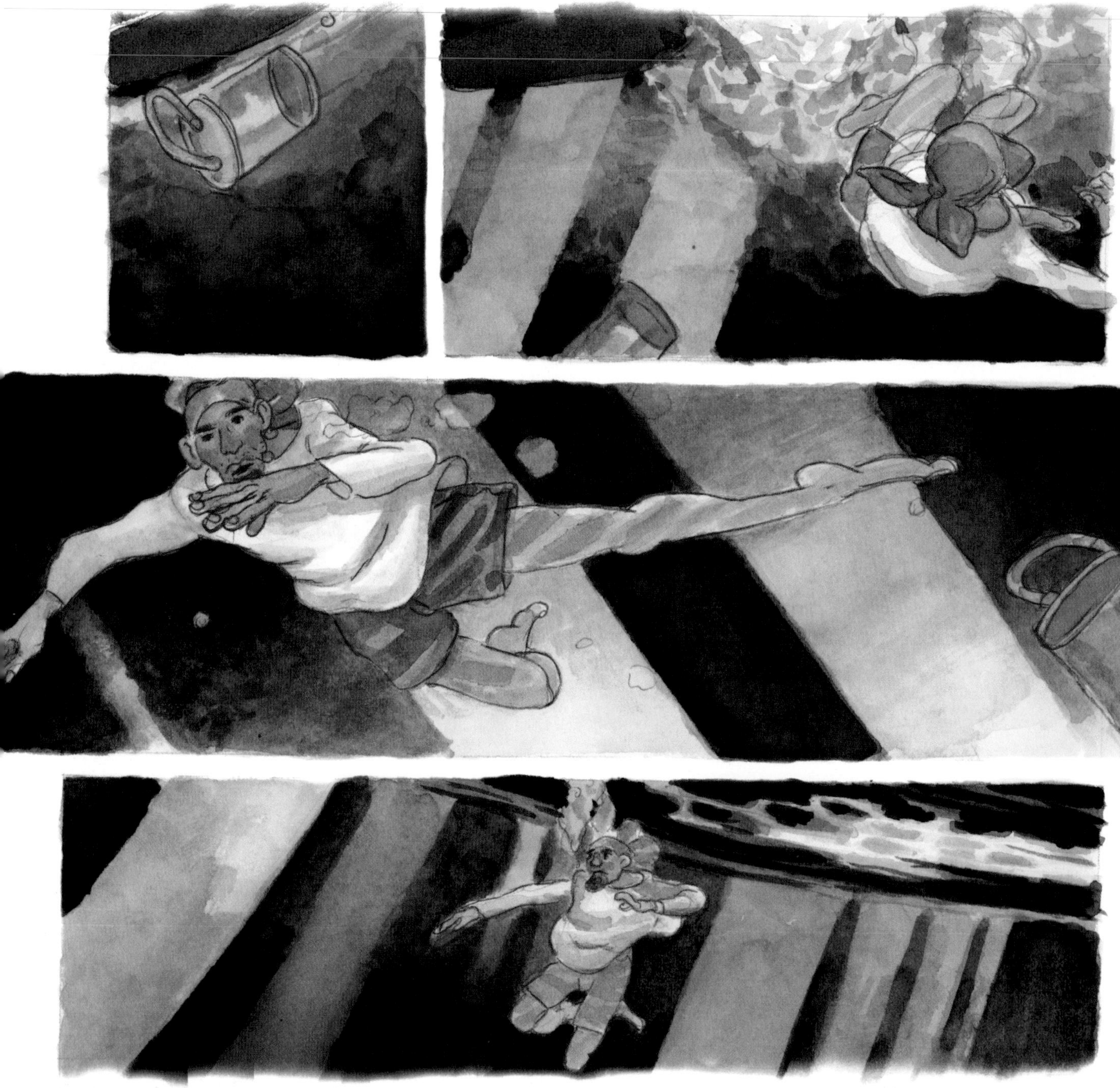

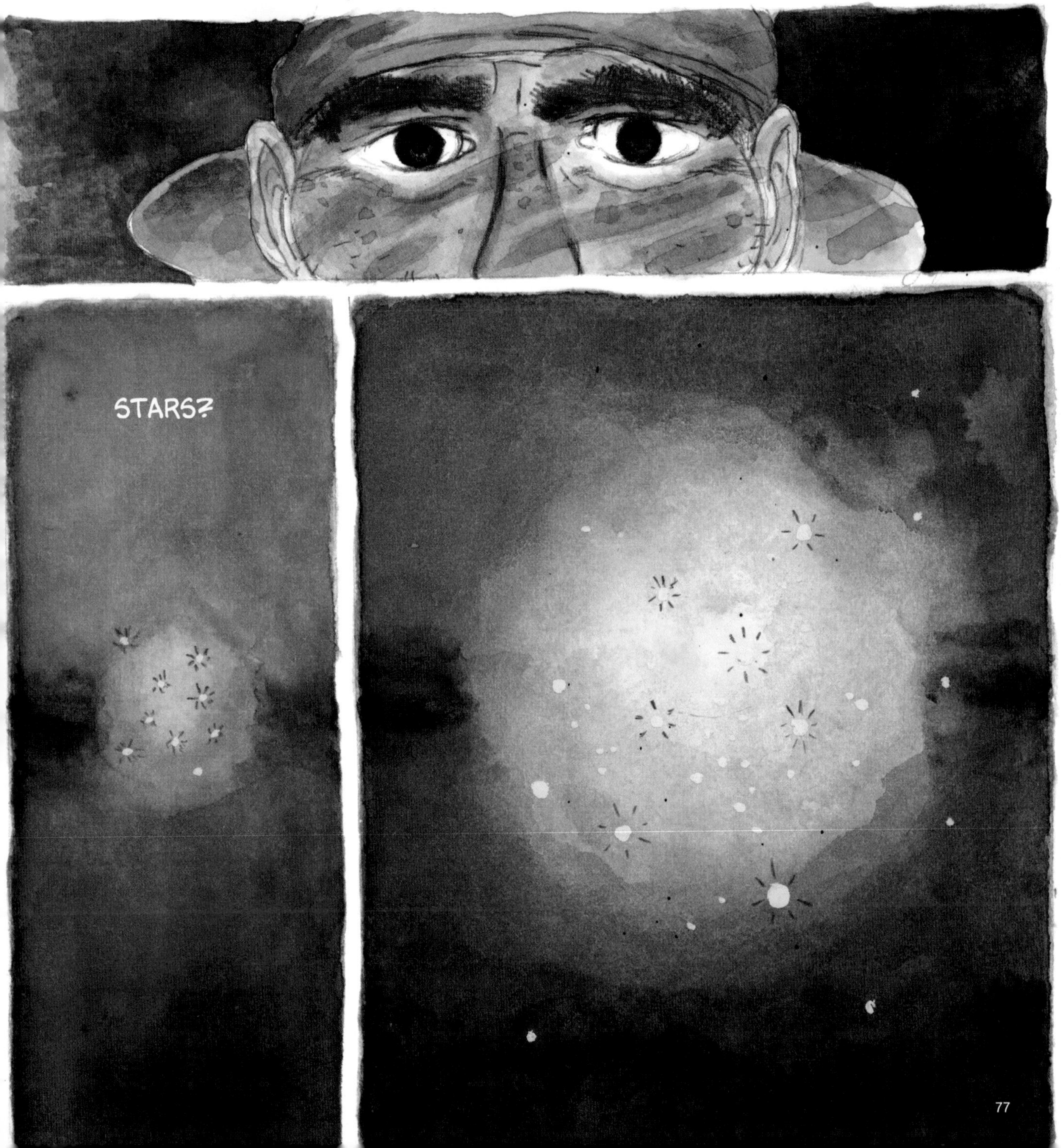
STARS?

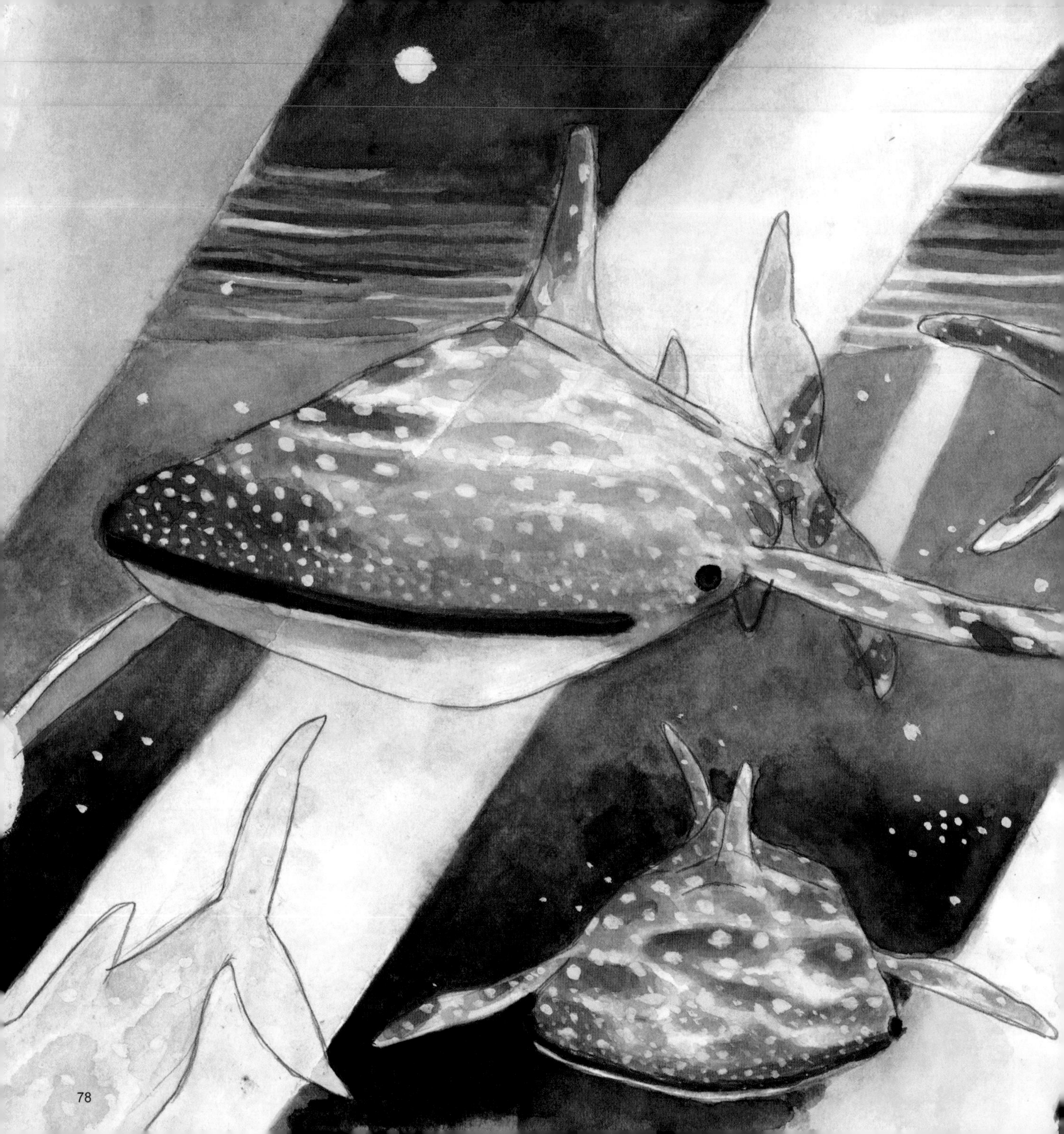

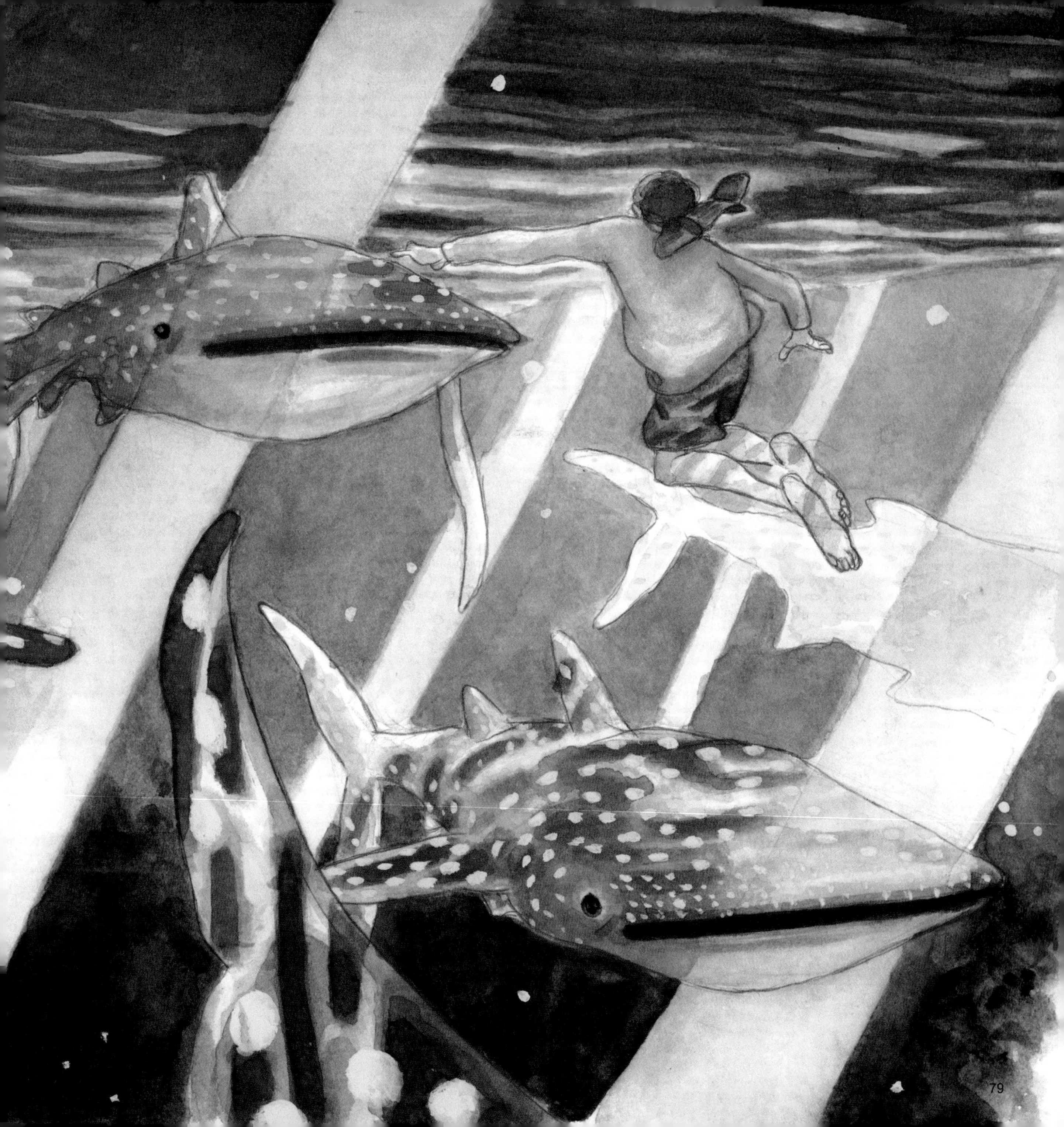

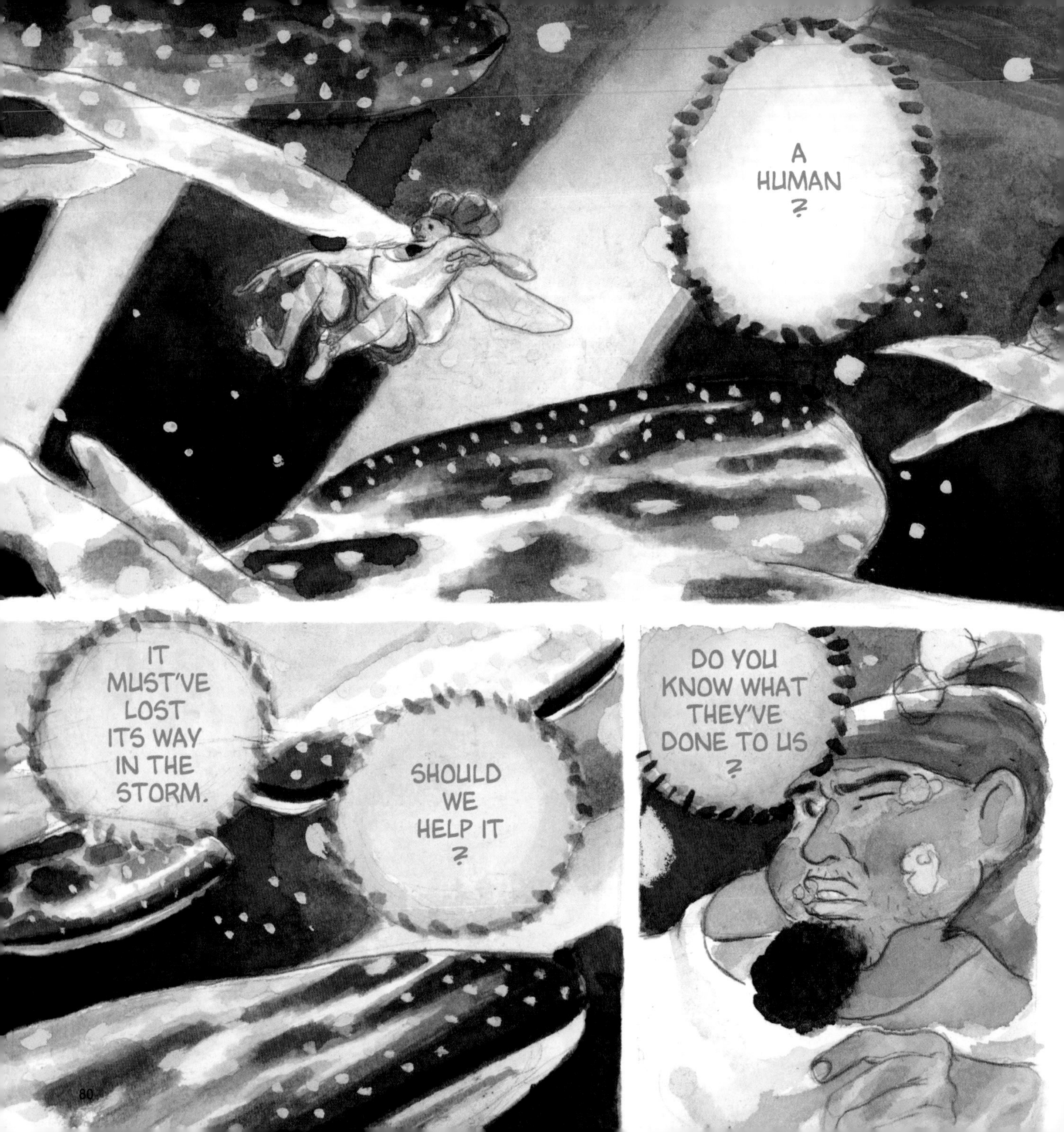
A HUMAN ?
IT MUST'VE LOST ITS WAY IN THE STORM.
SHOULD WE HELP IT ?
DO YOU KNOW WHAT THEY'VE DONE TO US ?

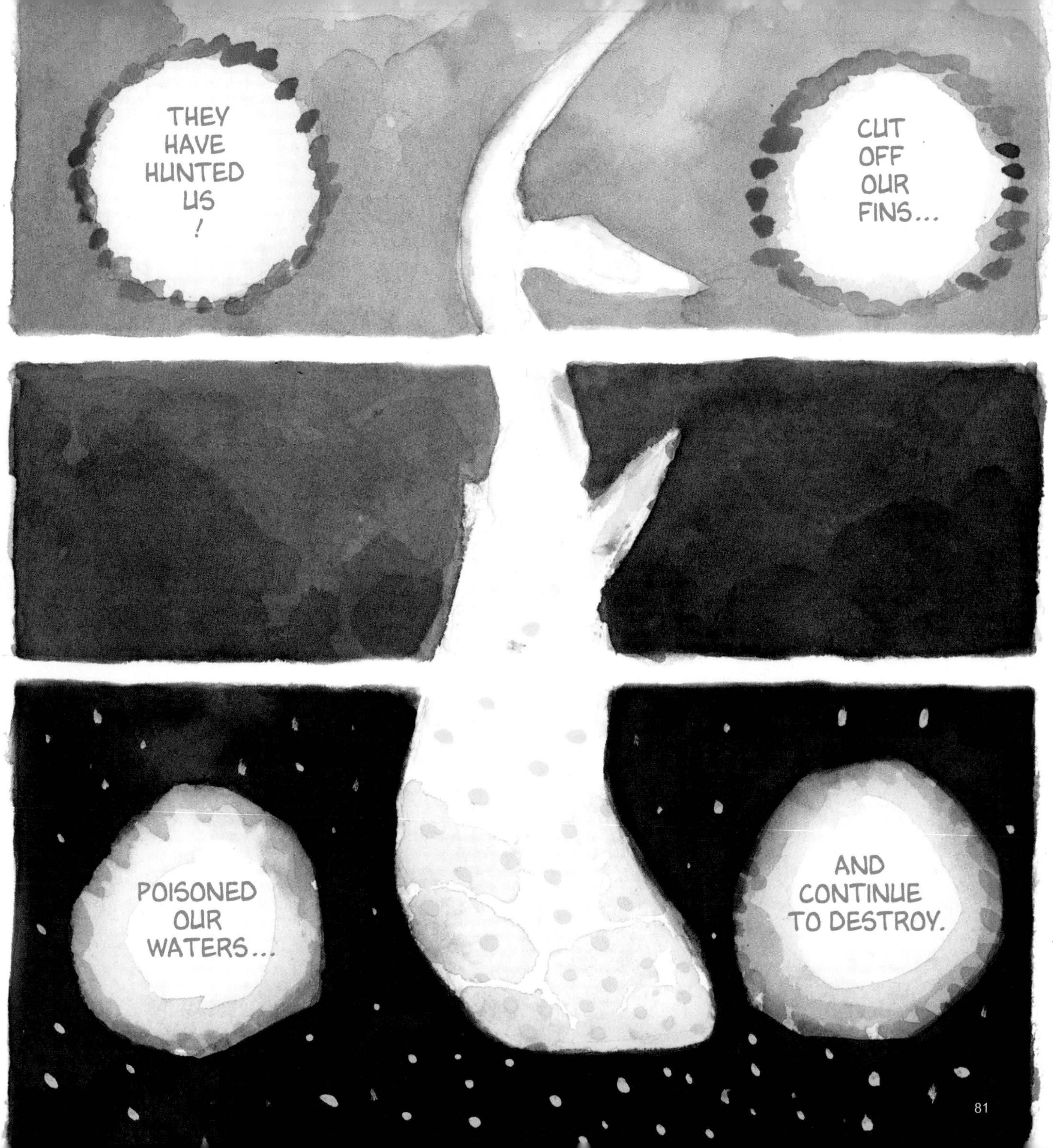
THEY HAVE HUNTED US !
CUT OFF OUR FINS...
POISONED OUR WATERS...
AND CONTINUE TO DESTROY.

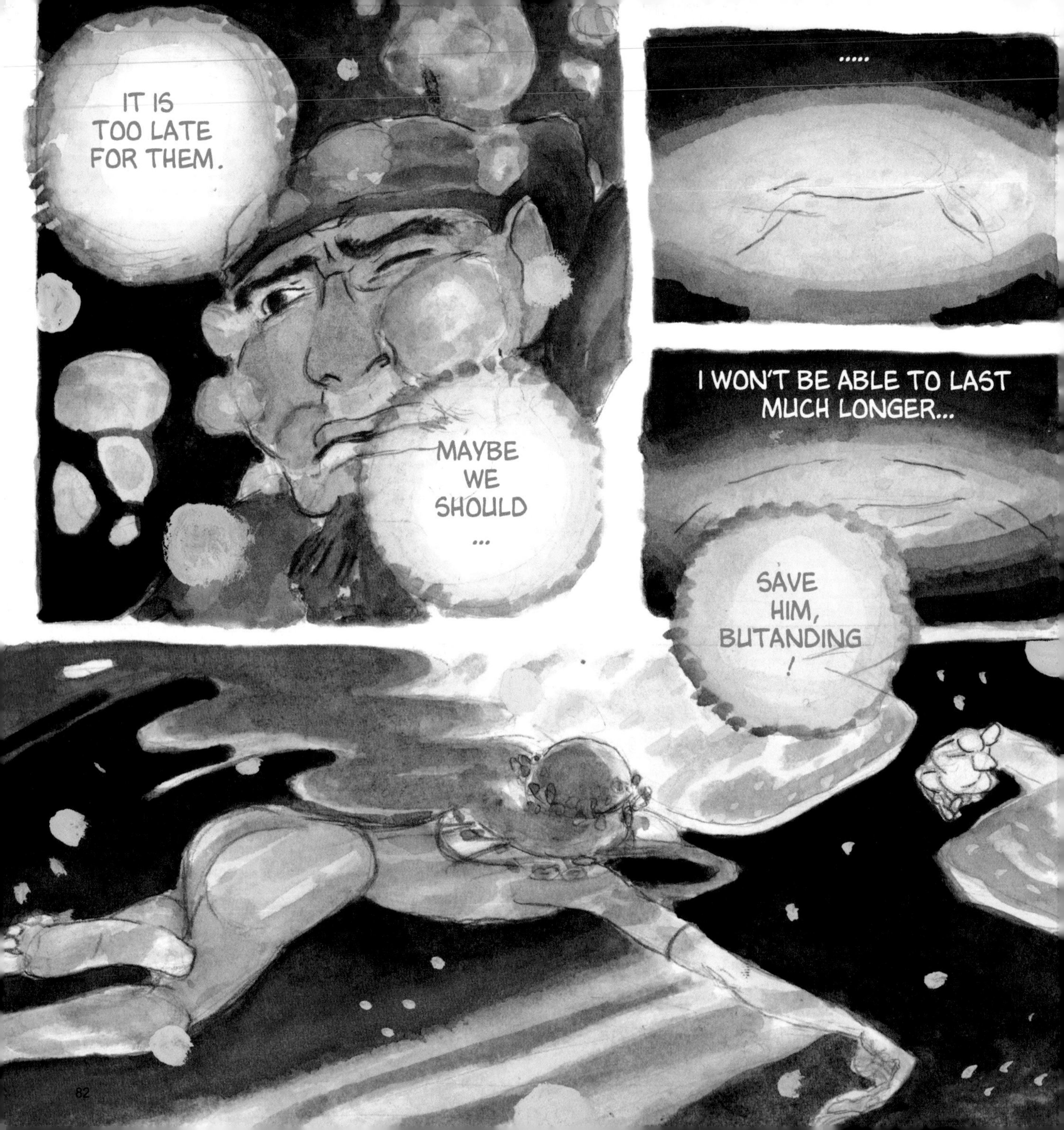
IT IS TOO LATE FOR THEM.
MAYBE WE SHOULD ...
.....
I WON'T BE ABLE TO LAST MUCH LONGER...
SAVE HIM, BUTANDING!

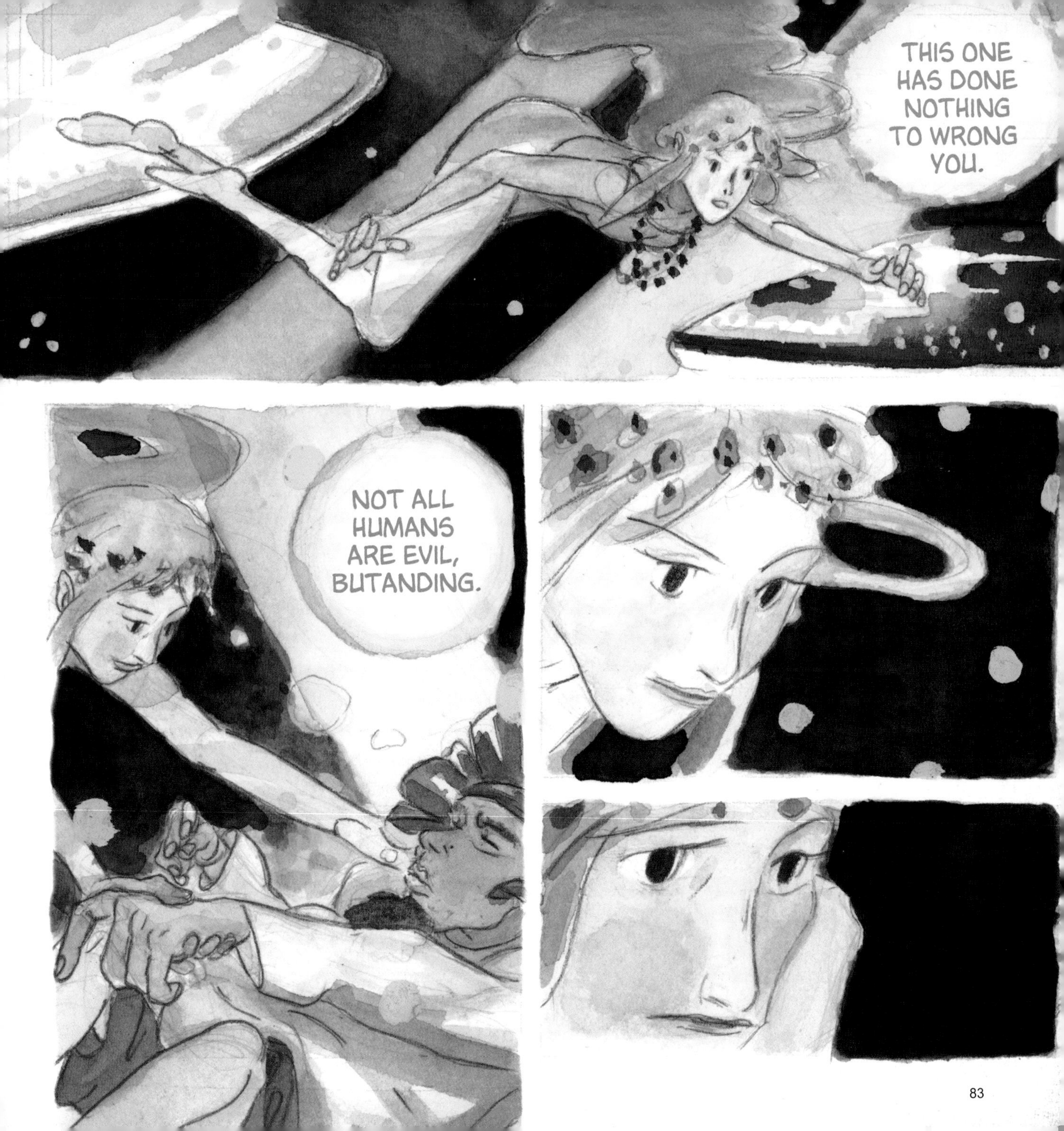
THIS ONE HAS DONE NOTHING TO WRONG YOU.
NOT ALL HUMANS ARE EVIL, BUTANDING.

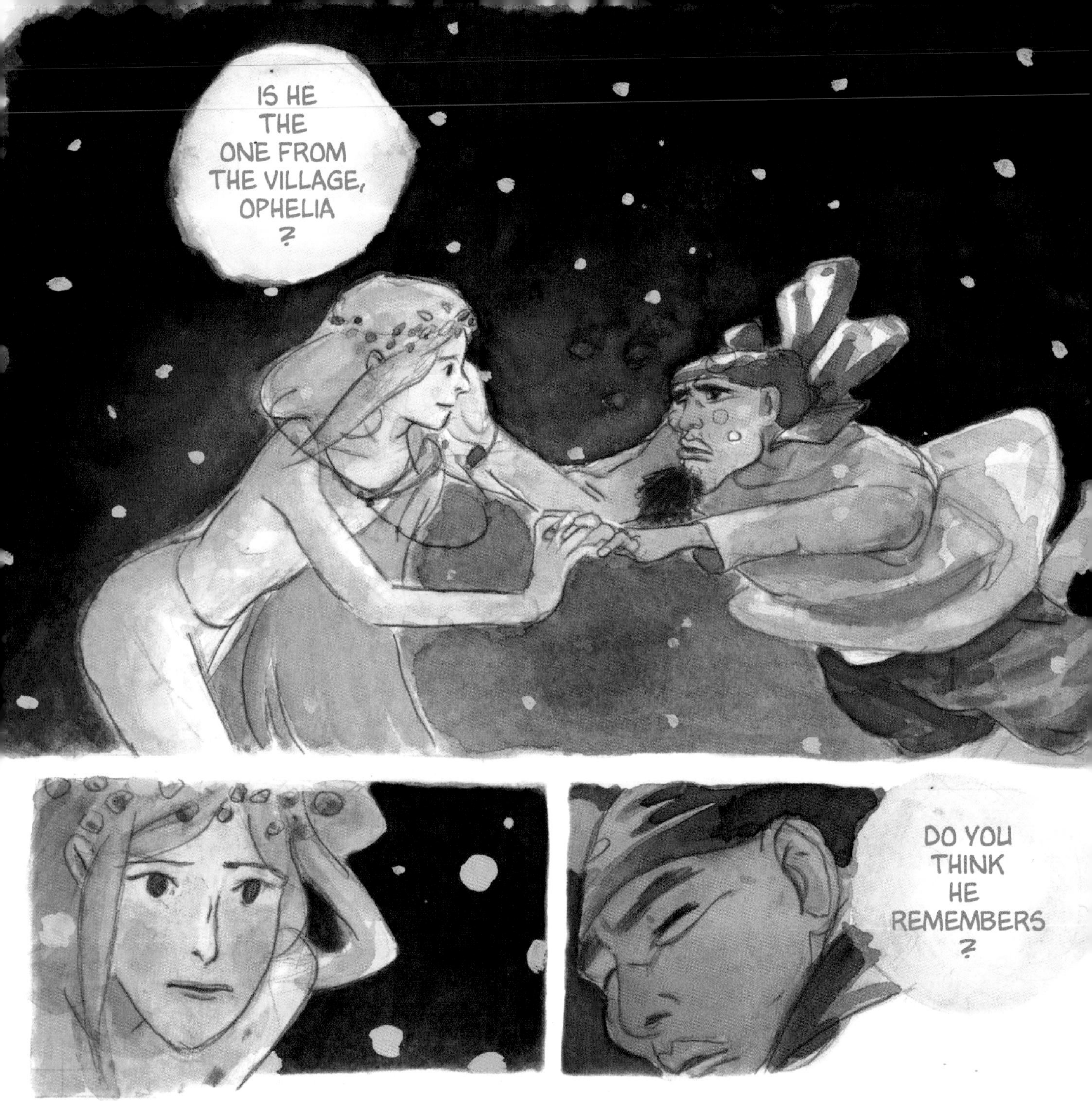
IS HE THE ONE FROM THE VILLAGE, OPHELIA ?
DO YOU THINK HE REMEMBERS ?

WE WILL
GIVE THE
HUMAN
A
CHANCE.

BUT WE
WILL NOT BE
THE ONES TO
SAVE THESE
WATERS.

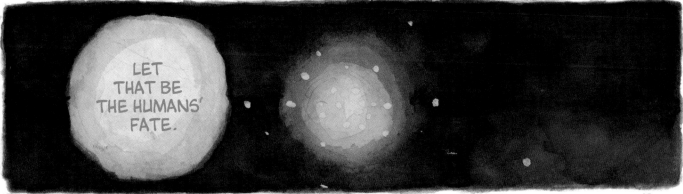

LET
THAT BE
THE HUMANS'
FATE.

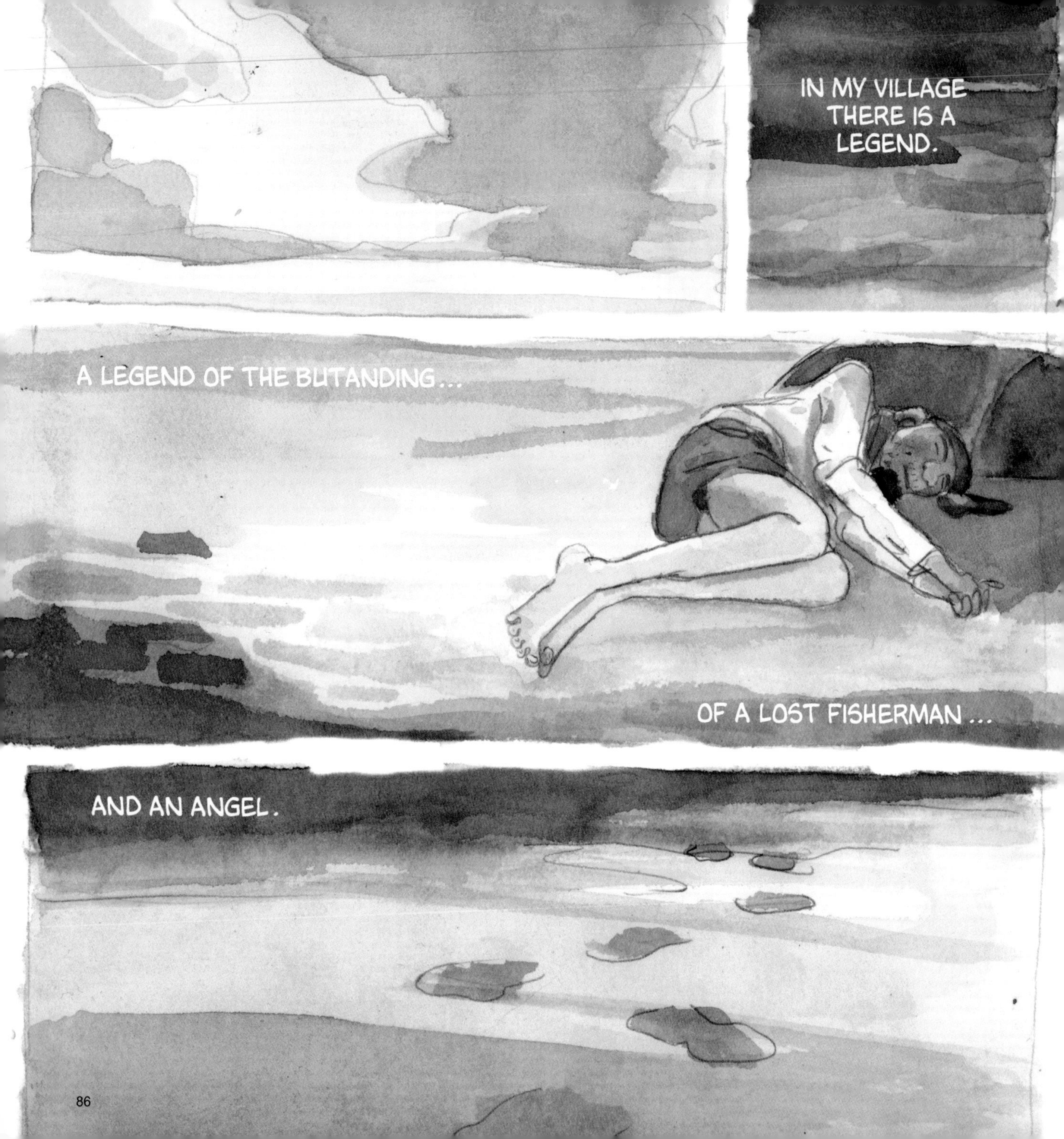
IN MY VILLAGE THERE IS A LEGEND.
A LEGEND OF THE BUTANDING...
OF A LOST FISHERMAN ...
AND AN ANGEL.

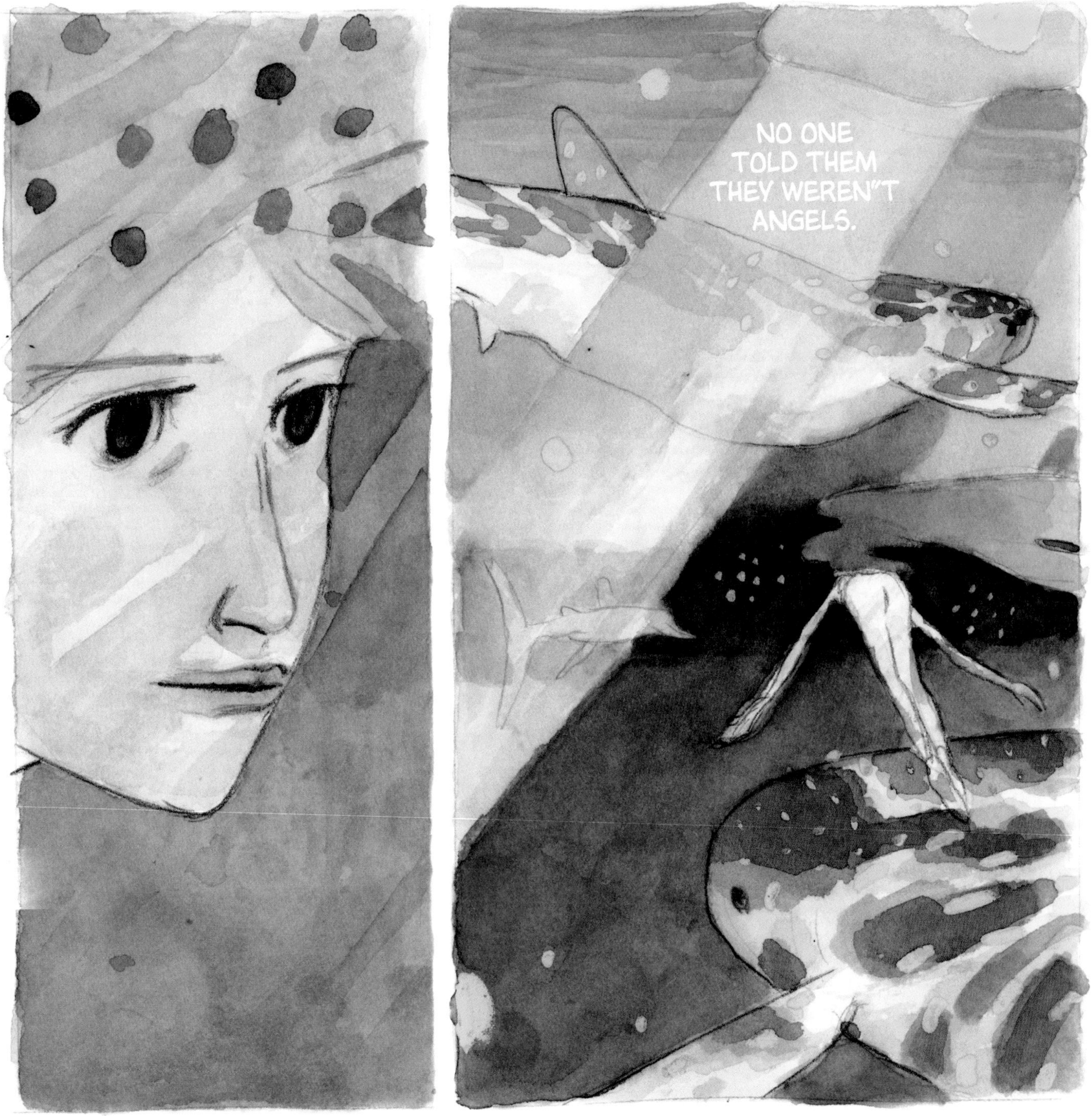
NO ONE TOLD THEM THEY WEREN"T ANGELS.

Poseidon's Steed

Story and Art by Steve Loya
Lettering by Matt Dembicki

THEY ARE SMALL AND DOCILE, but their image represents one of strength and power among ancient civilizations such as those of the Greeks and Romans. Perhaps more than any other sea animal, seahorses are revered for their unparalleled looks and their ties to mythology—after all, these were the creatures that the god of the sea, Poseidon, chose to pull his chariot.

Their unique adaptations do indeed make them seem almost magical. Seahorses change color to blend into their surroundings. They grow appendages to mix in with algae. They let organisms settle on them just to make them look like they're part of the environment. In fact, sometimes the only way you can find a seahorse is by noticing its tail anchored to a sea plant.

Perhaps most remarkably, it is the female that deposits eggs into the male's pouch, where he carries them—both before and after they hatch.

In addition to their long tradition as symbols of strength in Western culture, seahorses are highly valued as a powerful ingredient in non-Western medicine. It has been estimated that millions are used for this purpose every year—and this doesn't include those sold throughout the world as "souvenirs." A huge percentage of the seahorses captured and killed are pregnant males, whose offspring never have the chance to hatch and survive in the wild.

This slaughter, combined with habitat destruction and pollution, are forces that even the seahorse's "magic" can't withstand.

OUR BOWED HEADS REFLECT,
ON SPIRALS, BRITTLE BODIES,
FLOATING QUESTION MARKS.
--SIMON CLARKE

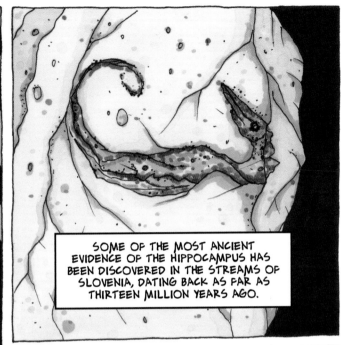

SOME OF THE MOST ANCIENT
EVIDENCE OF THE HIPPOCAMPUS HAS
BEEN DISCOVERED IN THE STREAMS OF
SLOVENIA, DATING BACK AS FAR AS
THIRTEEN MILLION YEARS AGO.

DESPITE THE
WIDESPREAD
PRESENCE AND
TRACK-RECORD
FOR SURVIVAL OF
THIS UNIQUE FISH,
IT STILL CARRIES
AN AURA OF
MYSTERY, AND A
HISTORY FILLED
WITH LEGEND AND
MYTH.

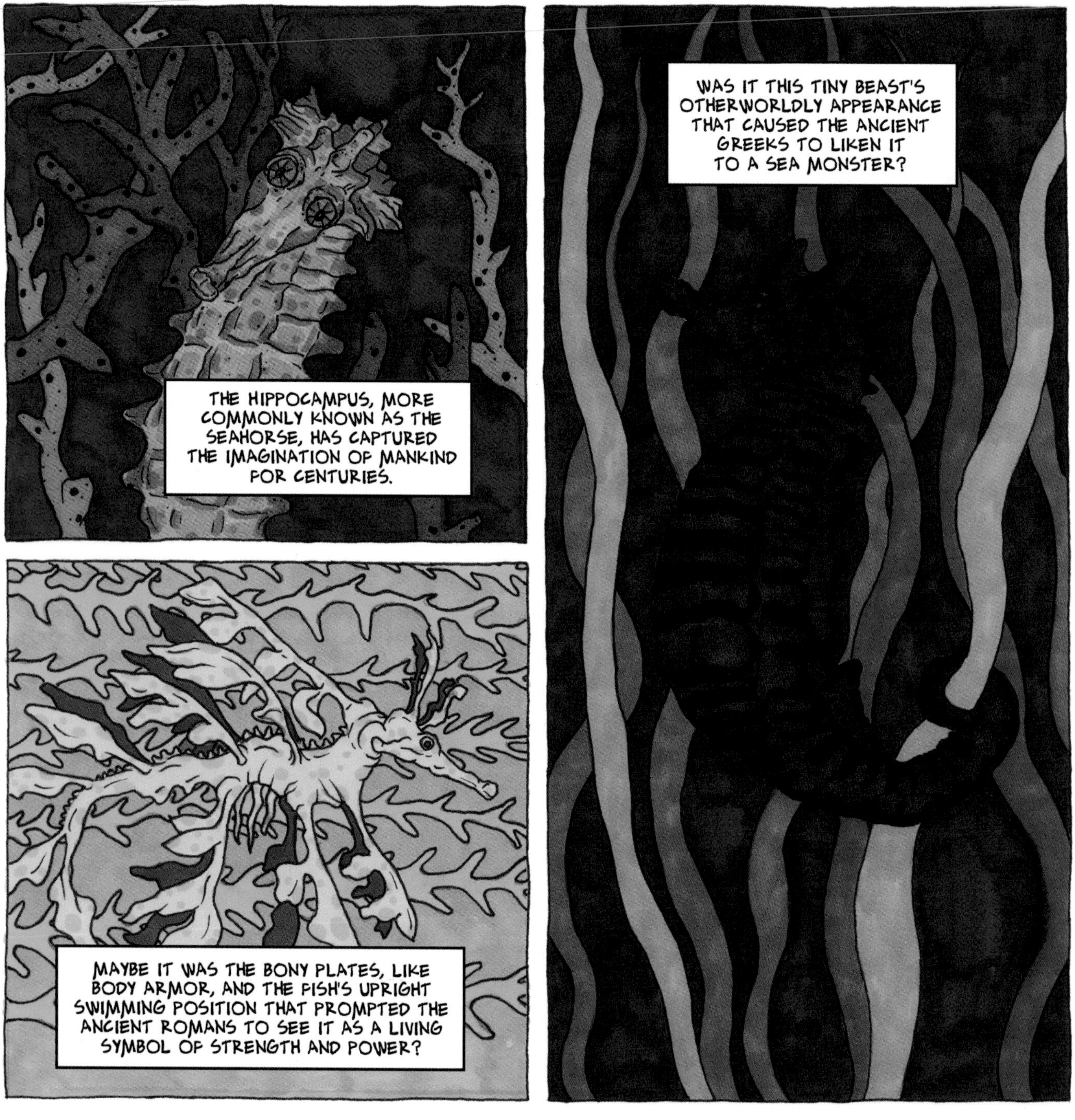
THE HIPPOCAMPUS, MORE COMMONLY KNOWN AS THE SEAHORSE, HAS CAPTURED THE IMAGINATION OF MANKIND FOR CENTURIES.
WAS IT THIS TINY BEAST'S OTHERWORLDLY APPEARANCE THAT CAUSED THE ANCIENT GREEKS TO LIKEN IT TO A SEA MONSTER?
MAYBE IT WAS THE BONY PLATES, LIKE BODY ARMOR, AND THE FISH'S UPRIGHT SWIMMING POSITION THAT PROMPTED THE ANCIENT ROMANS TO SEE IT AS A LIVING SYMBOL OF STRENGTH AND POWER?

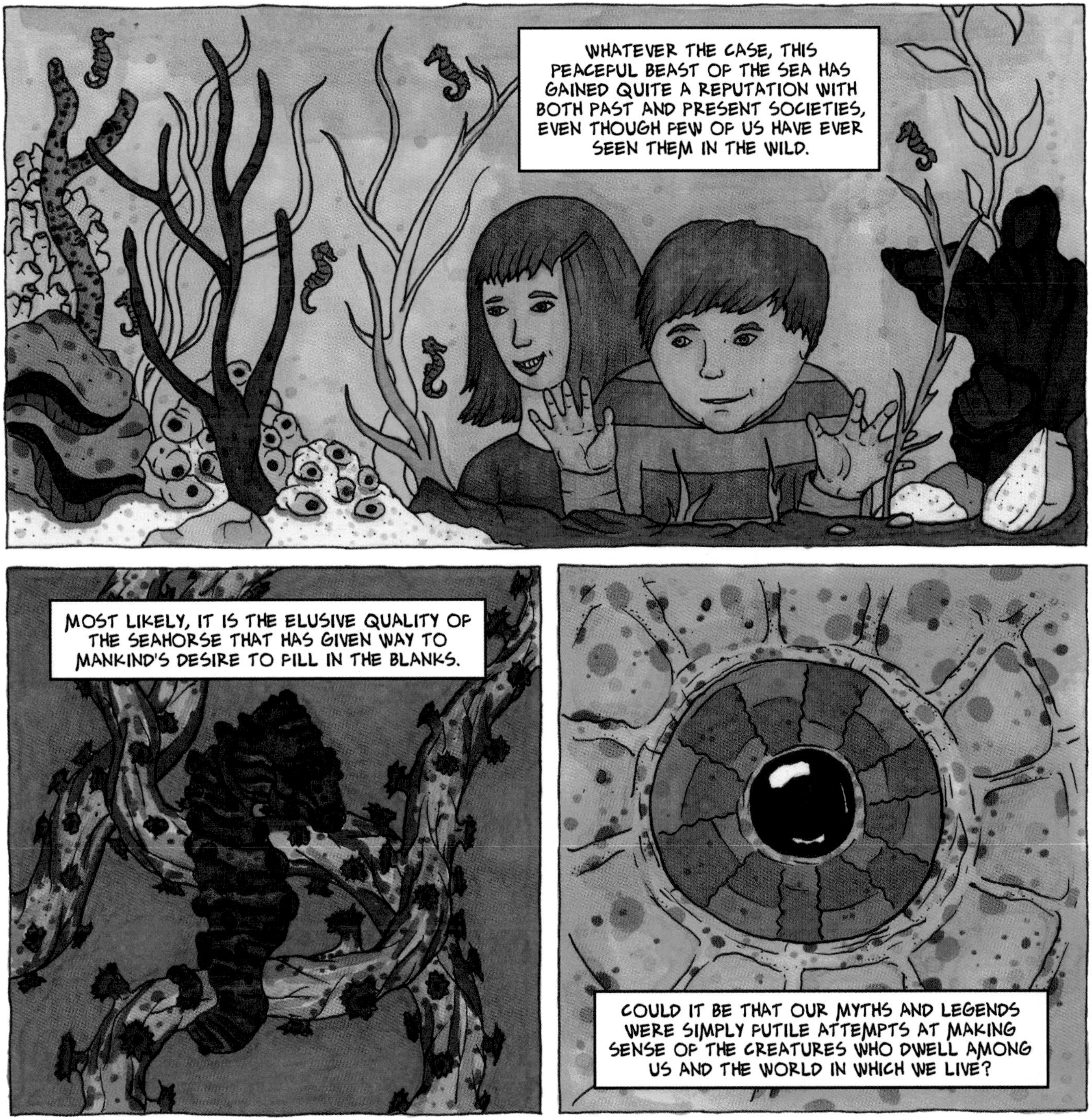
WHATEVER THE CASE, THIS PEACEFUL BEAST OF THE SEA HAS GAINED QUITE A REPUTATION WITH BOTH PAST AND PRESENT SOCIETIES, EVEN THOUGH FEW OF US HAVE EVER SEEN THEM IN THE WILD.
MOST LIKELY, IT IS THE ELUSIVE QUALITY OF THE SEAHORSE THAT HAS GIVEN WAY TO MANKIND'S DESIRE TO FILL IN THE BLANKS.
COULD IT BE THAT OUR MYTHS AND LEGENDS WERE SIMPLY FUTILE ATTEMPTS AT MAKING SENSE OF THE CREATURES WHO DWELL AMONG US AND THE WORLD IN WHICH WE LIVE?

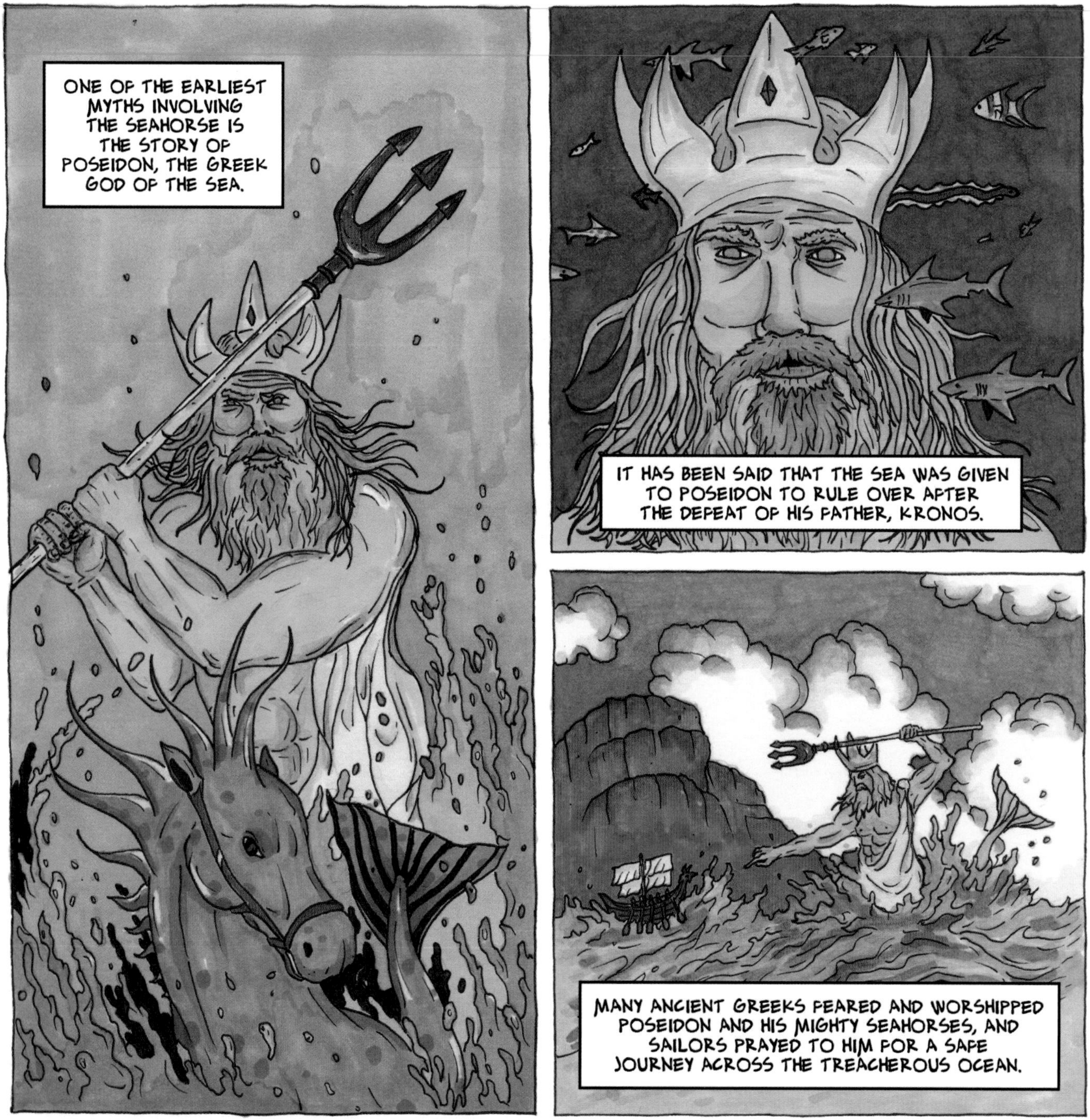
ONE OF THE EARLIEST MYTHS INVOLVING THE SEAHORSE IS THE STORY OF POSEIDON, THE GREEK GOD OF THE SEA.
IT HAS BEEN SAID THAT THE SEA WAS GIVEN TO POSEIDON TO RULE OVER AFTER THE DEFEAT OF HIS FATHER, KRONOS.
MANY ANCIENT GREEKS FEARED AND WORSHIPPED POSEIDON AND HIS MIGHTY SEAHORSES, AND SAILORS PRAYED TO HIM FOR A SAFE JOURNEY ACROSS THE TREACHEROUS OCEAN.

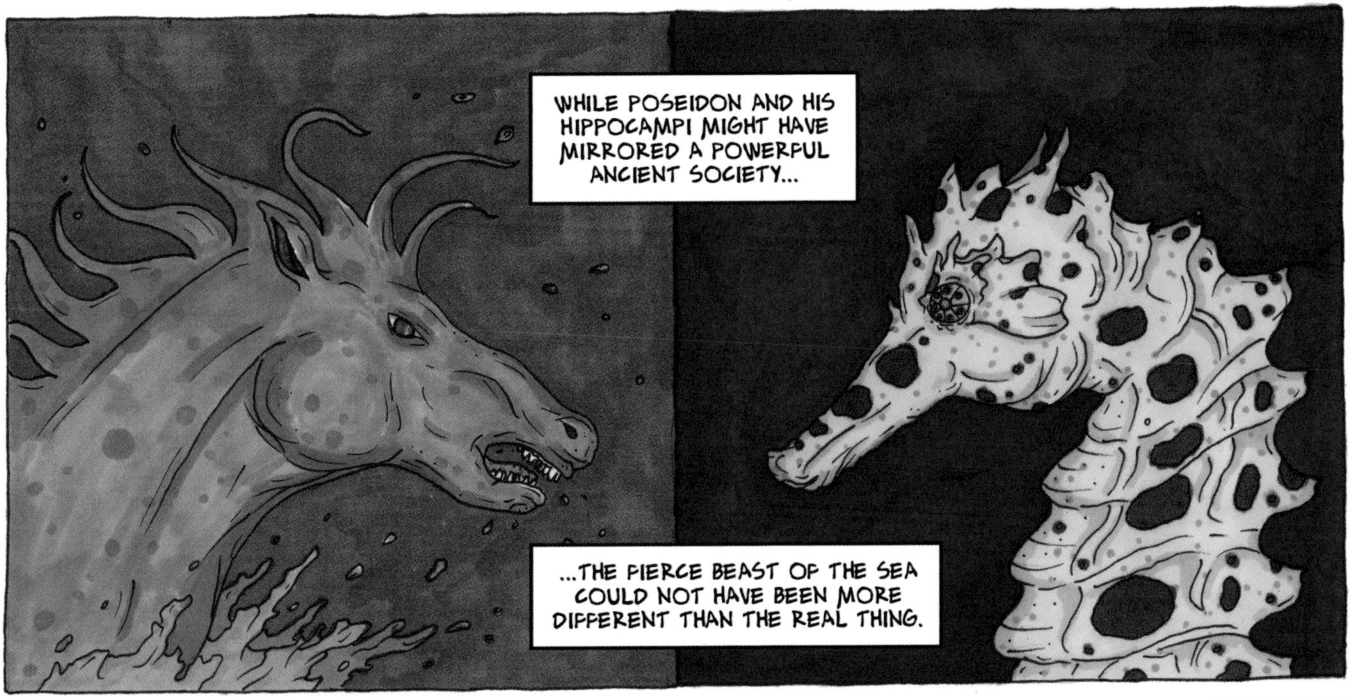
WHILE POSEIDON AND HIS HIPPOCAMPI MIGHT HAVE MIRRORED A POWERFUL ANCIENT SOCIETY...
...THE FIERCE BEAST OF THE SEA COULD NOT HAVE BEEN MORE DIFFERENT THAN THE REAL THING.

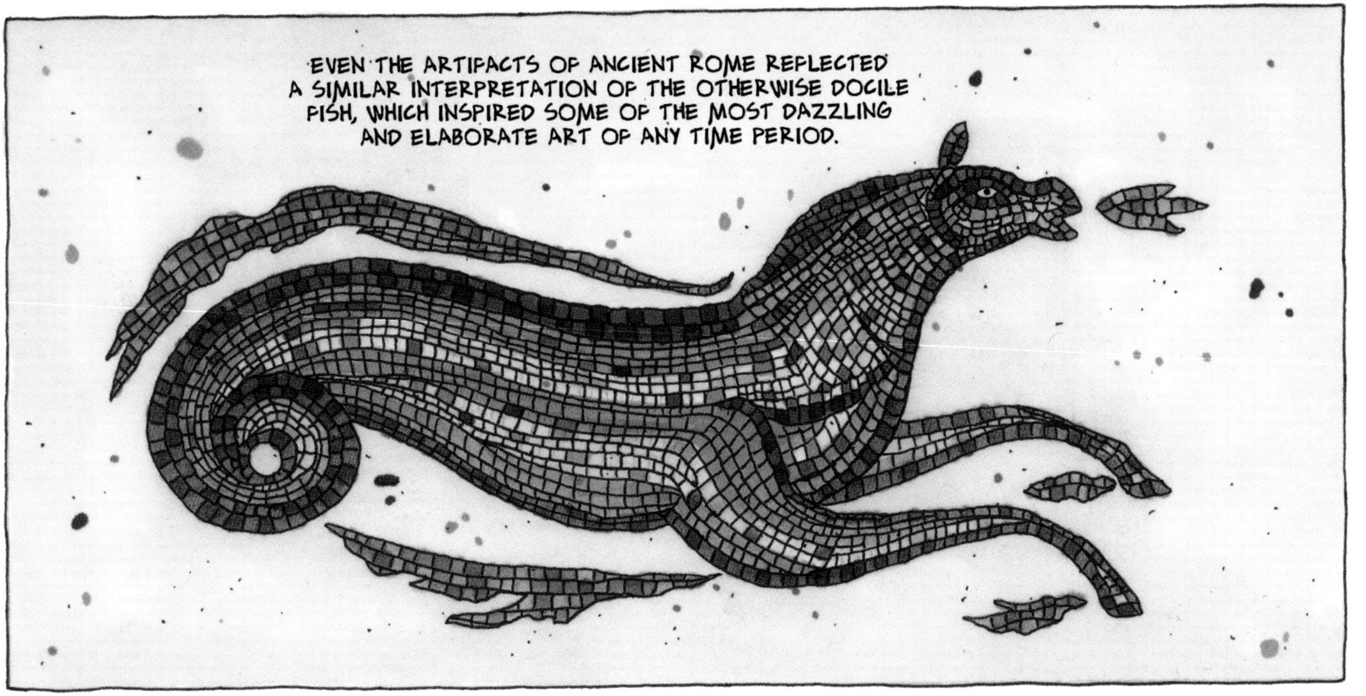
EVEN THE ARTIFACTS OF ANCIENT ROME REFLECTED A SIMILAR INTERPRETATION OF THE OTHERWISE DOCILE FISH, WHICH INSPIRED SOME OF THE MOST DAZZLING AND ELABORATE ART OF ANY TIME PERIOD.

SOMETIMES, THE CULTURE ITSELF WAS AS MYSTERIOUS AS THE ANIMALS DEPICTED IN ITS SYMBOLS.

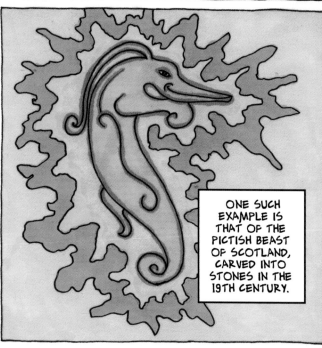

ONE SUCH EXAMPLE IS THAT OF THE PICTISH BEAST OF SCOTLAND, CARVED INTO STONES IN THE 19TH CENTURY.

THE MEANING OF THIS CURIOUS SYMBOL IS UNCERTAIN, BUT SOME SAY IT RESEMBLES A SEAHORSE. OTHERS THINK IT REPRESENTS THE LEGENDARY BEAST LIVING IN LOCH NESS.

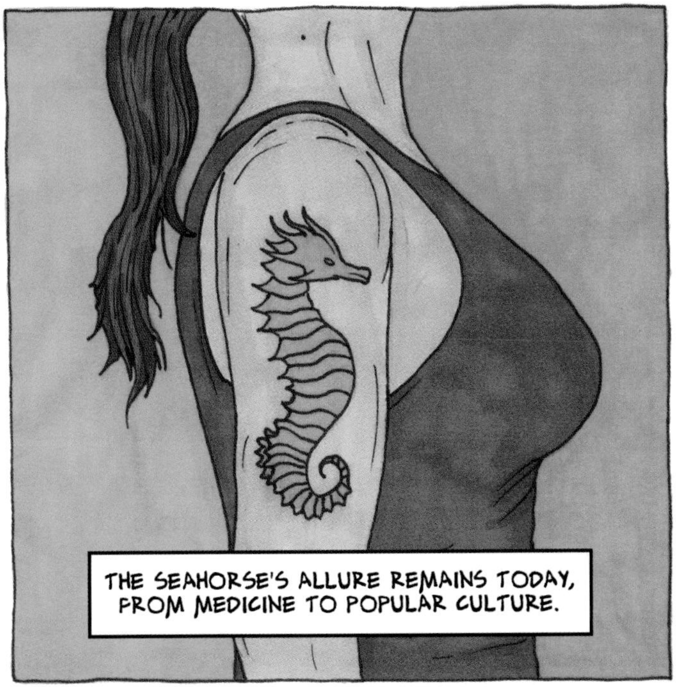
THE SEAHORSE'S ALLURE REMAINS TODAY, FROM MEDICINE TO POPULAR CULTURE.

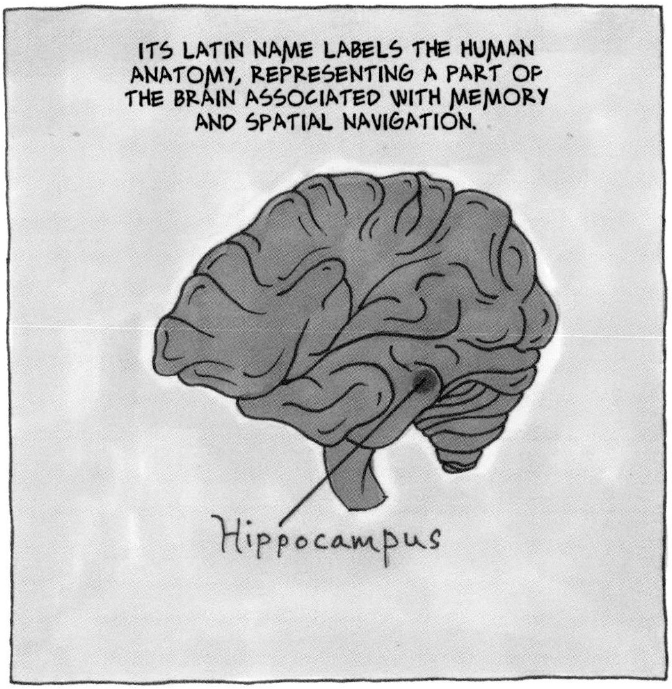
ITS LATIN NAME LABELS THE HUMAN ANATOMY, REPRESENTING A PART OF THE BRAIN ASSOCIATED WITH MEMORY AND SPATIAL NAVIGATION.
Hippocampus

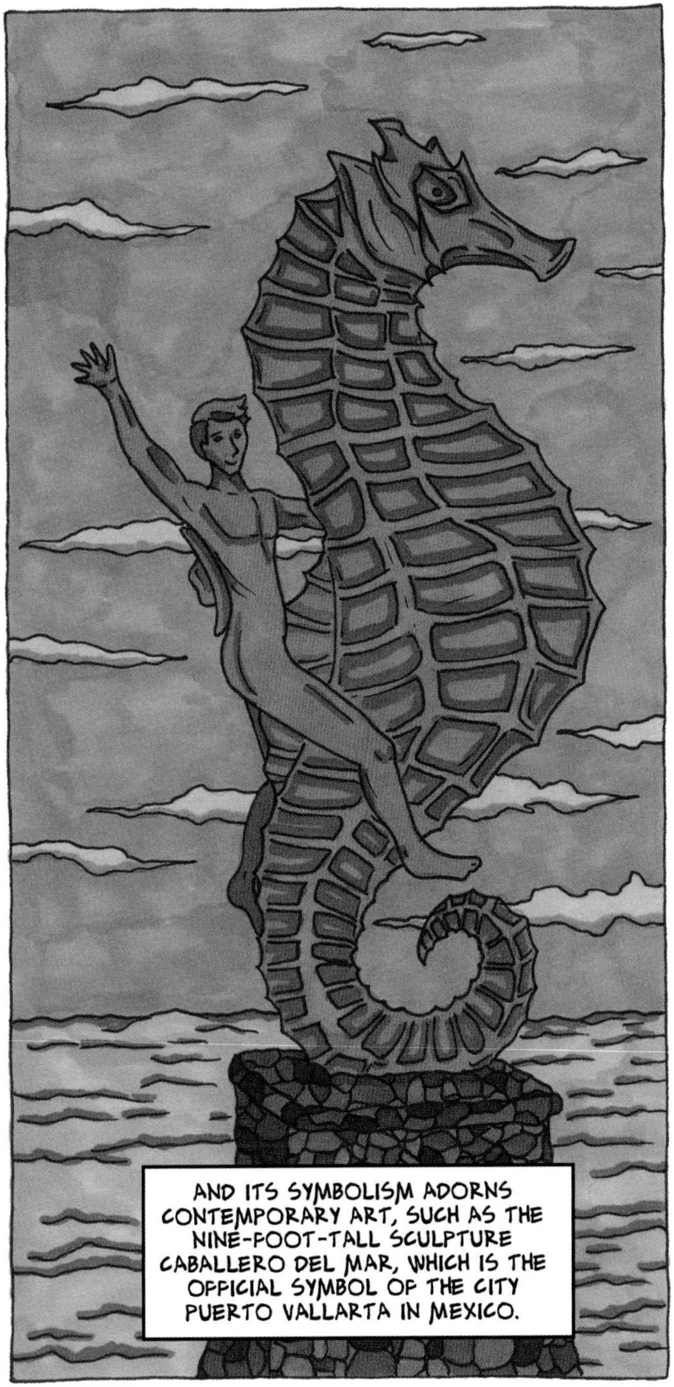
AND ITS SYMBOLISM ADORNS CONTEMPORARY ART, SUCH AS THE NINE-FOOT-TALL SCULPTURE CABALLERO DEL MAR, WHICH IS THE OFFICIAL SYMBOL OF THE CITY PUERTO VALLARTA IN MEXICO.

ONE OF THE MOST COMMON SYMBOLS ASSOCIATED WITH THE SEAHORSE IS THAT OF FERTILITY AND FATHERHOOD.

IT IS THE MALE SEAHORSE WHO GIVES BIRTH, INCUBATING THE FEMALE'S EGGS...

...ADDING YET ANOTHER DISTINCT QUALITY TO THIS UNUSUAL, ALIEN-LIKE FISH.

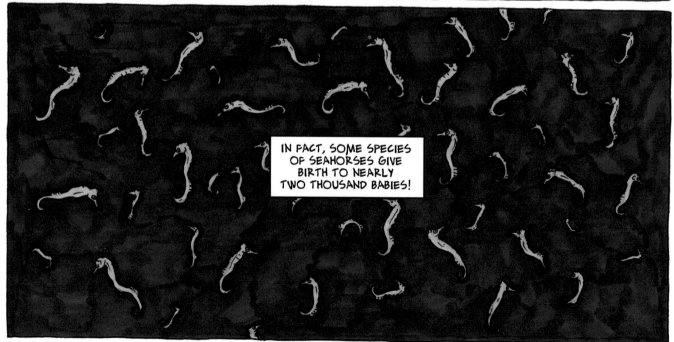

IN FACT, SOME SPECIES OF SEAHORSES GIVE BIRTH TO NEARLY TWO THOUSAND BABIES!

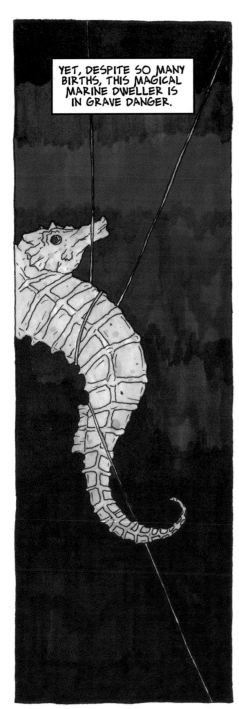

YET, DESPITE SO MANY BIRTHS, THIS MAGICAL MARINE DWELLER IS IN GRAVE DANGER.

POLLUTION, HABITAT DESTRUCTION, THE SOUVENIR TRADE, SHRIMP TRAWLS, AND USE IN TRADITIONAL CHINESE MEDICINE...

...CONTRIBUTE TO THE DEATH OF TENS OF MILLIONS OF SEA-HORSES EACH YEAR.

IT IS THE PERCEIVED MAGICAL QUALITY THAT SEAHORSES POSSESS THAT CAN SERVE AS THEIR OWN WORST ENEMY.

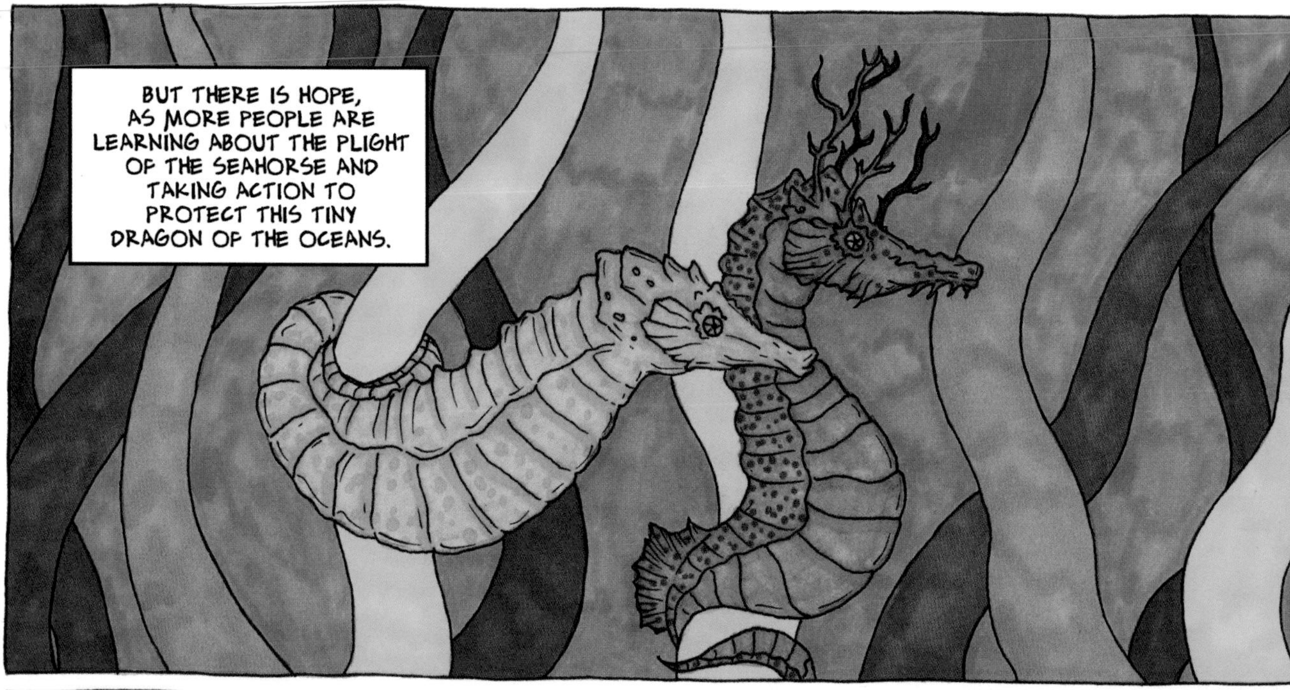
BUT THERE IS HOPE, AS MORE PEOPLE ARE LEARNING ABOUT THE PLIGHT OF THE SEAHORSE AND TAKING ACTION TO PROTECT THIS TINY DRAGON OF THE OCEANS.

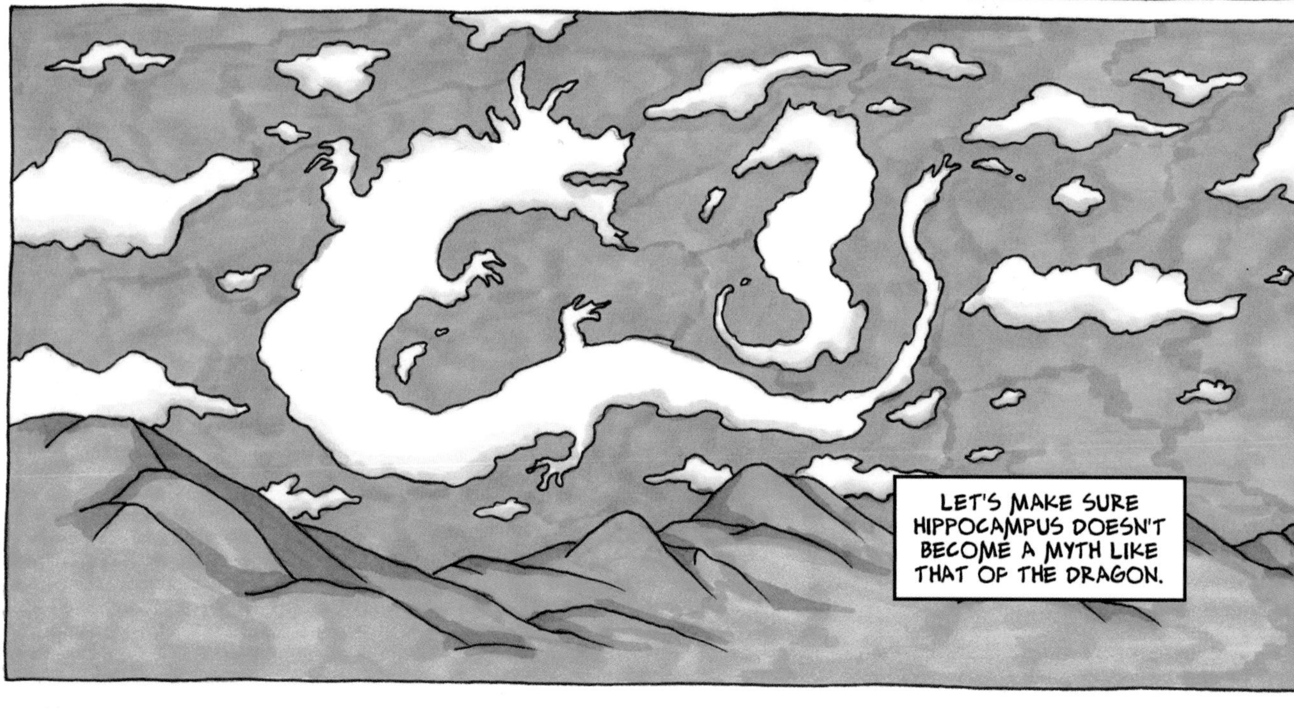
LET'S MAKE SURE HIPPOCAMPUS DOESN'T BECOME A MYTH LIKE THAT OF THE DRAGON.

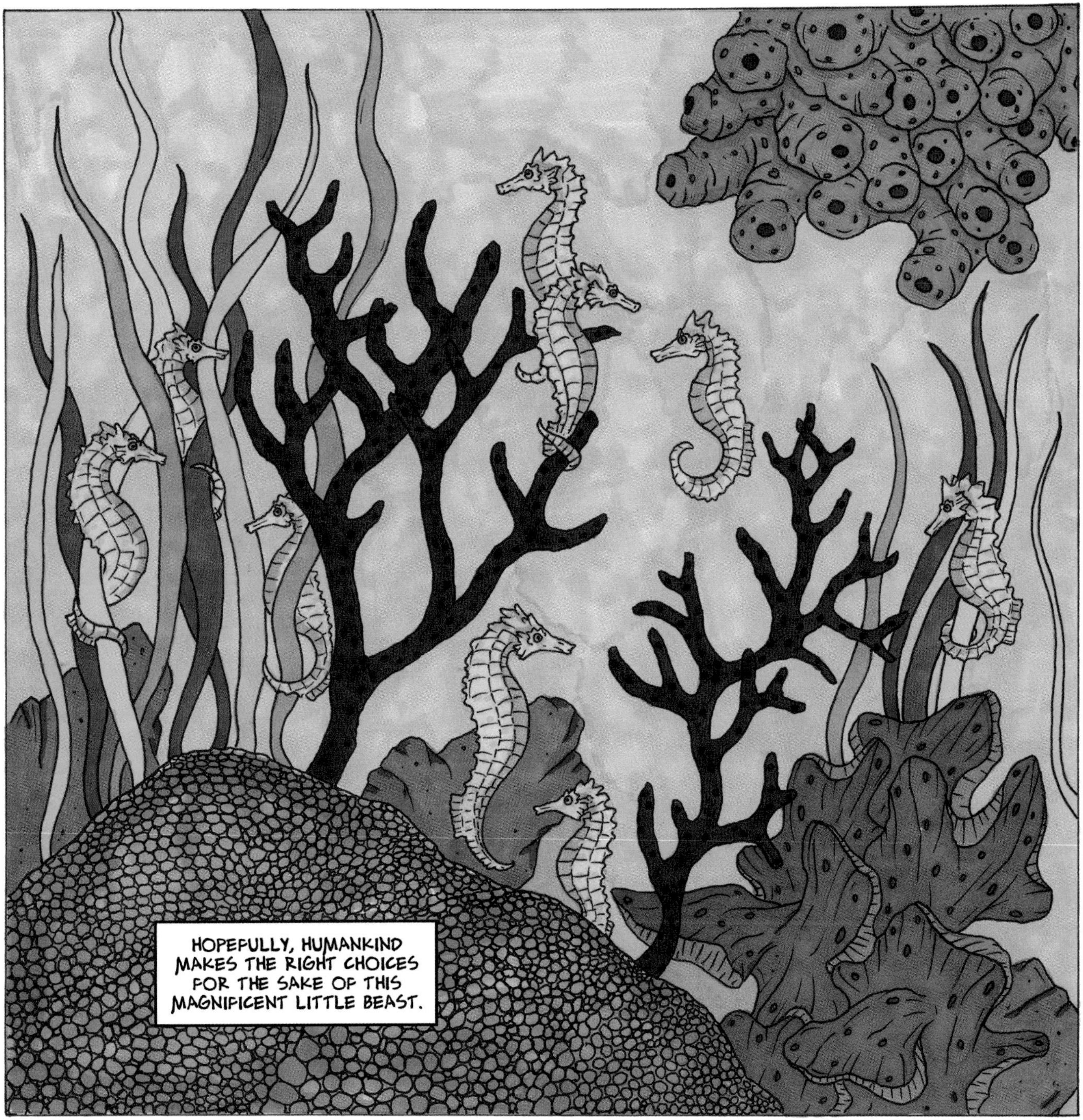
HOPEFULLY, HUMANKIND MAKES THE RIGHT CHOICES FOR THE SAKE OF THIS MAGNIFICENT LITTLE BEAST.

Raw Power

Story and Art by JF Frankel

CONSIDER THE UNIQUE POSITION of the bluefin tuna. A voracious predator patrolling atop the food chain. A coursing torpedo of finely tuned muscle. A marvel of submarine elegance. A wild animal relentlessly pursued at great expense by human hunters. A delicacy in bite-size chunks dipped in soy sauce and wasabi paste.

Consider the recent history of human-bluefin relations. Fifty years ago, this fish was undesirable. The Japanese had no taste for it. Sport fishermen valued the fight but discarded the carcass or sold it for cat food. They disparaged it with the unappetizing term "horse mackerel." But then a rapid confluence of technological advances in refrigeration, shipping, and fishing; cultural acceptance of red meat; and entrepreneurial spirit transformed the bluefin into an irresistible fortune beneath the waves. Before long, the fish became worth thousands—even millions—of dollars to fishermen, and the hunt was really on. Because of their dizzying value, fishermen have hunted them relentlessly, with a disastrous result: the fish are disappearing, and fast. With the loss of the bluefin, an entire ocean ecosystem could be toppled.

Consider the raw power of the bluefin tuna.

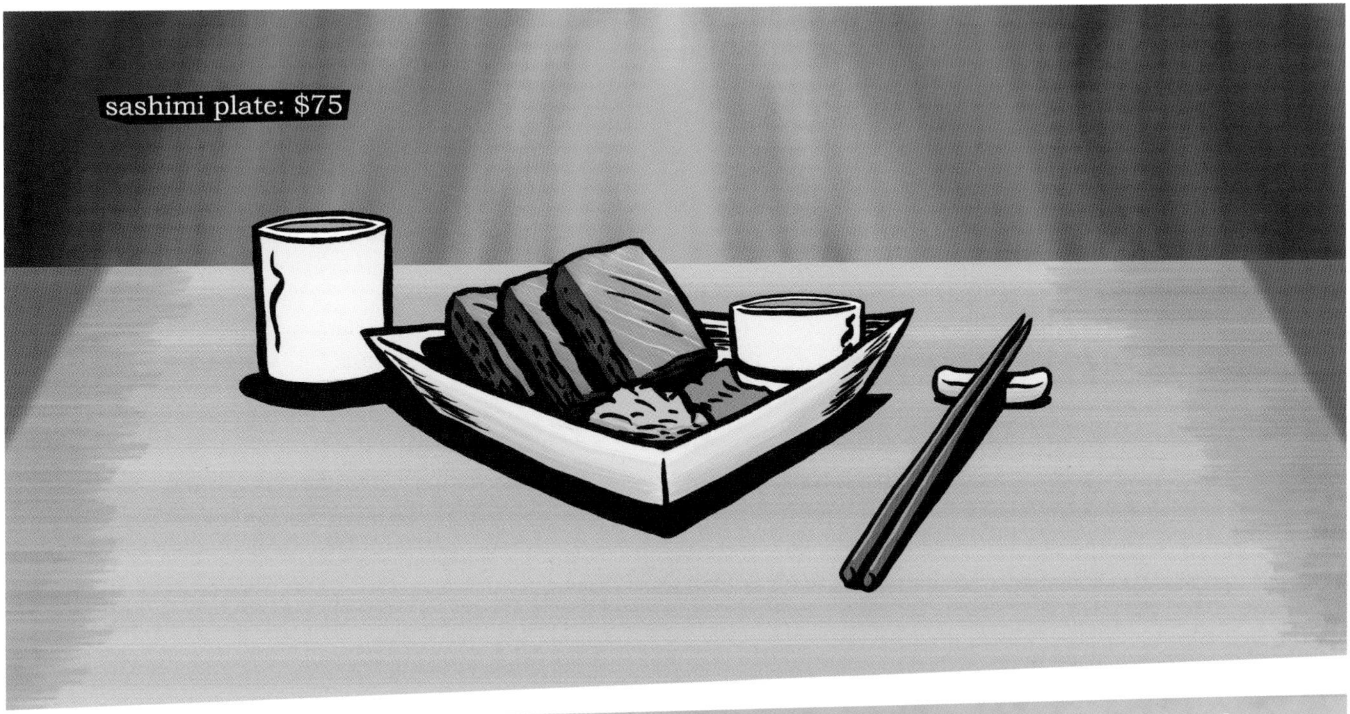
sashimi plate: $75

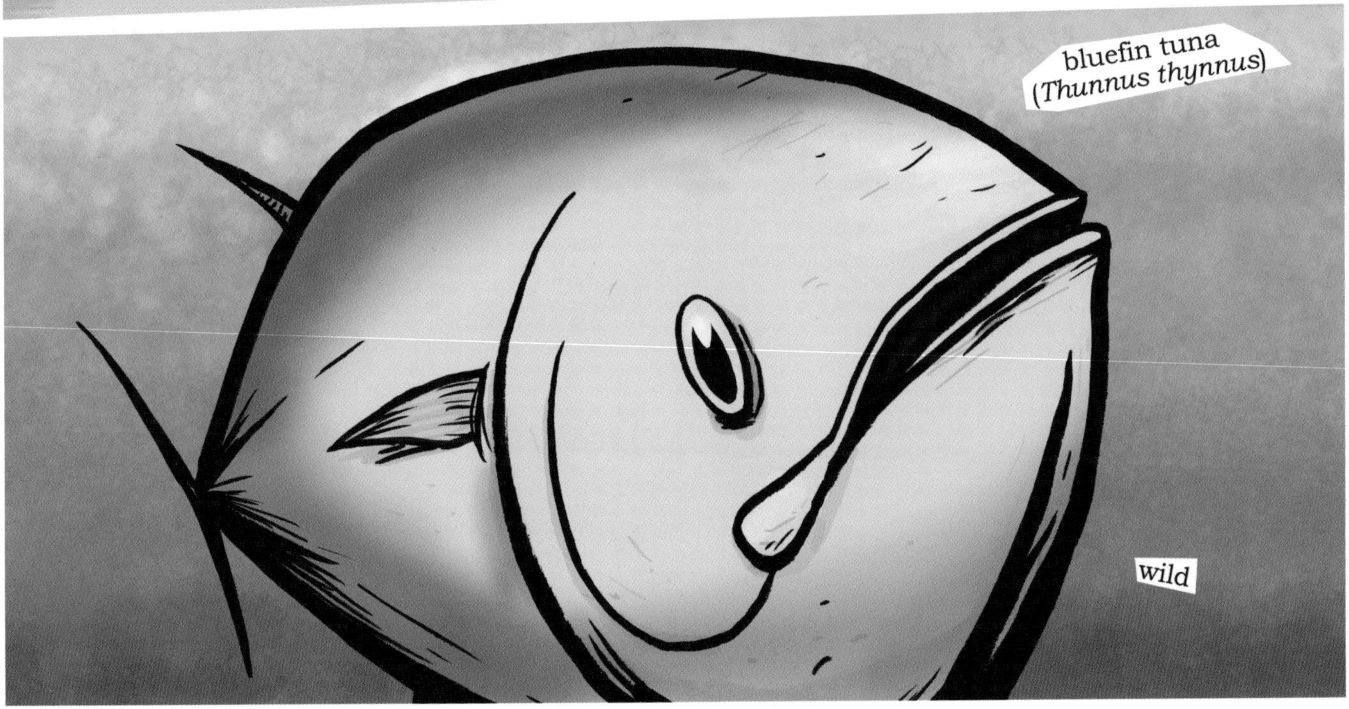
bluefin tuna
(Thunnus thynnus)
wild

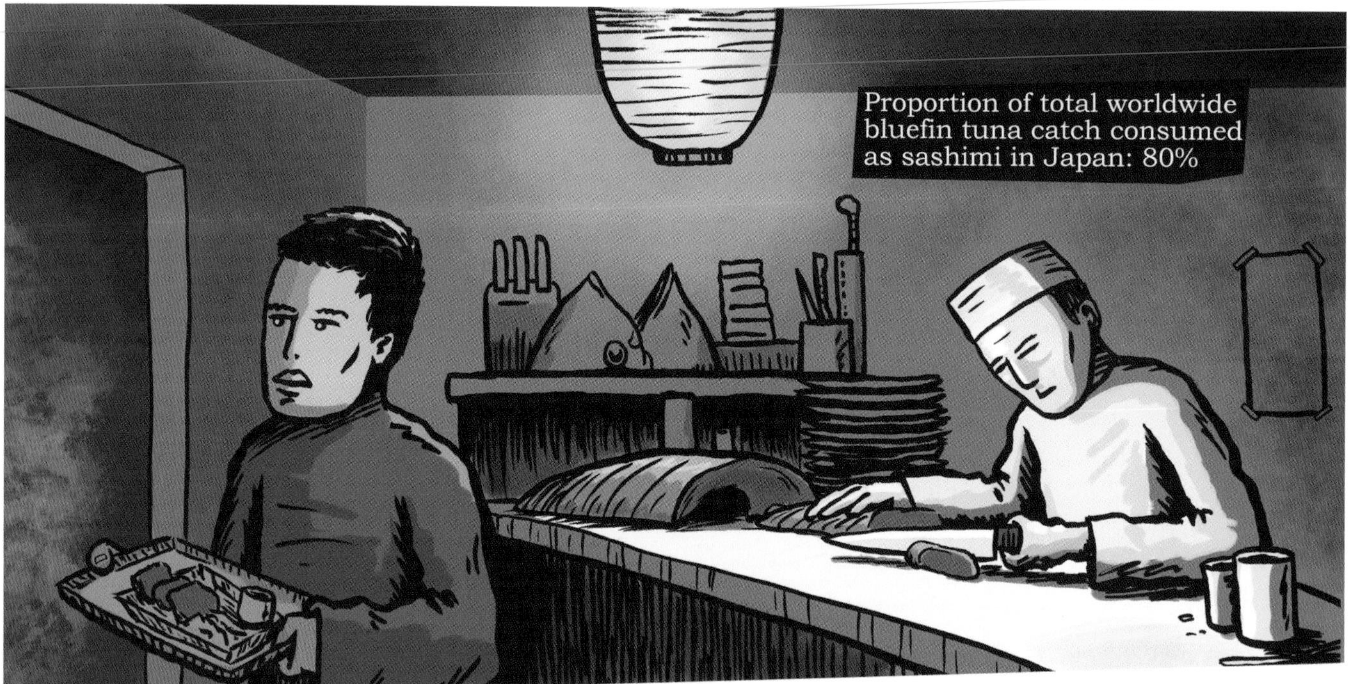
Proportion of total worldwide bluefin tuna catch consumed as sashimi in Japan: 80%

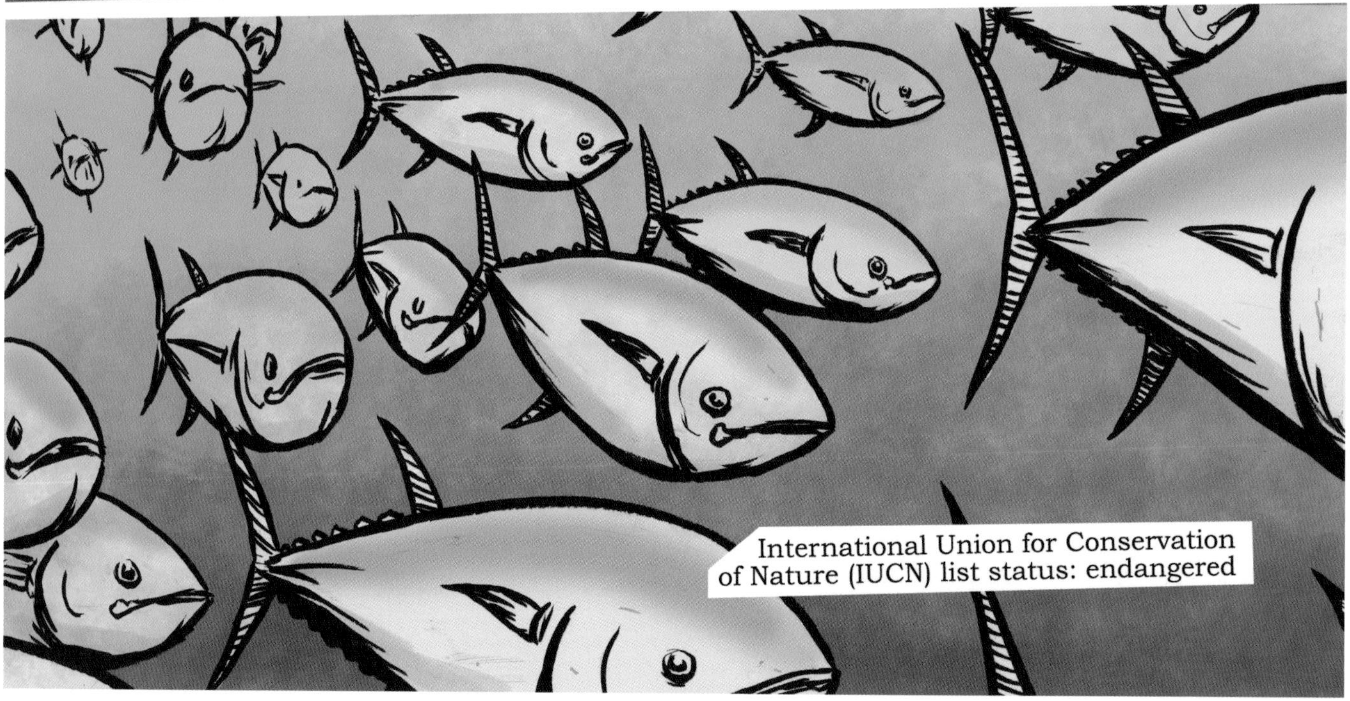
International Union for Conservation of Nature (IUCN) list status: endangered

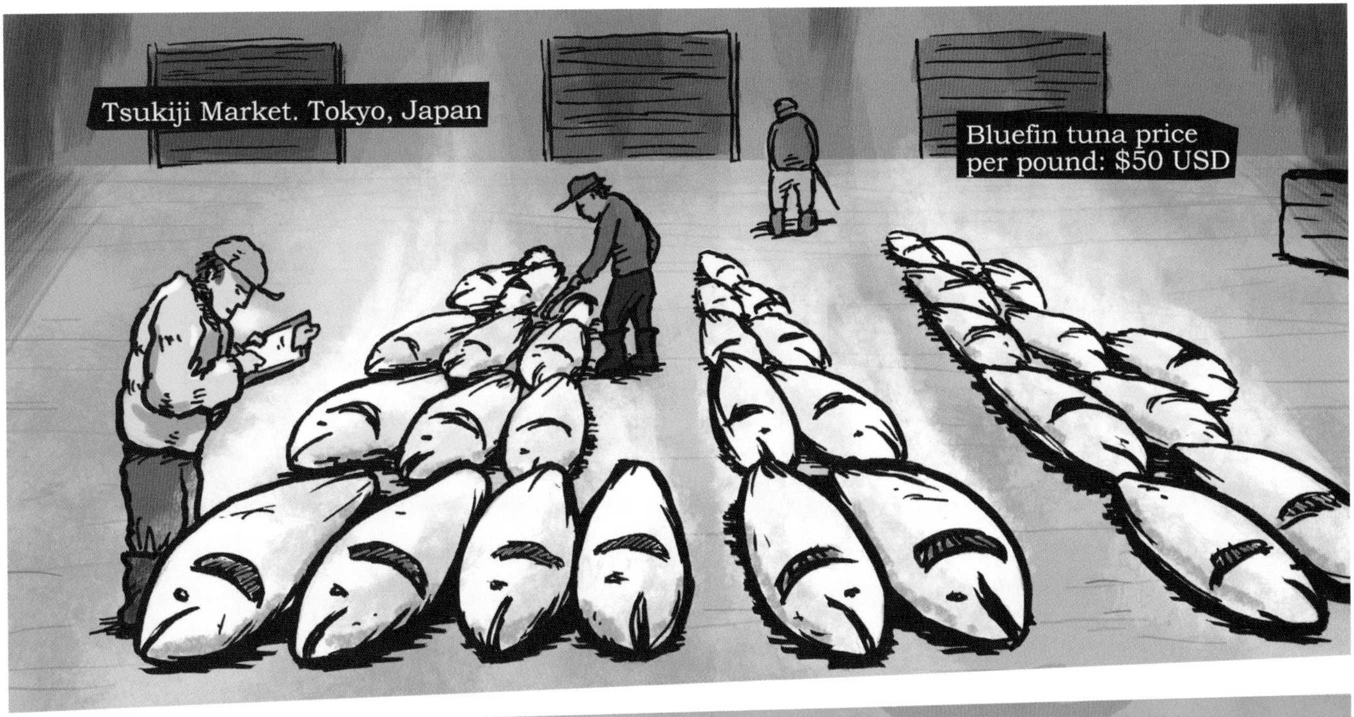
Tsukiji Market. Tokyo, Japan
Bluefin tuna price per pound: $50 USD

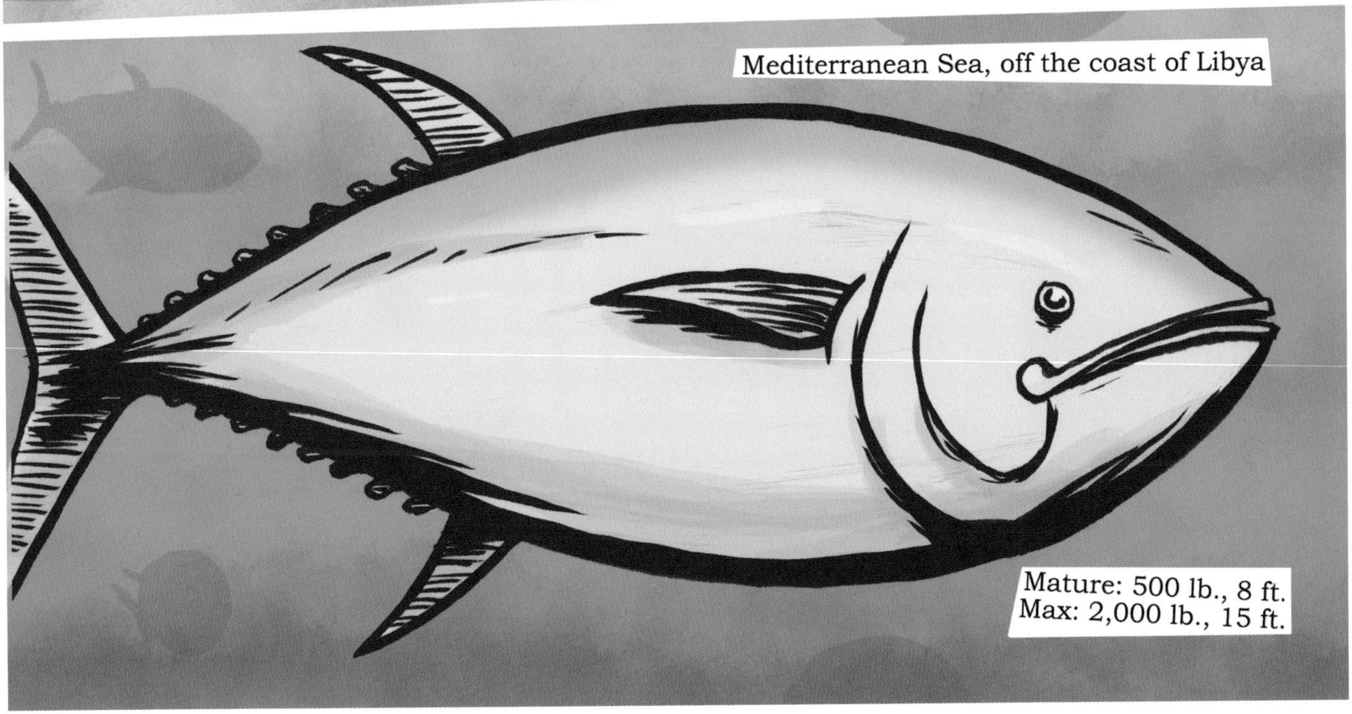
Mediterranean Sea, off the coast of Libya
Mature: 500 lb., 8 ft.
Max: 2,000 lb., 15 ft.

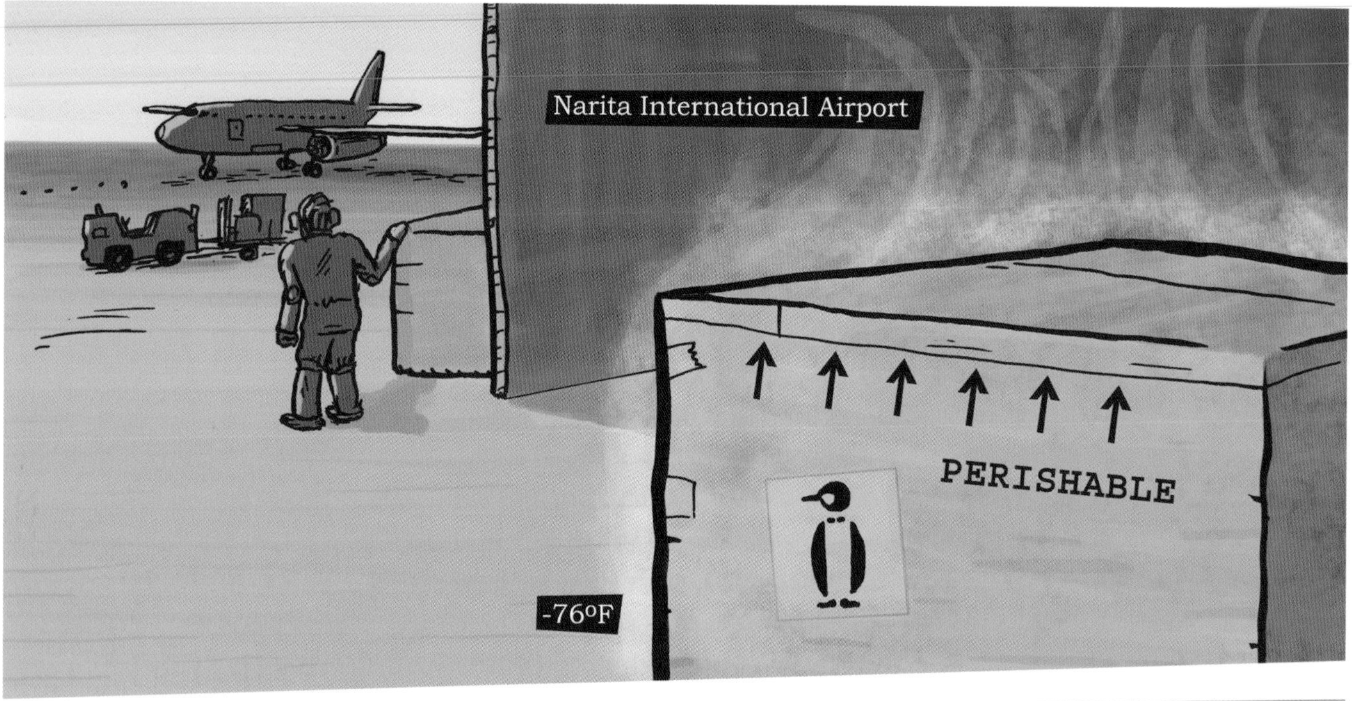
Narita International Airport
PERISHABLE
-76ºF

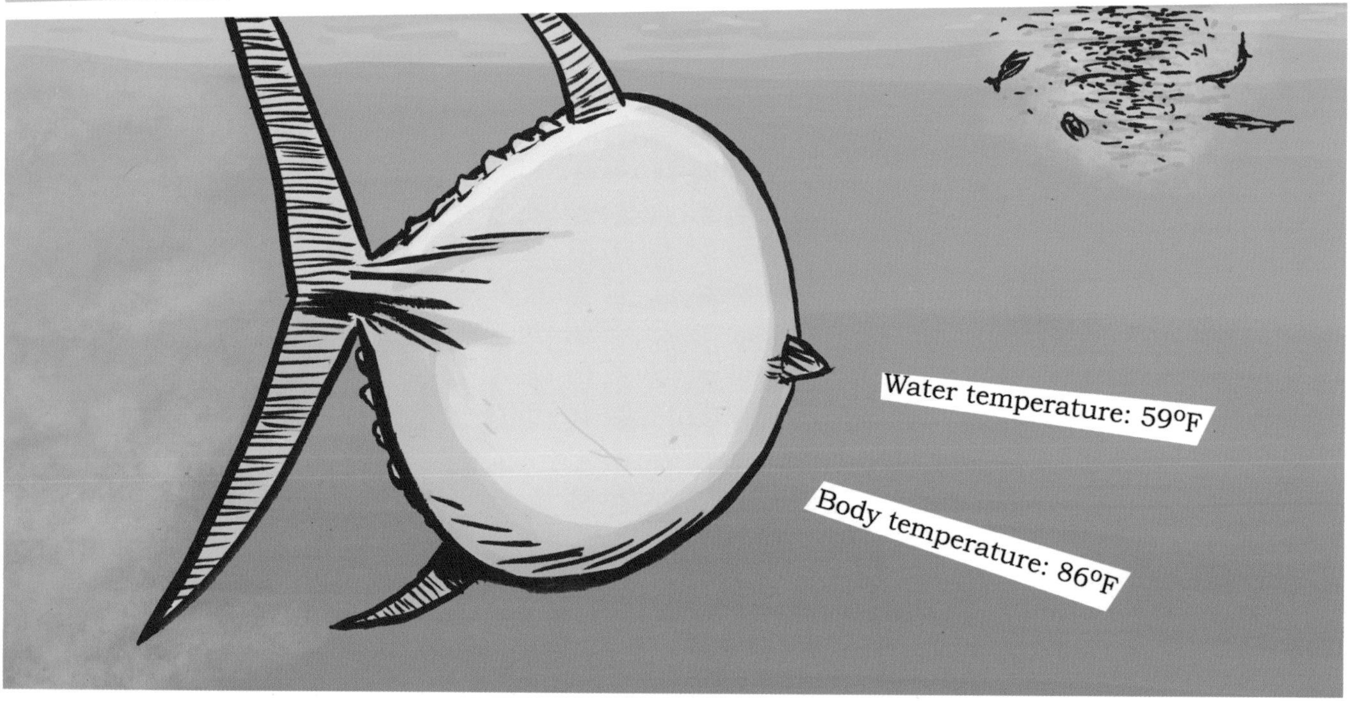
Water temperature: 59ºF
Body temperature: 86ºF

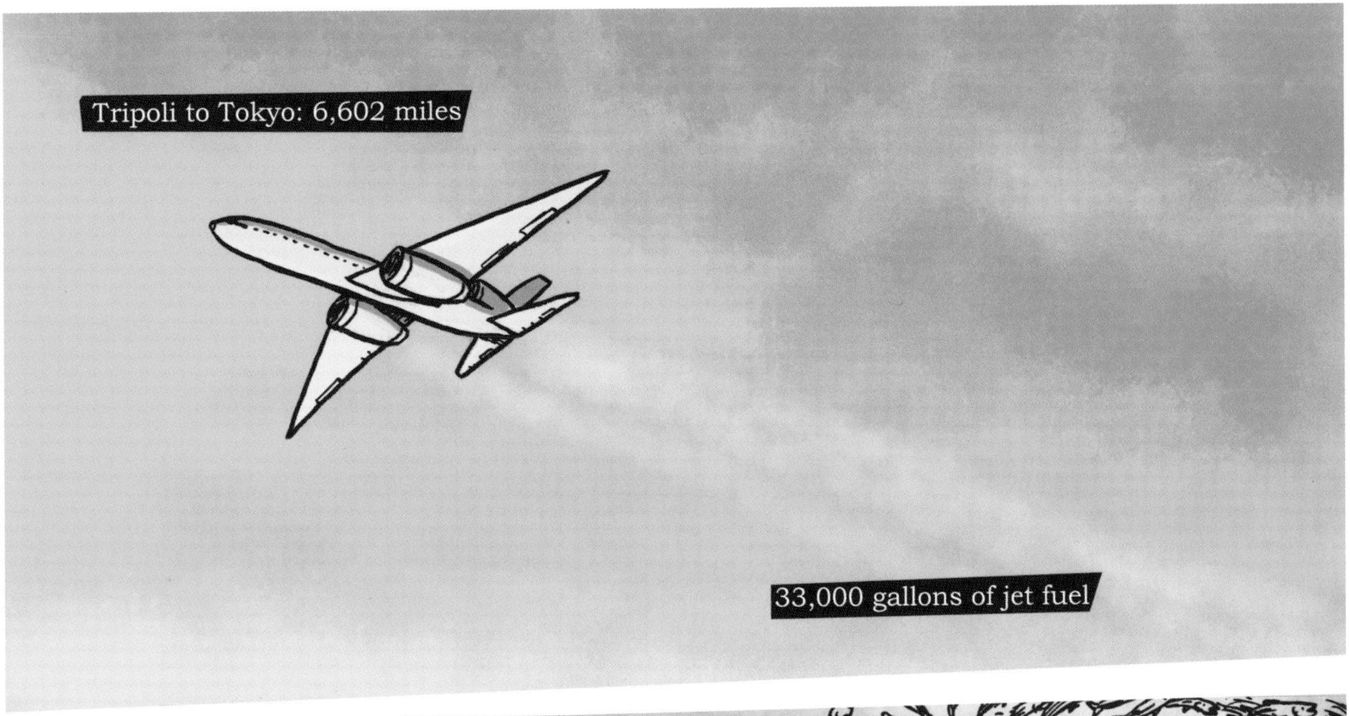
Tripoli to Tokyo: 6,602 miles
33,000 gallons of jet fuel

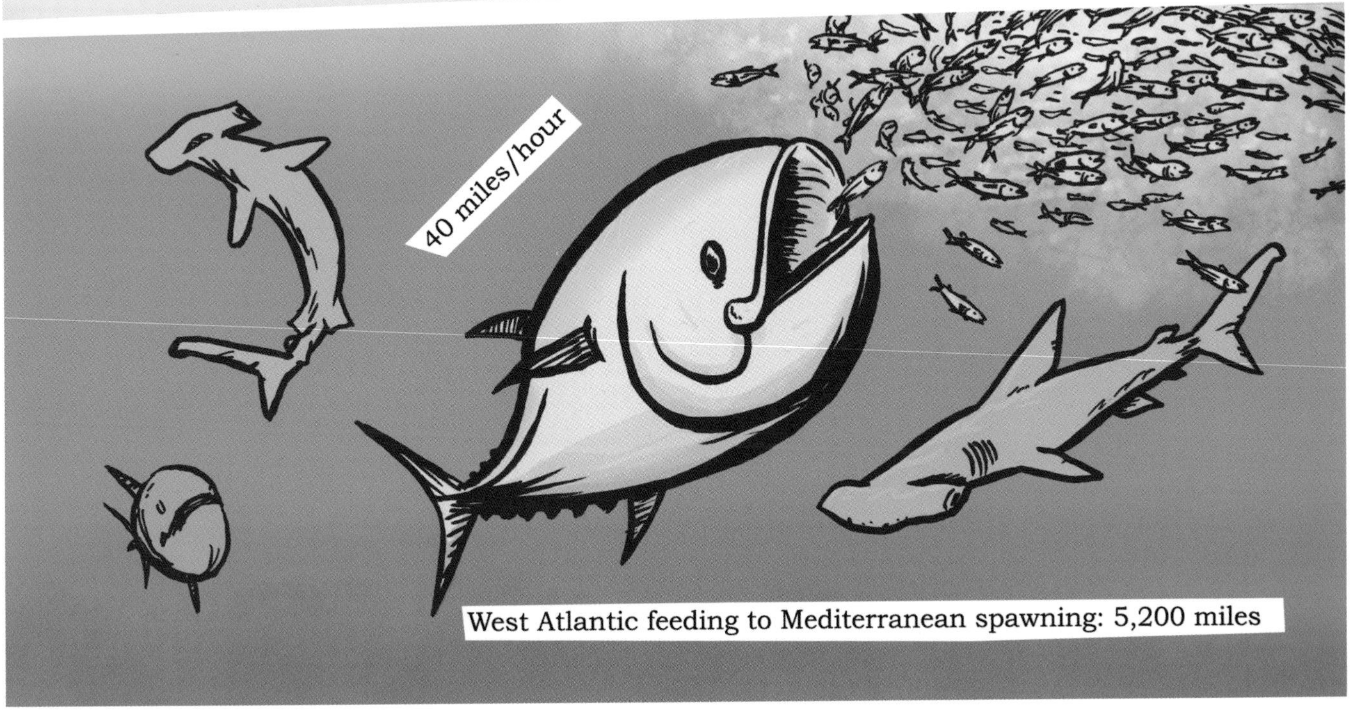
40 miles/hour
West Atlantic feeding to Mediterranean spawning: 5,200 miles

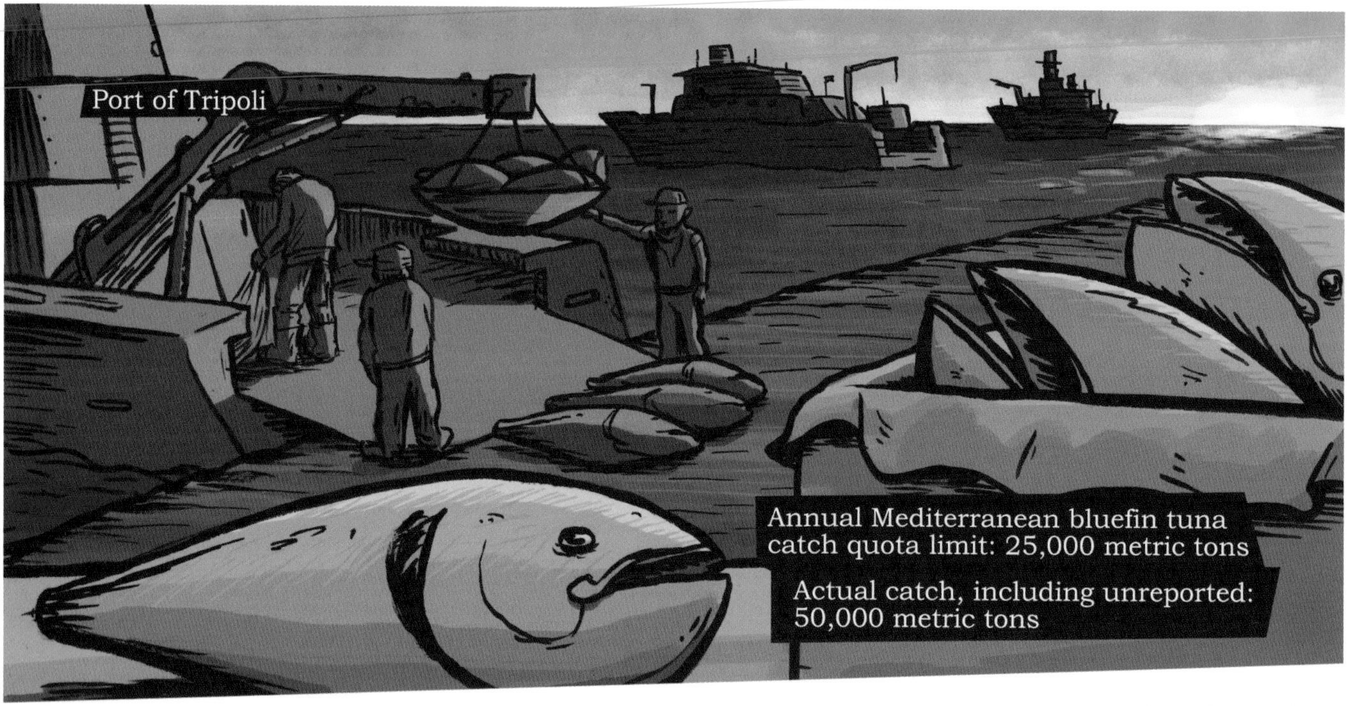
Port of Tripoli
Annual Mediterranean bluefin tuna catch quota limit: 25,000 metric tons
Actual catch, including unreported: 50,000 metric tons

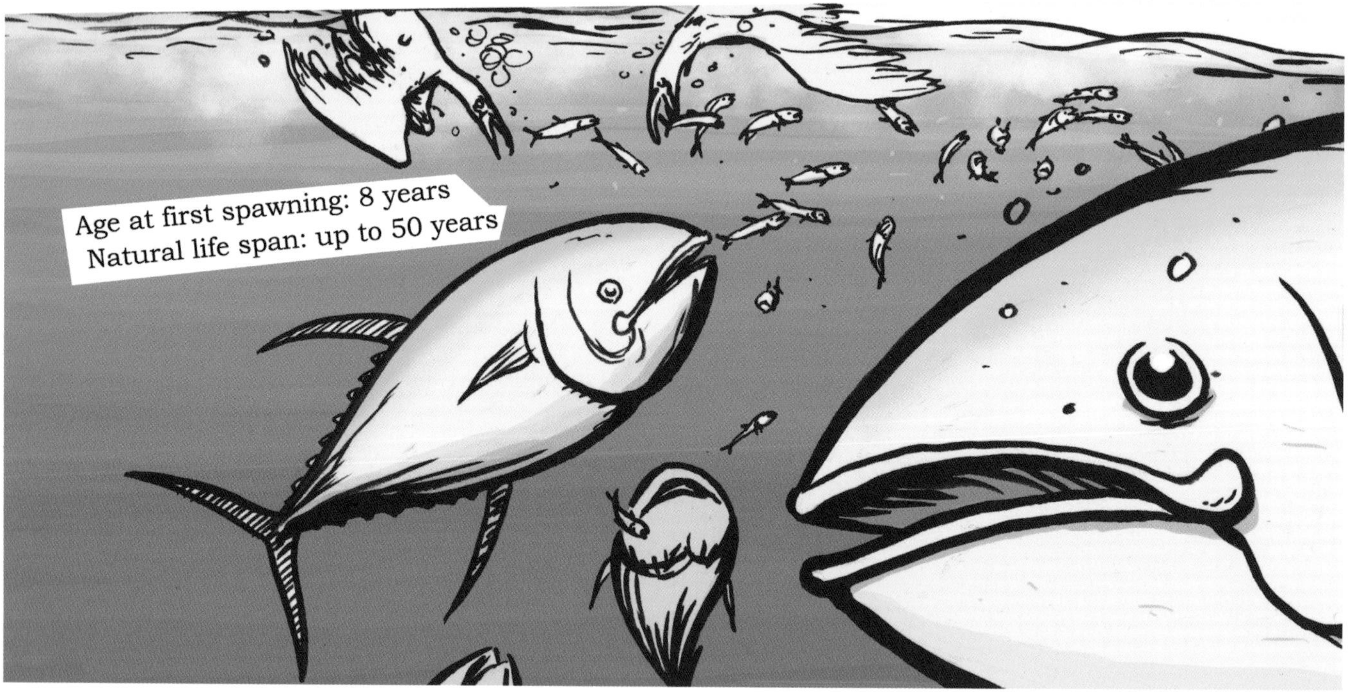
Age at first spawning: 8 years
Natural life span: up to 50 years

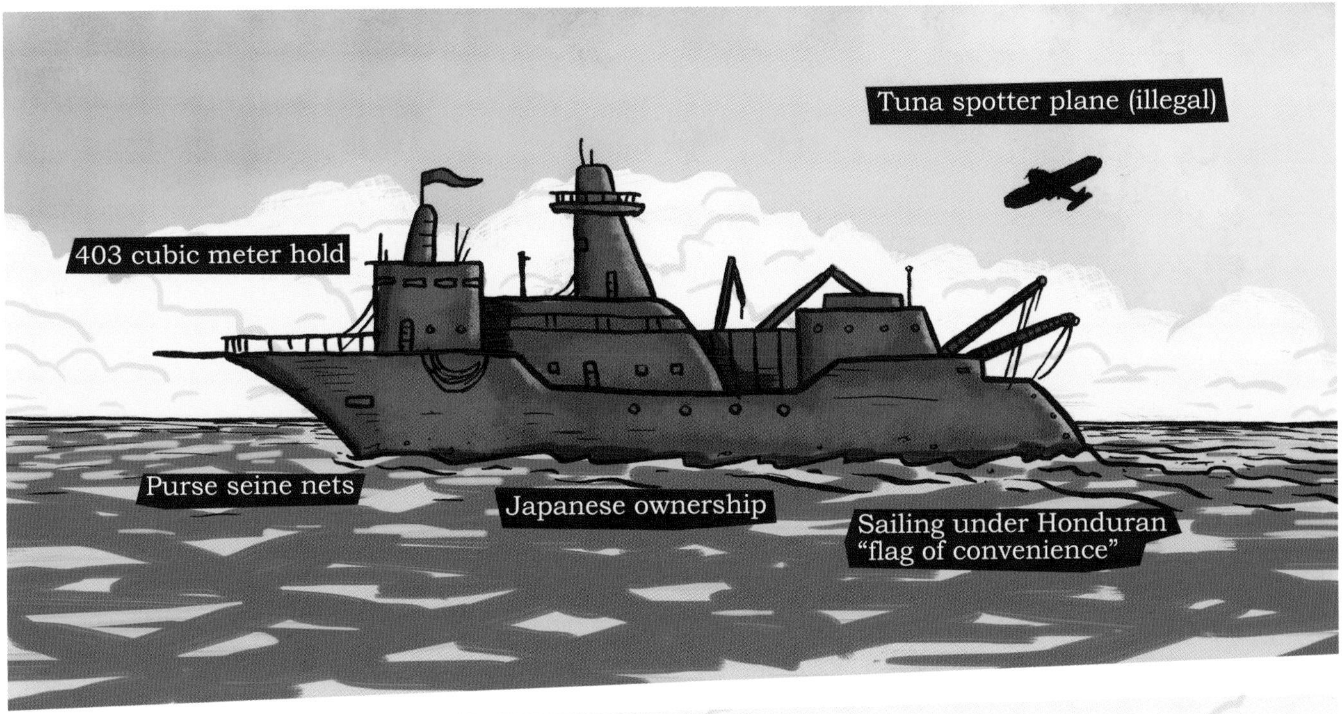
Tuna spotter plane (illegal)
403 cubic meter hold
Purse seine nets
Japanese ownership
Sailing under Honduran "flag of convenience"

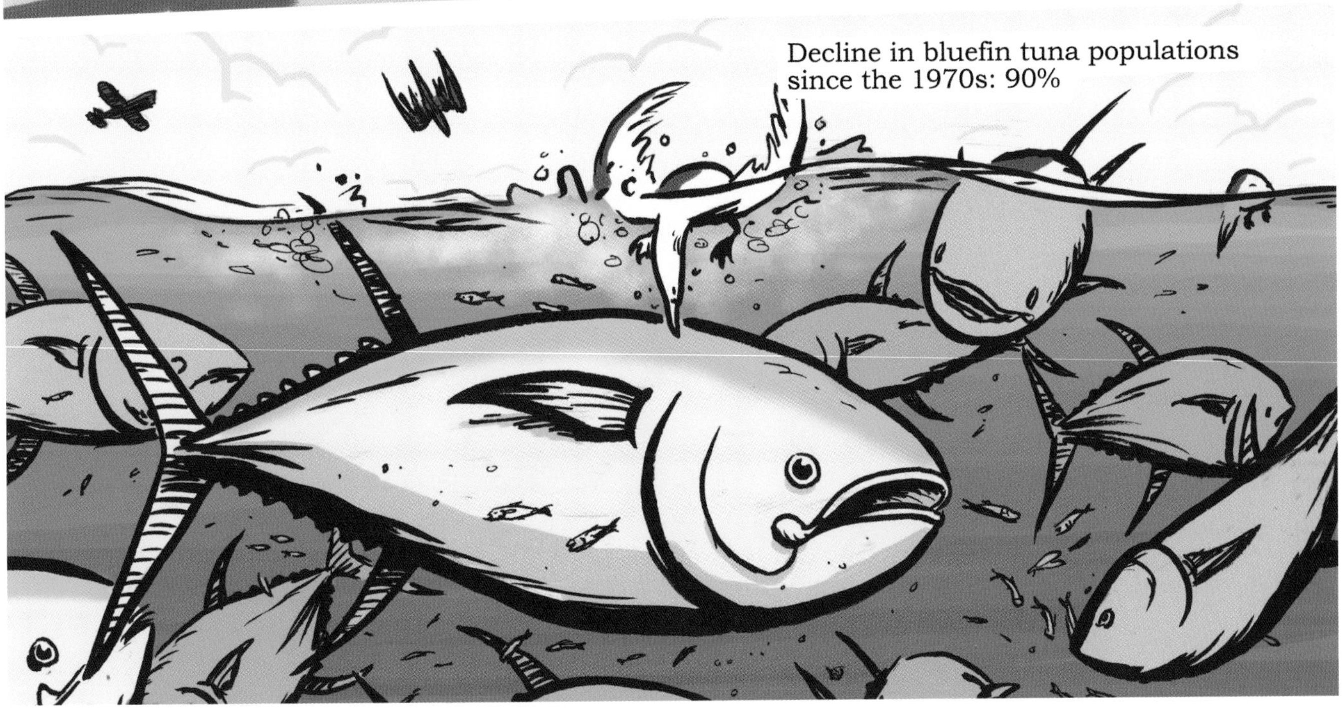
Decline in bluefin tuna populations since the 1970s: 90%

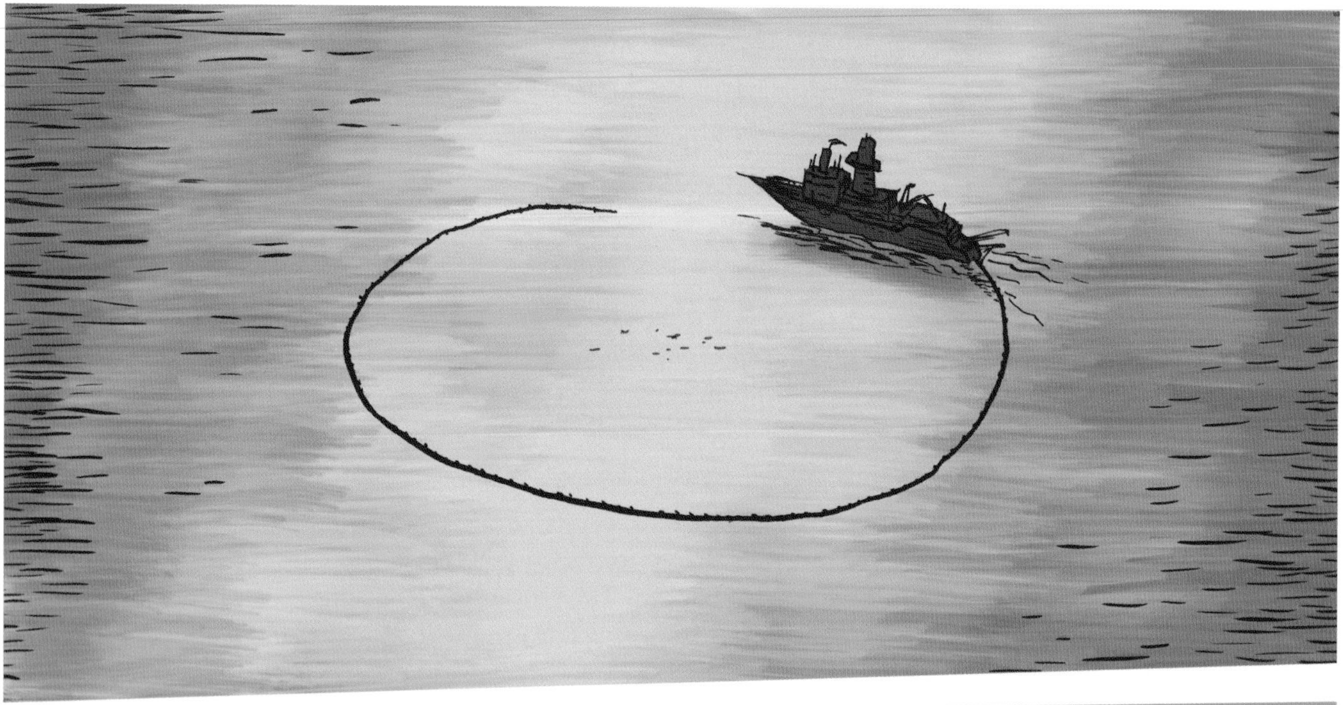

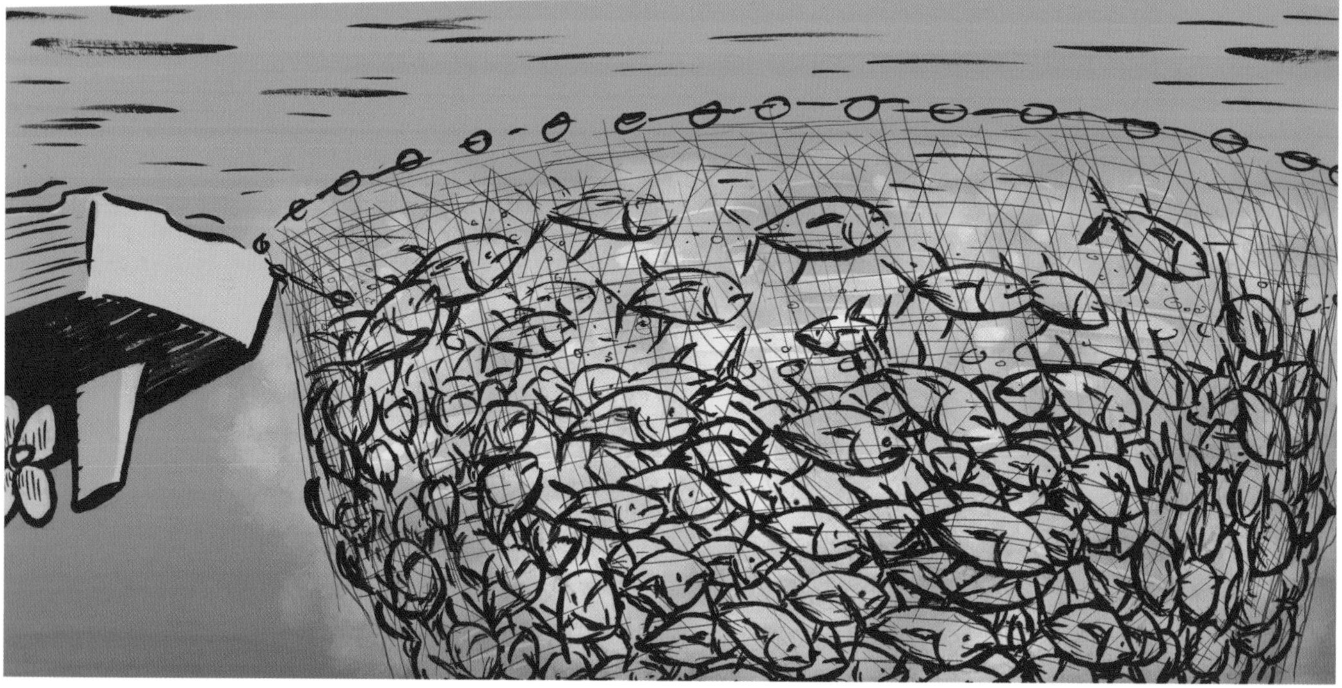

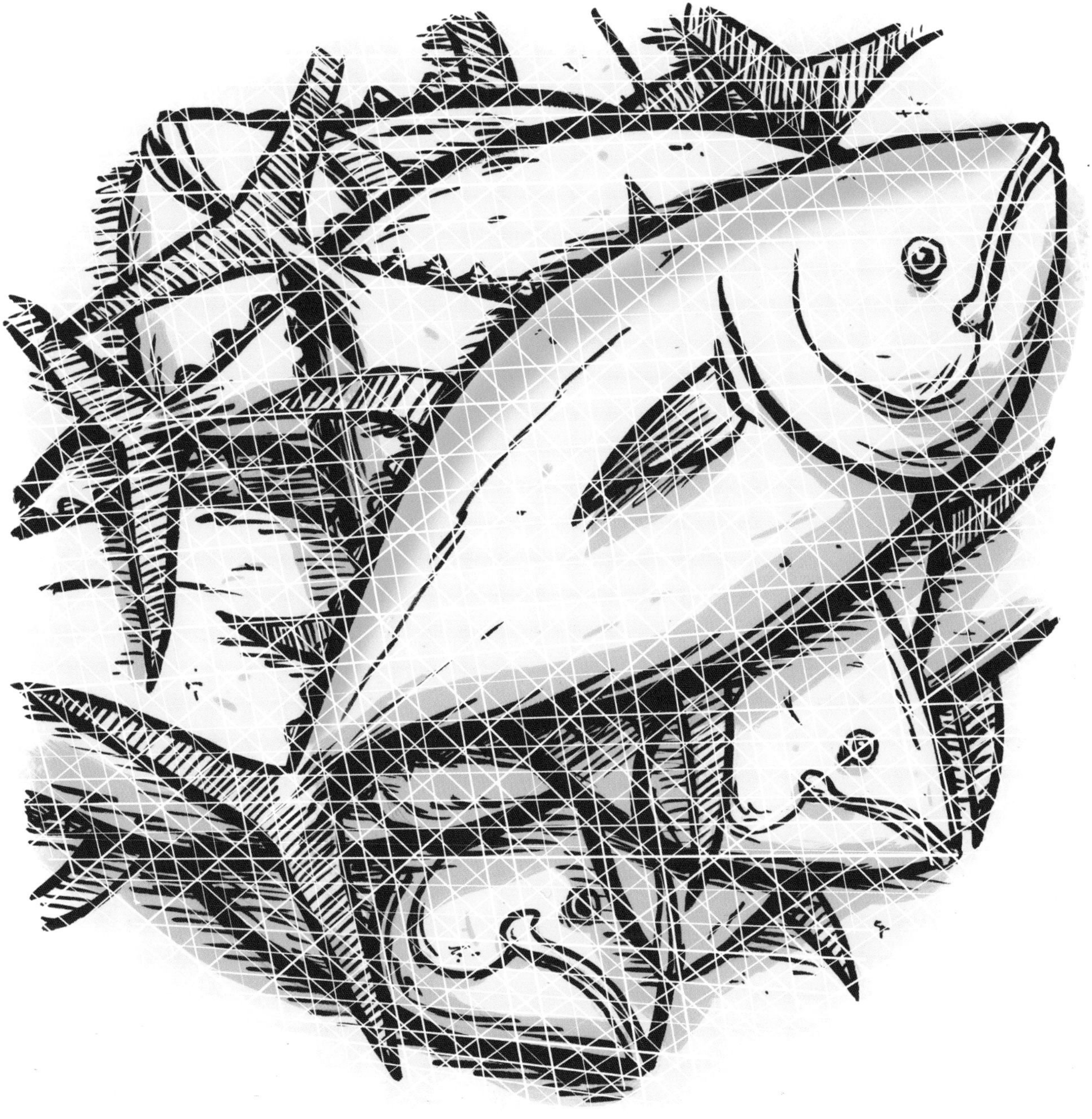

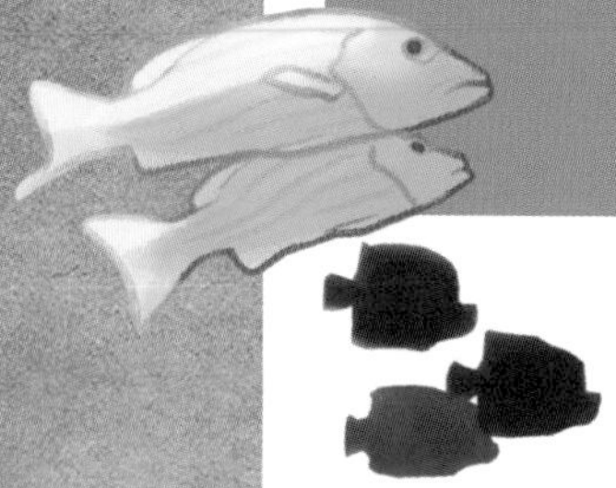

Atolls of the Maldives

Story by Kevin Panetta
Art by Paulina Ganucheau

CORAL REEFS ARE CITIES—vibrant and full of the hustle and bustle of city life. Home to a myriad of aquatic species, they are where animals eat, sleep, and play. Some coral reefs are bigger than some of the largest cities humans have ever built. The Great Barrier Reef in Australia, which can be seen from space, is the world's largest single structure that has been created by living organisms. It is 440 times larger than New York City!

Unfortunately, some of these underwater metropolises are becoming ghost towns. Environmental stresses, such as warming waters, are causing a phenomenon called "bleaching" where the coral expels algae that lives in coral tissues. In 2005, the United States lost half its coral reefs in the Caribbean in one year because of bleaching.

This story follows a young saddle butterflyfish who explores the dangers and delights of a reef system in the Indian Ocean.

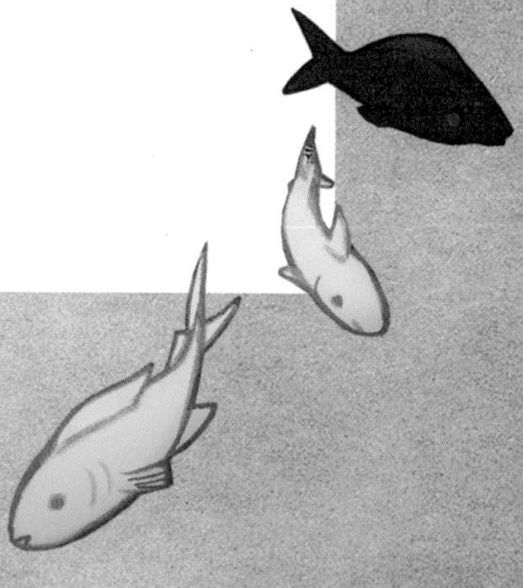

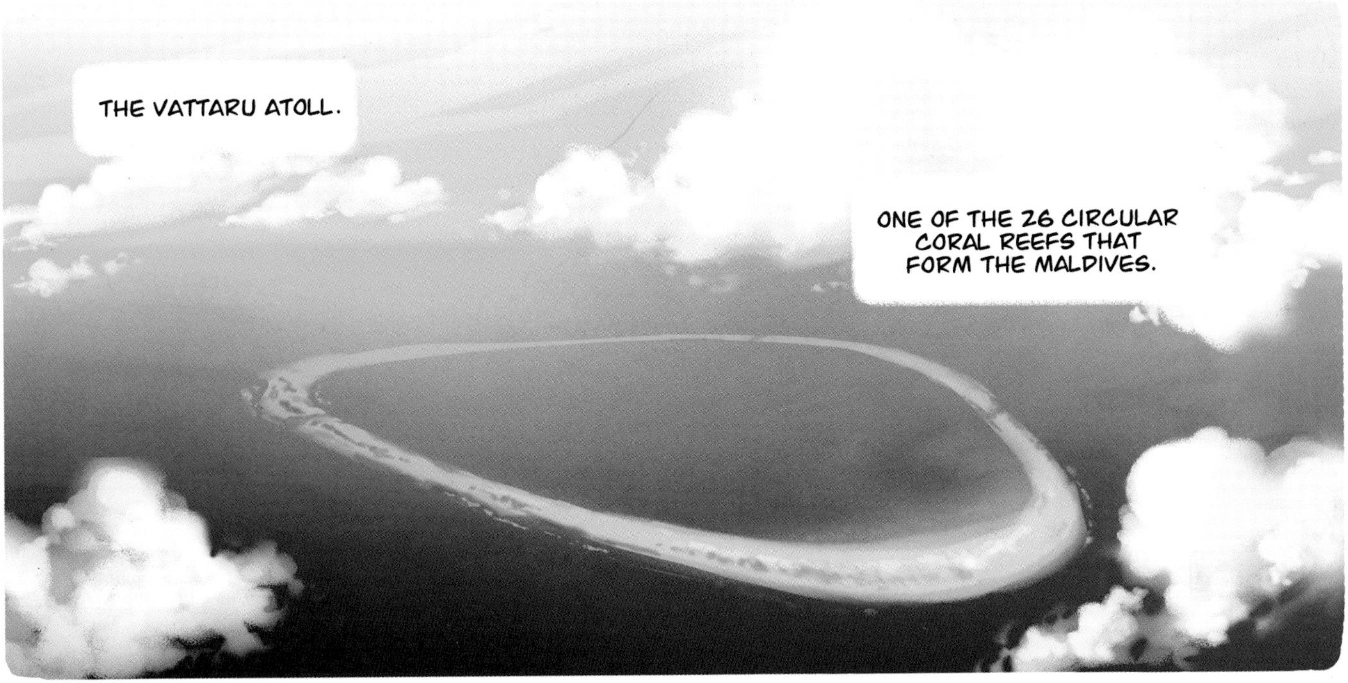
THE VATTARU ATOLL.
ONE OF THE 26 CIRCULAR CORAL REEFS THAT FORM THE MALDIVES.

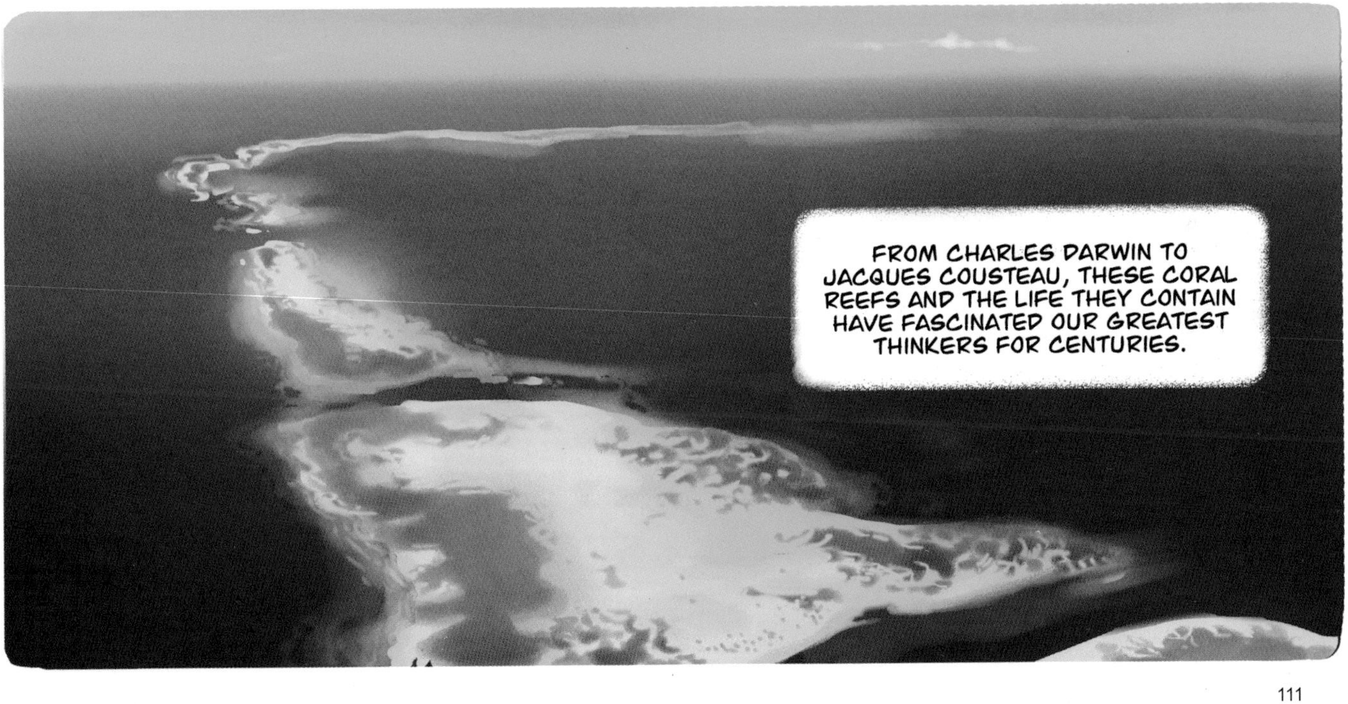
FROM CHARLES DARWIN TO JACQUES COUSTEAU, THESE CORAL REEFS AND THE LIFE THEY CONTAIN HAVE FASCINATED OUR GREATEST THINKERS FOR CENTURIES.

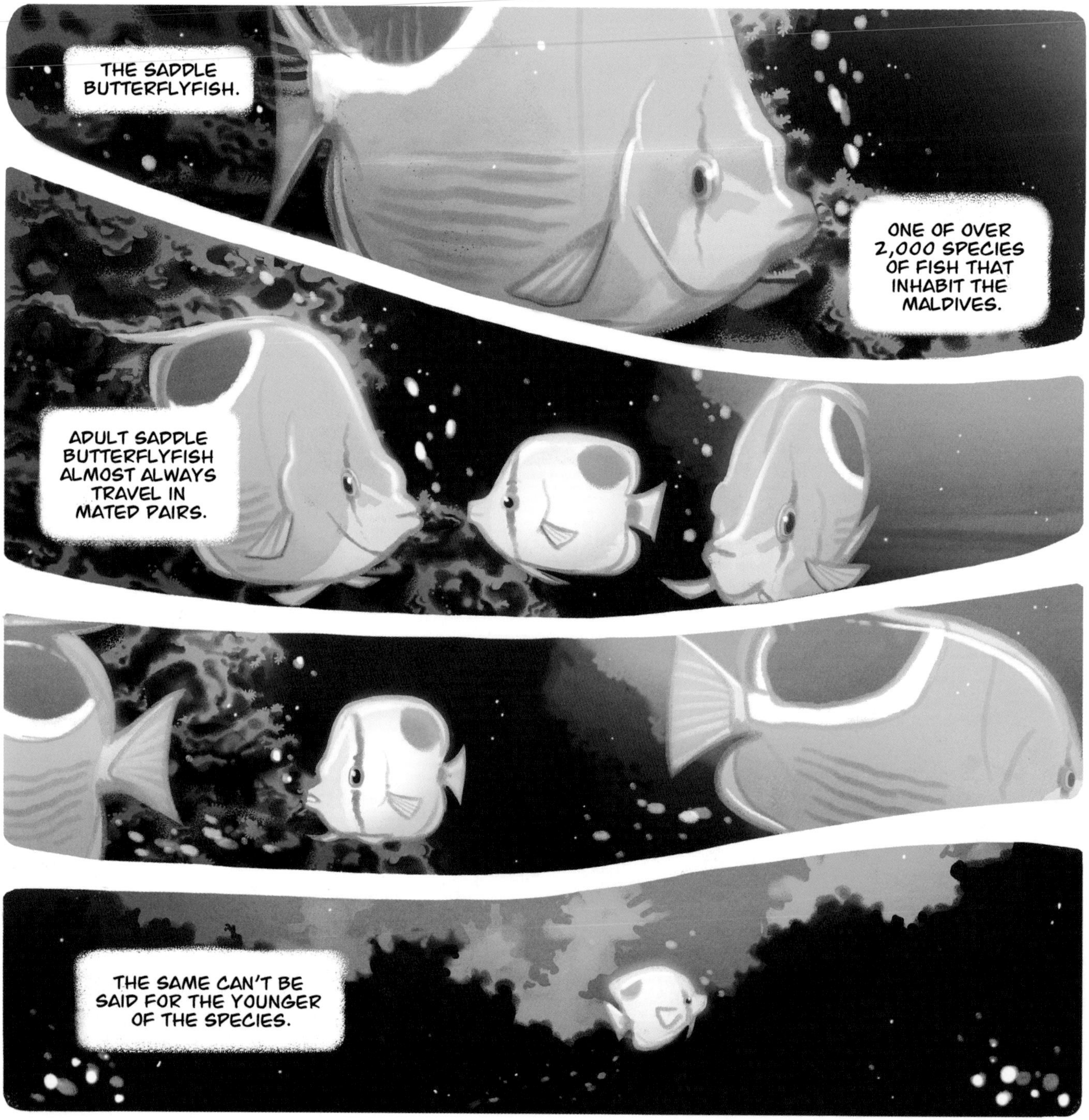
THE SADDLE BUTTERFLYFISH.
ONE OF OVER 2,000 SPECIES OF FISH THAT INHABIT THE MALDIVES.
ADULT SADDLE BUTTERFLYFISH ALMOST ALWAYS TRAVEL IN MATED PAIRS.
THE SAME CAN'T BE SAID FOR THE YOUNGER OF THE SPECIES.

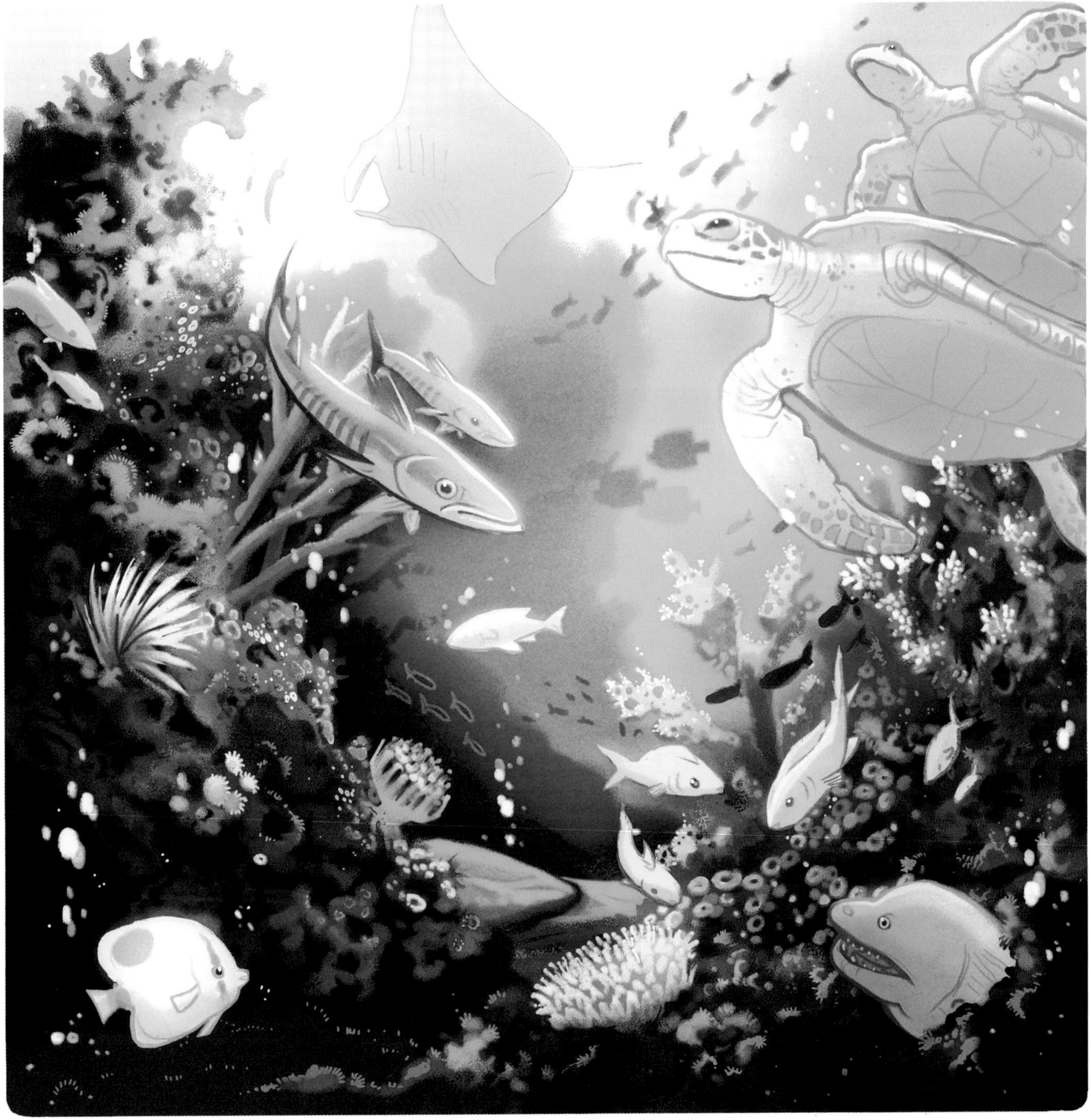

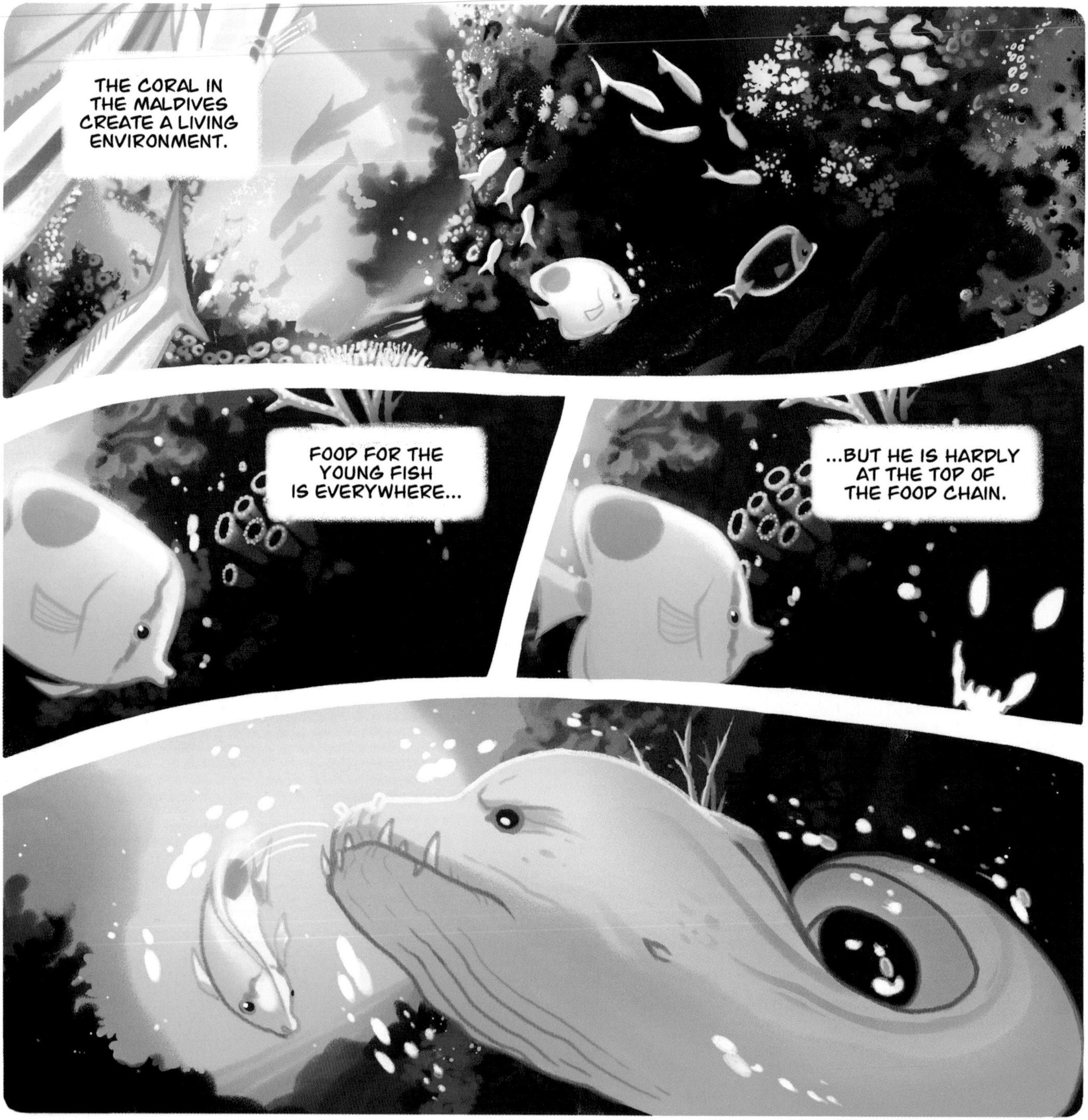
THE CORAL IN THE MALDIVES CREATE A LIVING ENVIRONMENT.
FOOD FOR THE YOUNG FISH IS EVERYWHERE...
...BUT HE IS HARDLY AT THE TOP OF THE FOOD CHAIN.

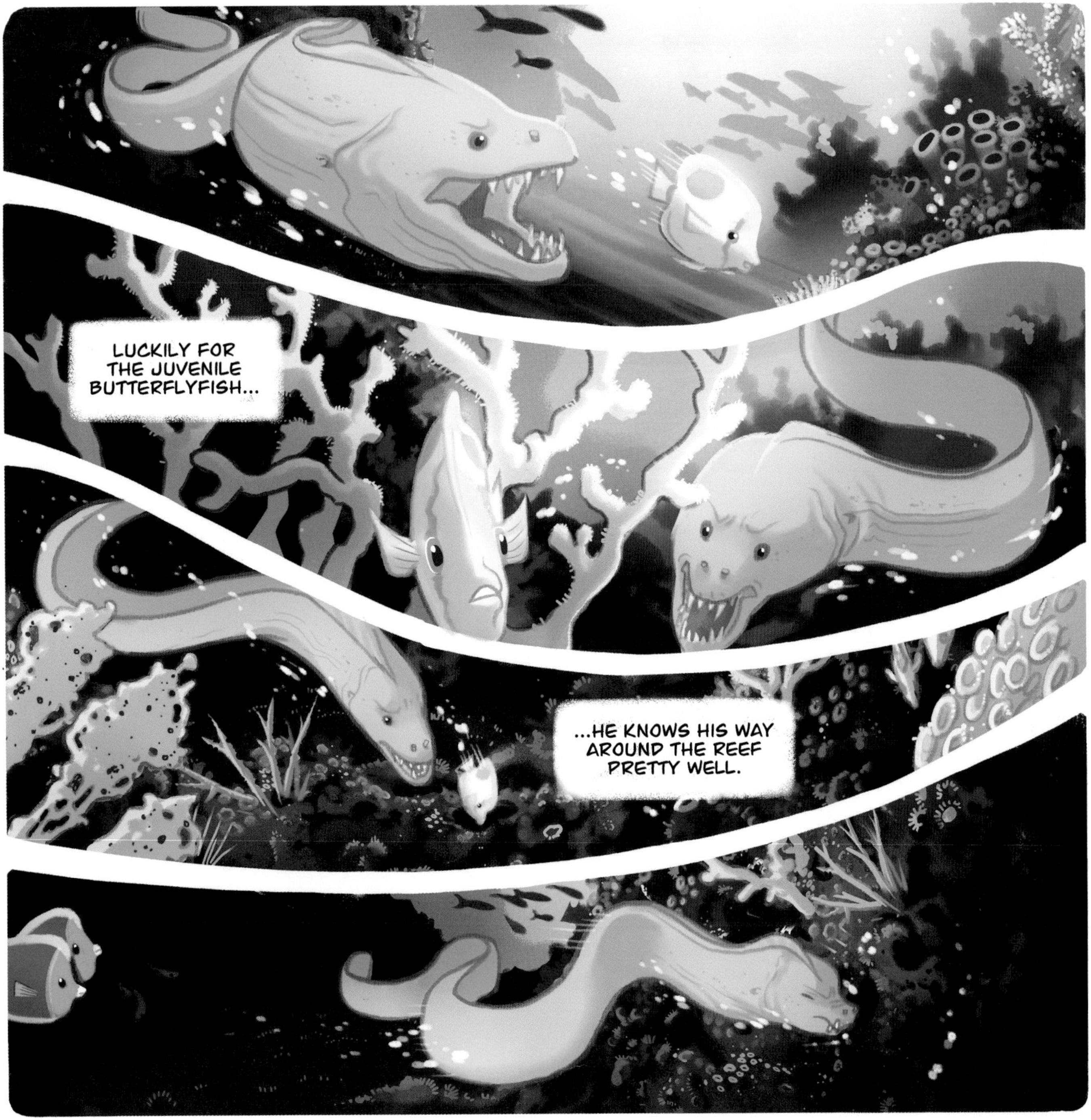
LUCKILY FOR THE JUVENILE BUTTERFLYFISH...
...HE KNOWS HIS WAY AROUND THE REEF PRETTY WELL.

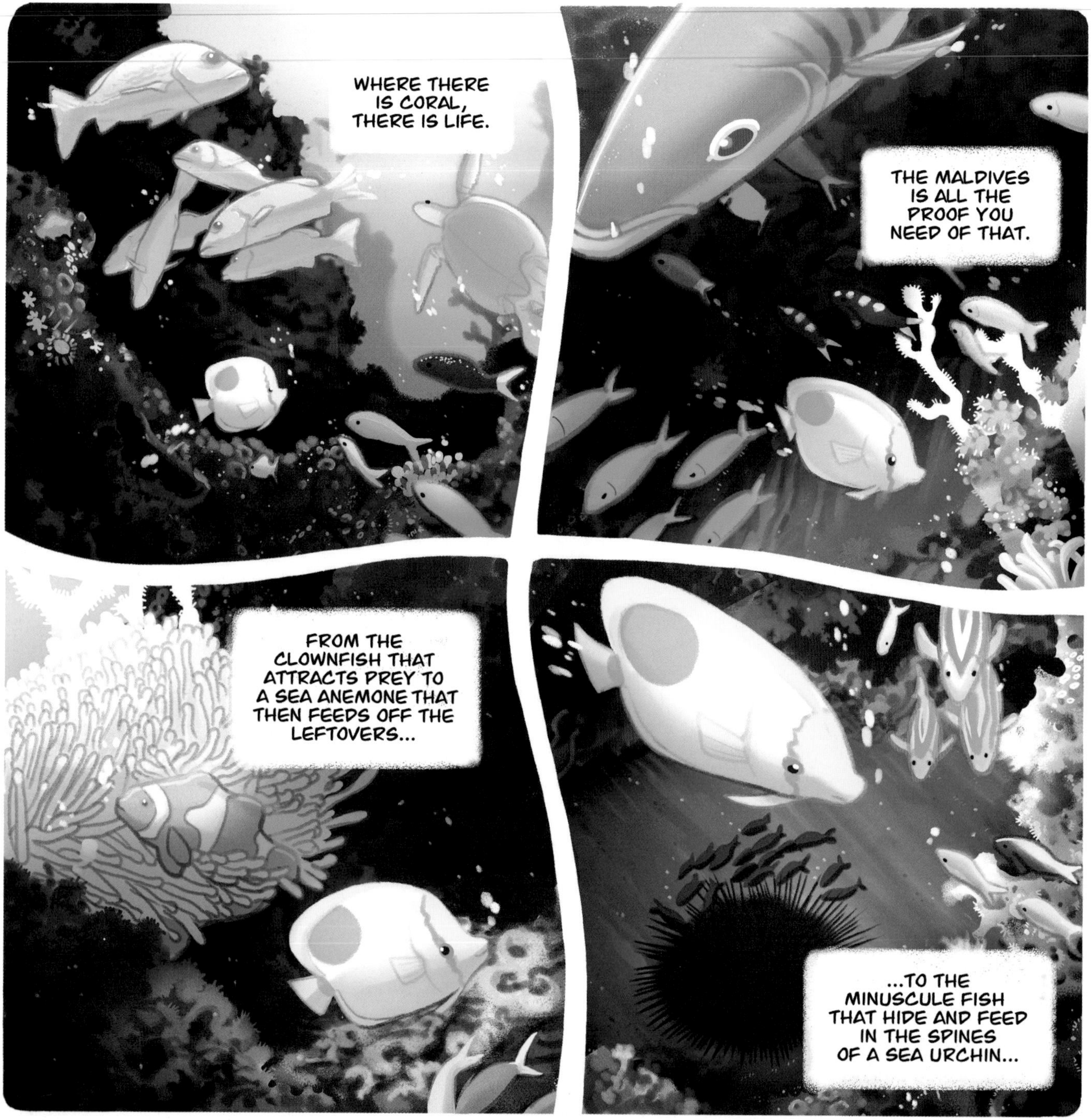
WHERE THERE IS CORAL, THERE IS LIFE.
THE MALDIVES IS ALL THE PROOF YOU NEED OF THAT.
FROM THE CLOWNFISH THAT ATTRACTS PREY TO A SEA ANEMONE THAT THEN FEEDS OFF THE LEFTOVERS...
...TO THE MINUSCULE FISH THAT HIDE AND FEED IN THE SPINES OF A SEA URCHIN...

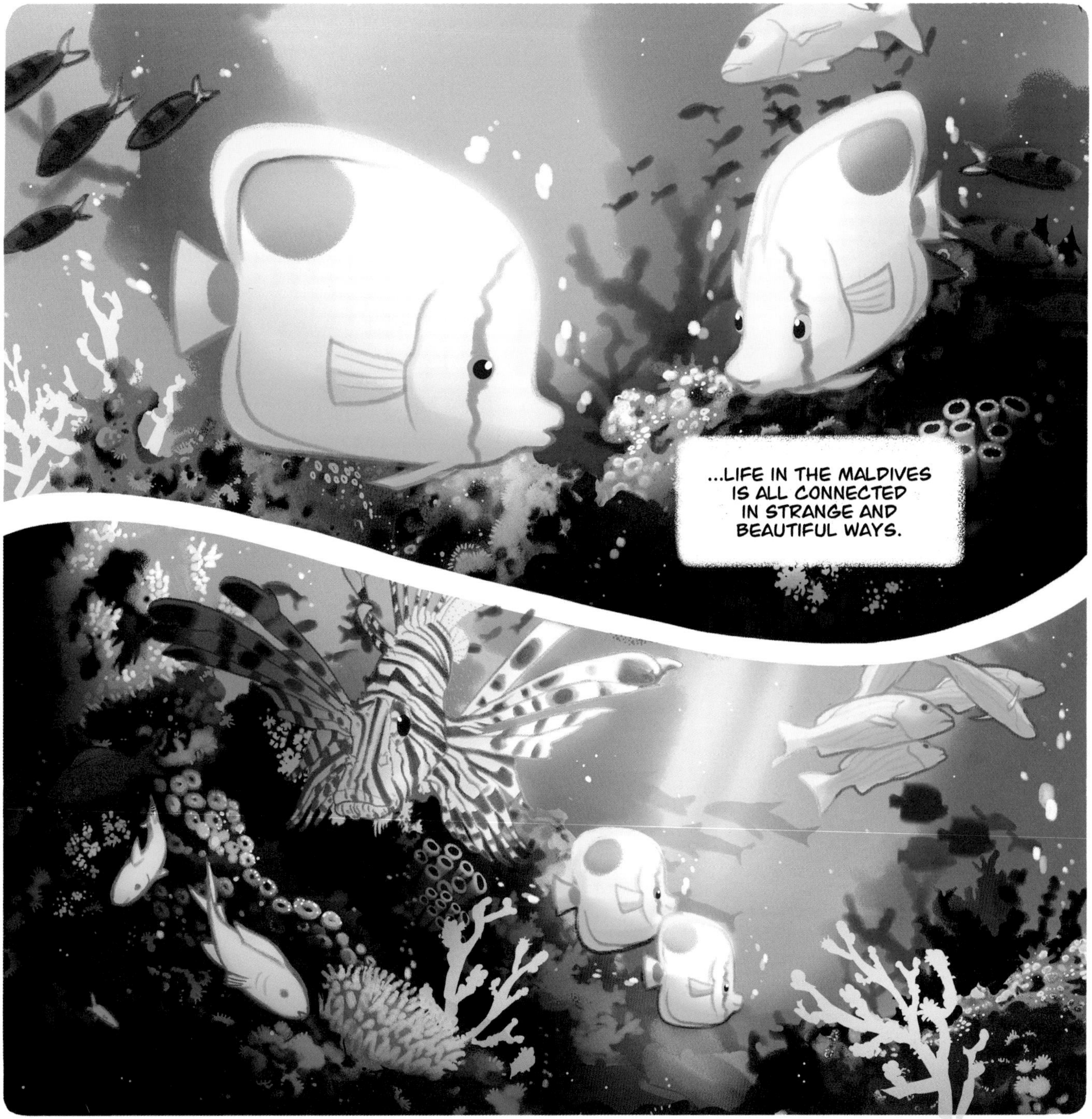
...LIFE IN THE MALDIVES IS ALL CONNECTED IN STRANGE AND BEAUTIFUL WAYS.

THE LADY OF THE SEA

Story and Art by Pat N. Lewis

ALSO KNOWN AS SEA COWS, manatees are large, mostly plant-eating aquatic mammals that swim with astonishing grace and ease. They are slow-moving, gentle creatures—and they even have a colorful folklore. When European explorers first ventured into the Americas, sailors often mistook manatees for beings that were half-human, half-fish: mermaids.

Apart from being mistaken for mermaids, these majestic mammals—which can live up to 60 years in the wild—have played other interesting and important roles in human culture.

In Africa, manatees were sacred, while in South America their meat and bones were used to treat ailments. In North America, Native Americans and early European settlers hunted manatees for their meat, hide, and bones.

Yet overhunting isn't the main reason that these shallow-water swimmers are on the endangered species list. Instead, it's mainly been carelessness. The chief causes of death for manatees include habitat destruction, pollution, and injuries from boats. In fact, watercraft collisions cause nearly 25 percent of all manatee deaths.

In recent years, there have been efforts to help these portly mammals, including the federal government and the state of Florida passing laws that make it illegal to harm manatees.

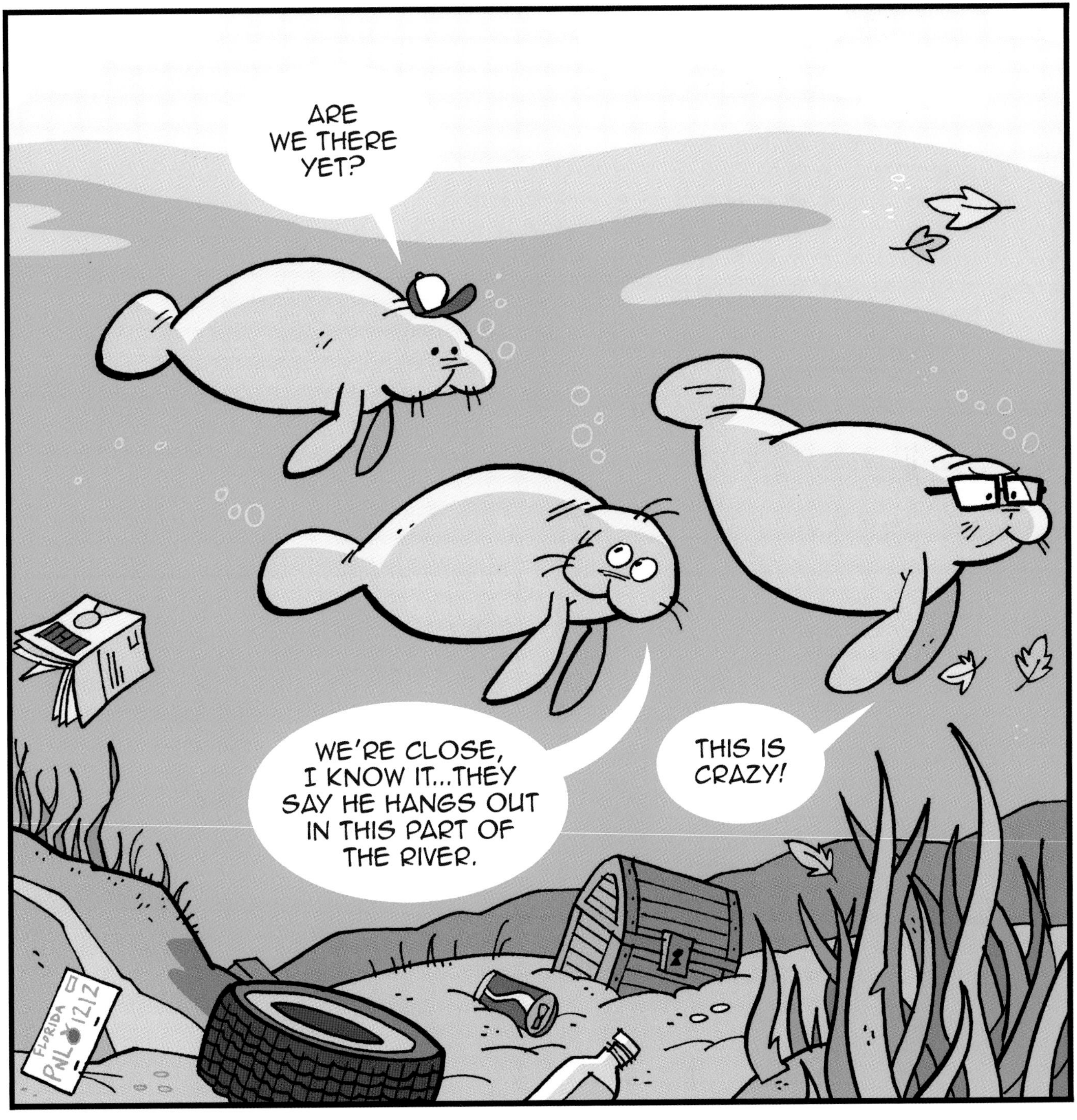
ARE WE THERE YET?
WE'RE CLOSE, I KNOW IT...THEY SAY HE HANGS OUT IN THIS PART OF THE RIVER.
THIS IS CRAZY!
FLORIDA
PNL 1212

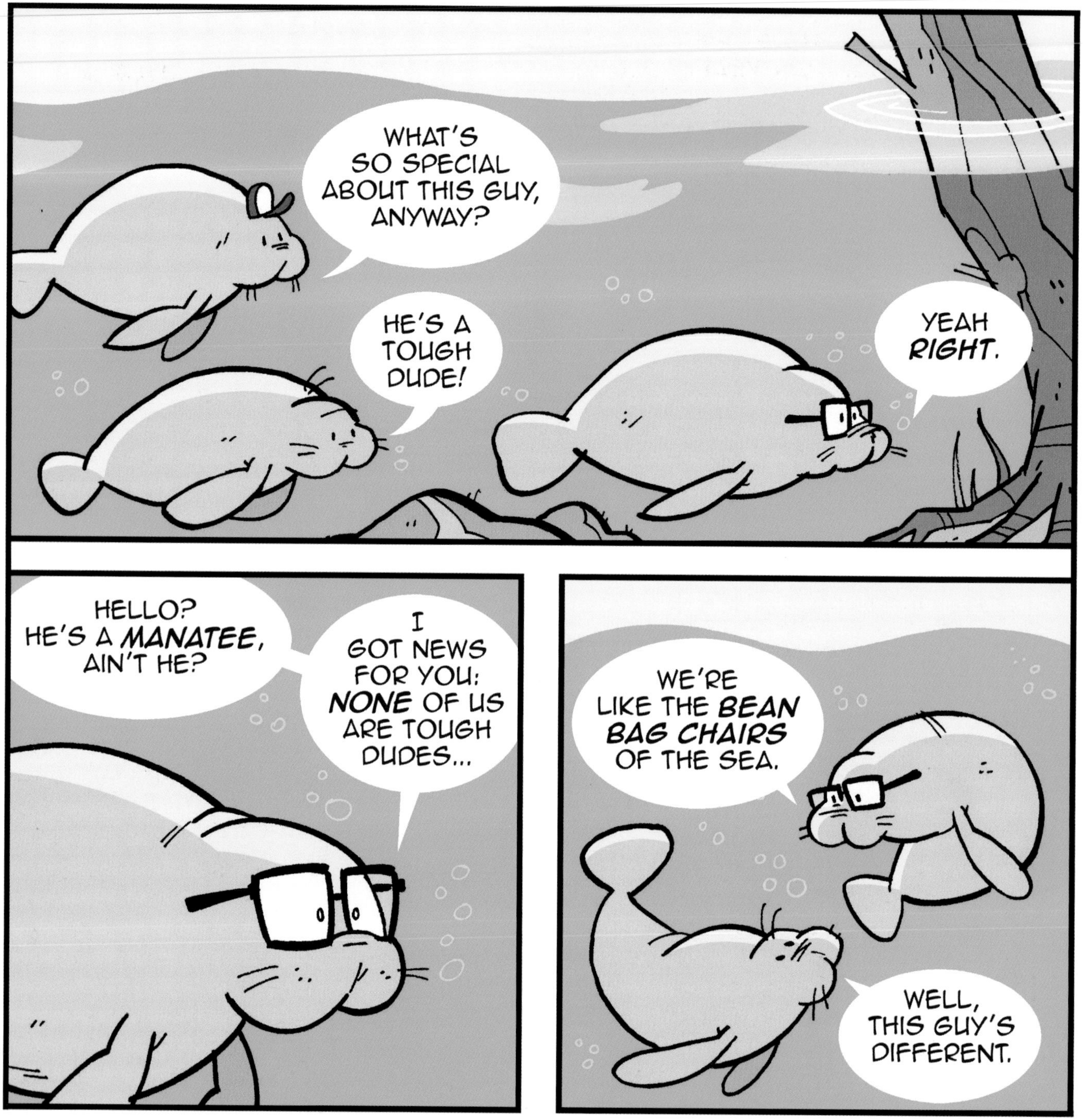
WHAT'S SO SPECIAL ABOUT THIS GUY, ANYWAY?
HE'S A TOUGH DUDE!
YEAH *RIGHT*.
HELLO? HE'S A *MANATEE*, AIN'T HE?
I GOT NEWS FOR YOU: *NONE* OF US ARE TOUGH DUDES...
WE'RE LIKE THE *BEAN BAG CHAIRS* OF THE SEA.
WELL, THIS GUY'S DIFFERENT.

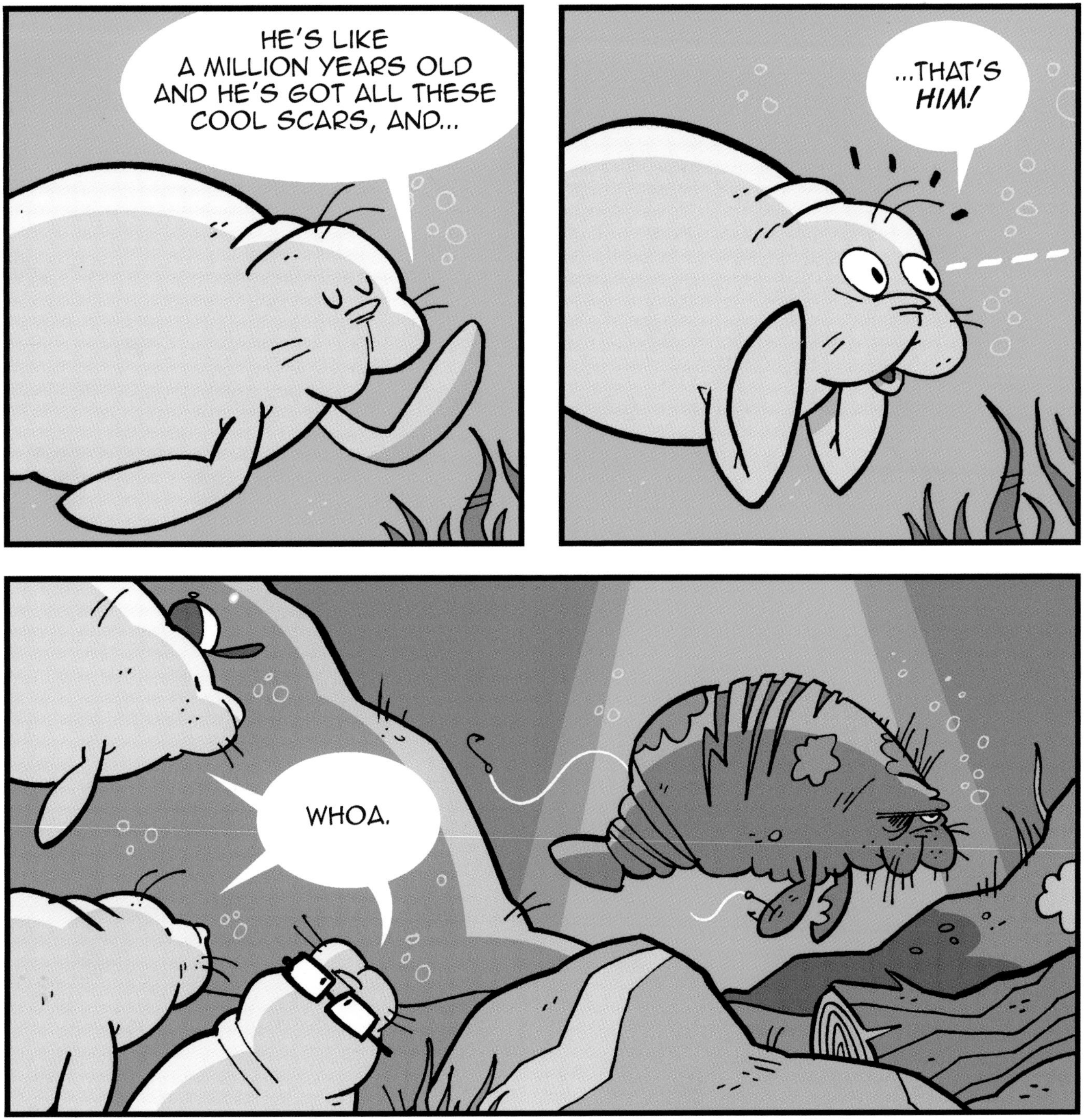
HE'S LIKE A MILLION YEARS OLD AND HE'S GOT ALL THESE COOL SCARS, AND...
...THAT'S *HIM!*
WHOA.

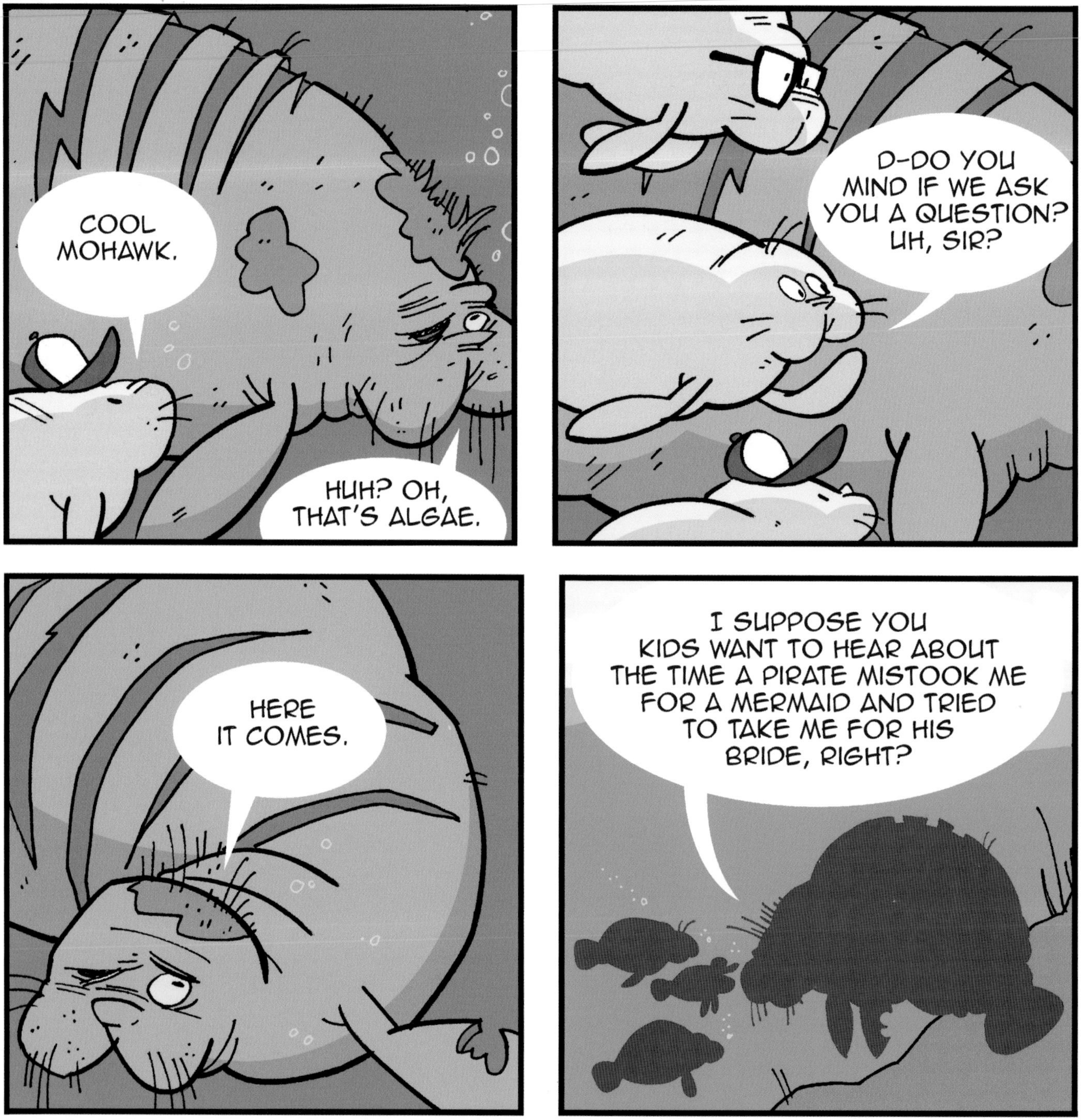
COOL MOHAWK.
HUH? OH, THAT'S ALGAE.
D-DO YOU MIND IF WE ASK YOU A QUESTION? UH, SIR?
HERE IT COMES.
I SUPPOSE YOU KIDS WANT TO HEAR ABOUT THE TIME A PIRATE MISTOOK ME FOR A MERMAID AND TRIED TO TAKE ME FOR HIS BRIDE, RIGHT?

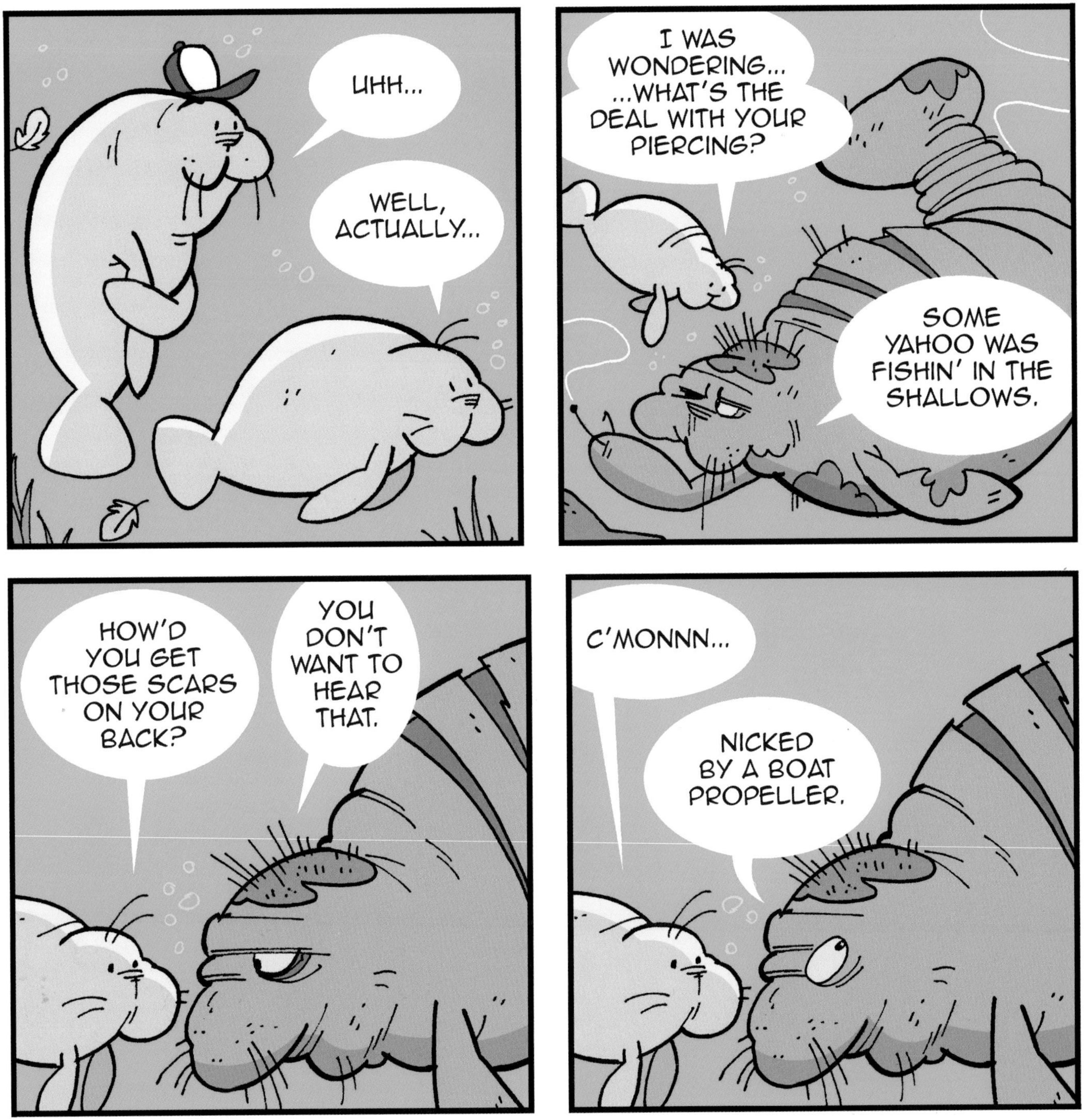
UHH...
WELL, ACTUALLY...
I WAS WONDERING... ...WHAT'S THE DEAL WITH YOUR PIERCING?
SOME YAHOO WAS FISHIN' IN THE SHALLOWS.
HOW'D YOU GET THOSE SCARS ON YOUR BACK?
YOU DON'T WANT TO HEAR THAT.
C'MONNN...
NICKED BY A BOAT PROPELLER.

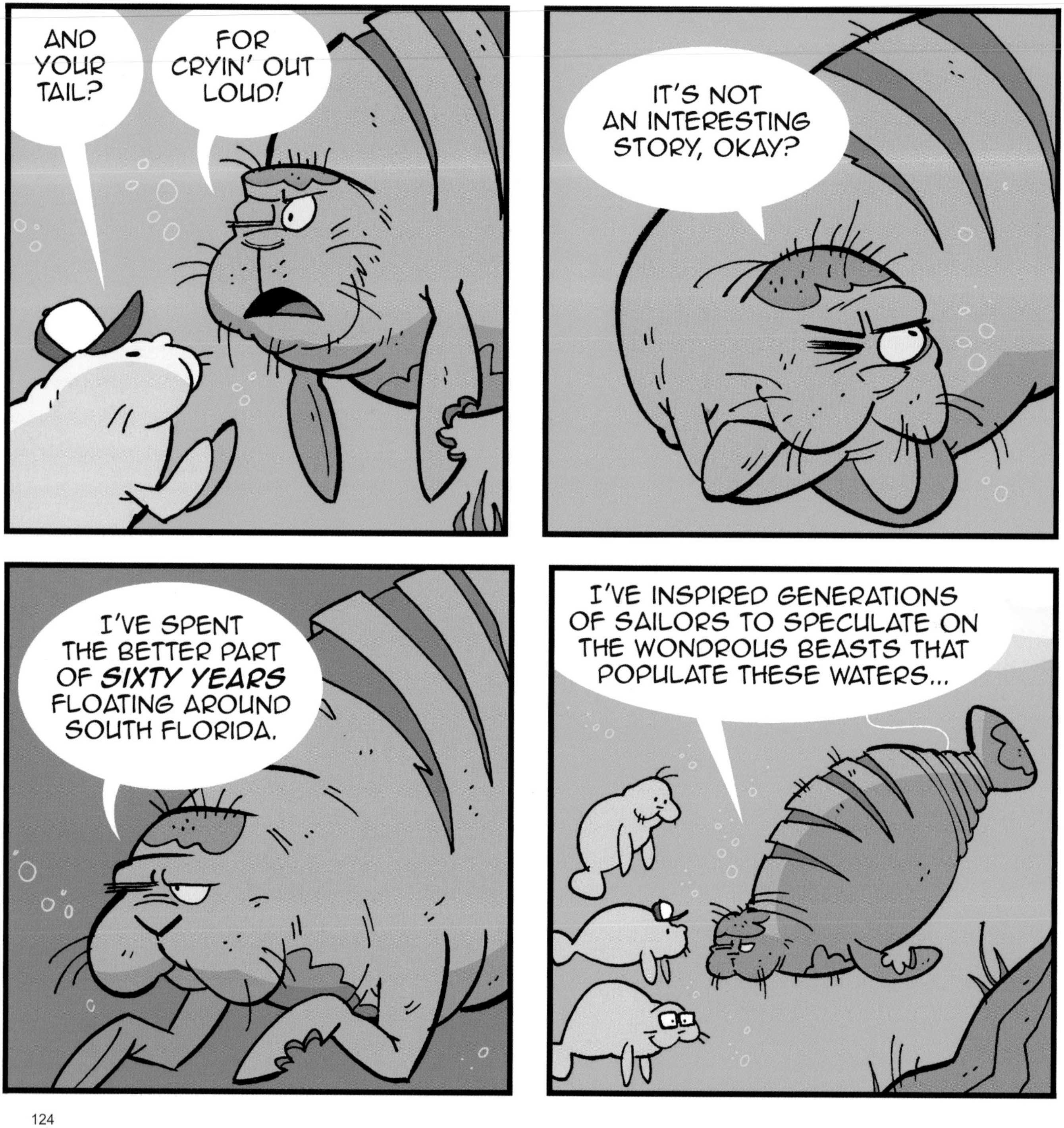
AND YOUR TAIL?
FOR CRYIN' OUT LOUD!
IT'S NOT AN INTERESTING STORY, OKAY?
I'VE SPENT THE BETTER PART OF *SIXTY YEARS* FLOATING AROUND SOUTH FLORIDA.
I'VE INSPIRED GENERATIONS OF SAILORS TO SPECULATE ON THE WONDROUS BEASTS THAT POPULATE THESE WATERS...

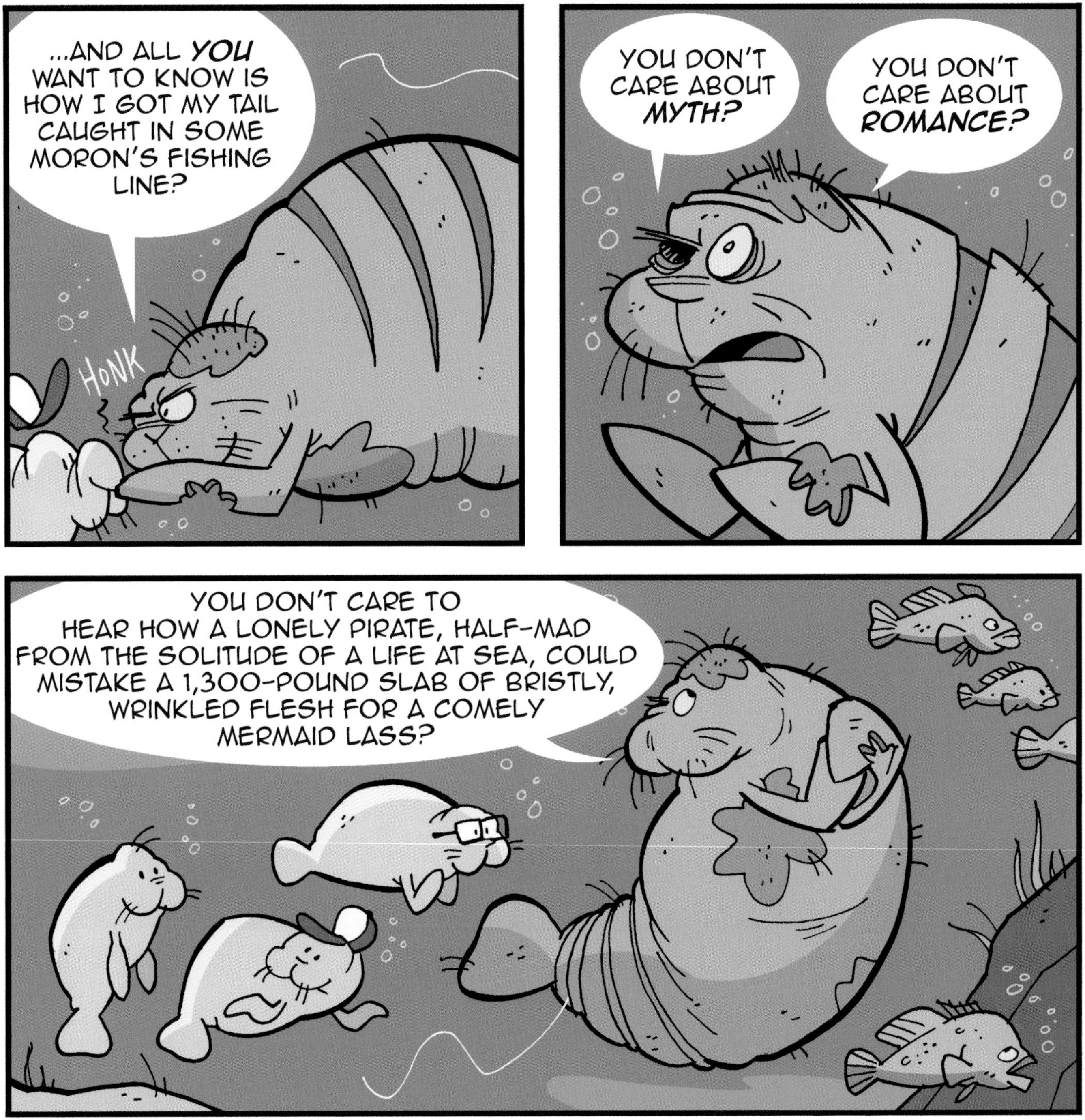
...AND ALL YOU WANT TO KNOW IS HOW I GOT MY TAIL CAUGHT IN SOME MORON'S FISHING LINE?
HONK
YOU DON'T CARE ABOUT MYTH?
YOU DON'T CARE ABOUT ROMANCE?
YOU DON'T CARE TO HEAR HOW A LONELY PIRATE, HALF-MAD FROM THE SOLITUDE OF A LIFE AT SEA, COULD MISTAKE A 1,300-POUND SLAB OF BRISTLY, WRINKLED FLESH FOR A COMELY MERMAID LASS?

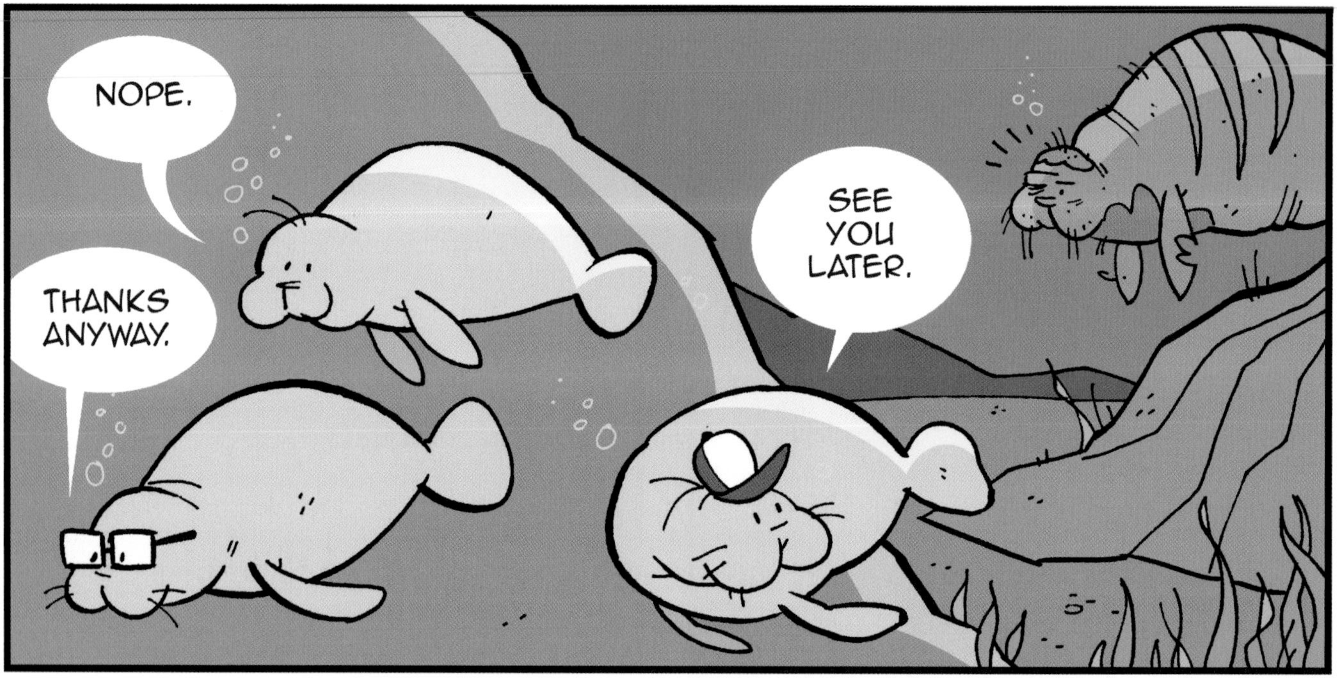
NOPE.
THANKS ANYWAY.
SEE YOU LATER.

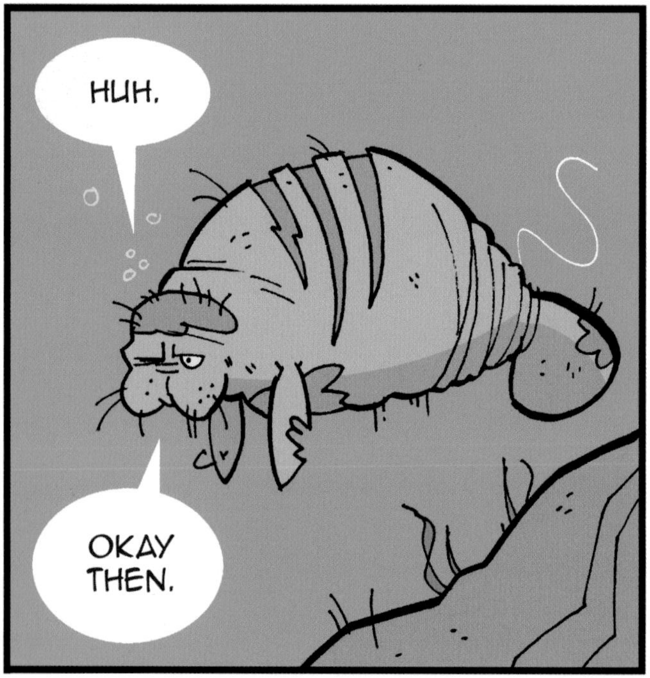
HUH.
OKAY THEN.

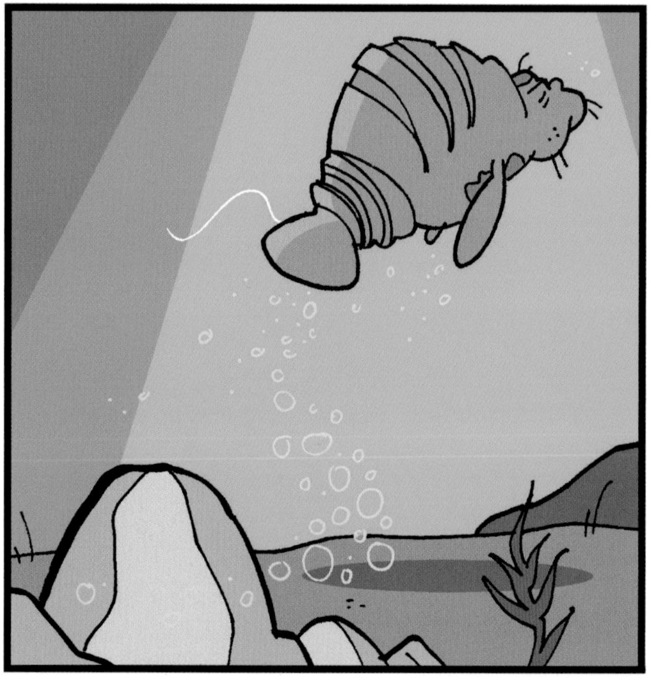

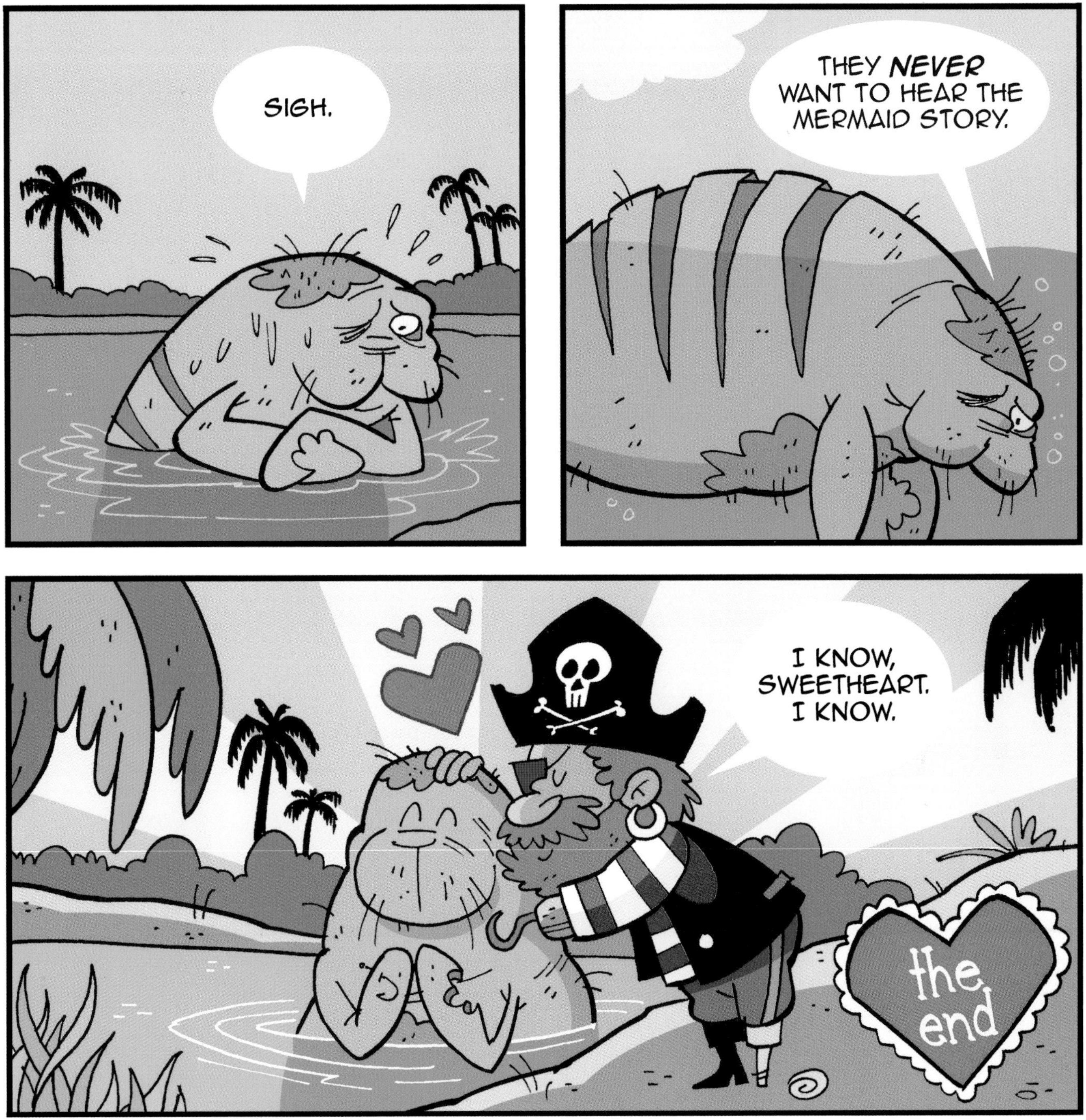
SIGH.
THEY NEVER WANT TO HEAR THE MERMAID STORY.
I KNOW, SWEETHEART. I KNOW.
the end

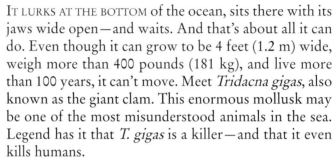

THE LEGEND OF T. GIGAS!

Story and Art by Brooke A. Allen
Lettering by Kevin Panetta

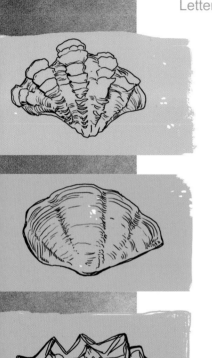

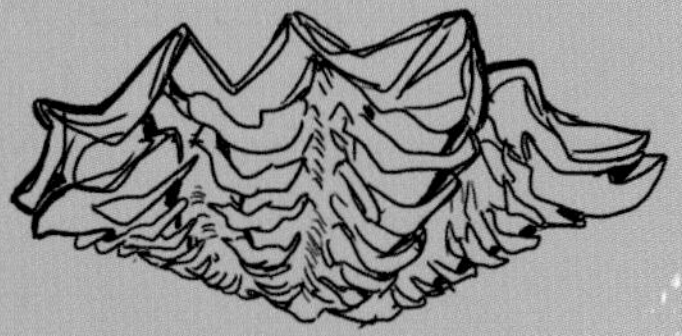

IT LURKS AT THE BOTTOM of the ocean, sits there with its jaws wide open—and waits. And that's about all it can do. Even though it can grow to be 4 feet (1.2 m) wide, weigh more than 400 pounds (181 kg), and live more than 100 years, it can't move. Meet *Tridacna gigas*, also known as the giant clam. This enormous mollusk may be one of the most misunderstood animals in the sea. Legend has it that *T. gigas* is a killer—and that it even kills humans.

You may have seen movies or read accounts of a diver brushing past the *Tridacna gigas*, only to have the shell clamp down on a leg or arm, causing the diver to drown. This, however, is impossible. In the first place, its shell closes far too slowly to trap a diver. Second, many are unable to close their shell entirely. And finally, giant clams don't eat humans. Their main food is the sugar and proteins produced by algae that live in them.

In fact, it is actually humans that are the killers in this case. The giant clam is hunted and eaten as a delicacy in Asia and certain parts of Europe, and its massive shells are sold as decorations. The adult clam's inability to move (when it is a larva, it can swim until it starts to develop a shell and sinks) may actually help researchers save it. Several government institutions and universities that are located near the warm, shallow waters of the Indian and South Pacific Oceans, where *T. gigas* makes its home, have started hatcheries to study, raise, and preserve the colossal clam.

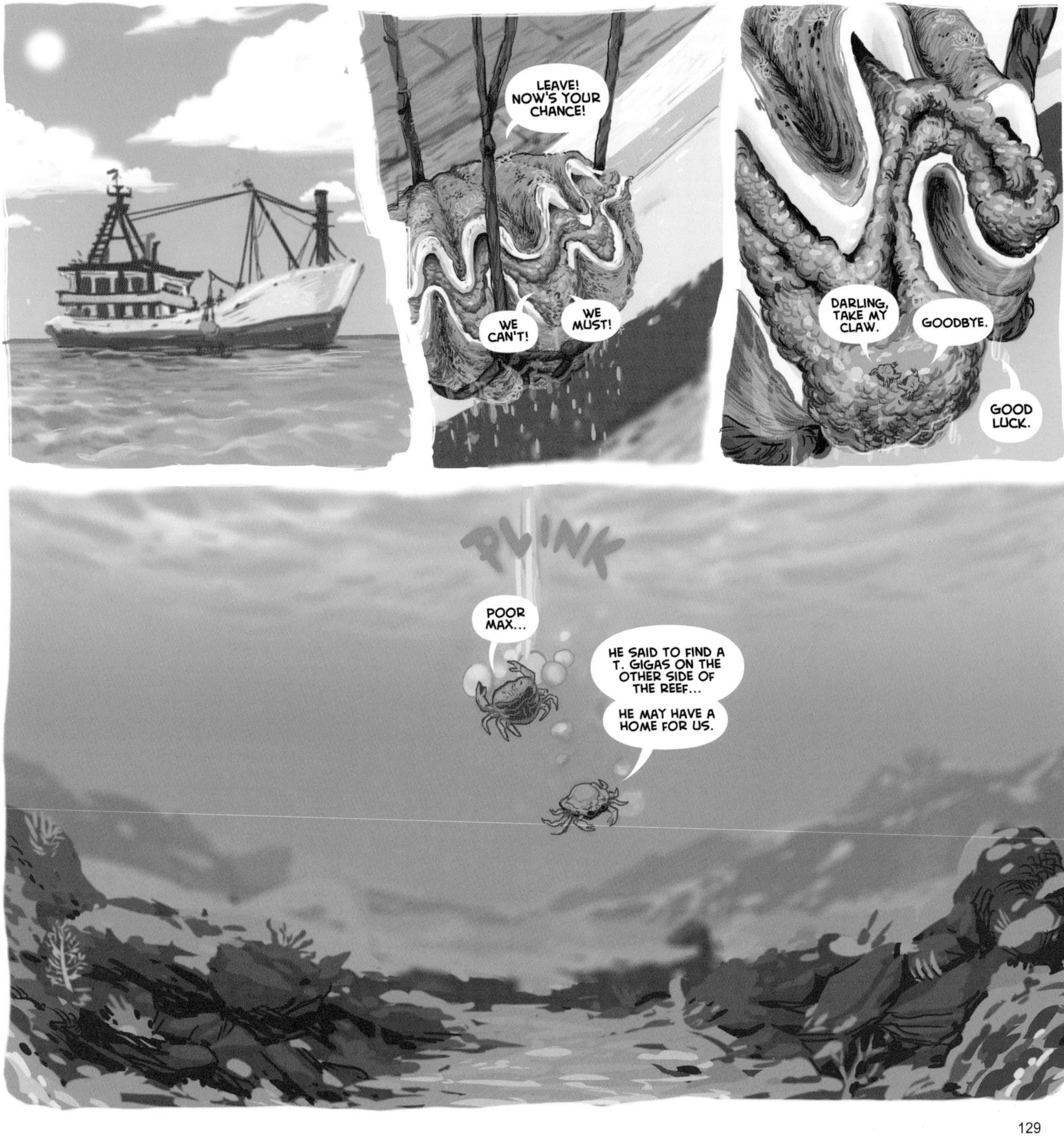
LEAVE! NOW'S YOUR CHANCE!
WE CAN'T!
WE MUST!
DARLING, TAKE MY CLAW.
GOODBYE.
GOOD LUCK.
PLINK
POOR MAX...
HE SAID TO FIND A T. GIGAS ON THE OTHER SIDE OF THE REEF...
HE MAY HAVE A HOME FOR US.

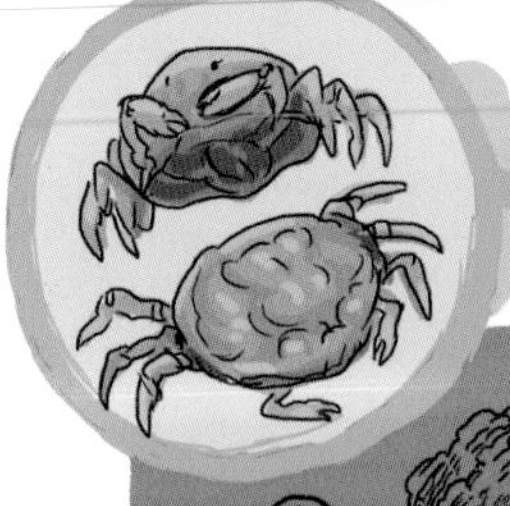

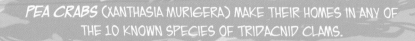

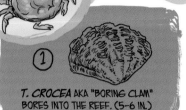

PEA CRABS (XANTHASIA MURIGERA) MAKE THEIR HOMES IN ANY OF THE 10 KNOWN SPECIES OF TRIDACNID CLAMS.

1

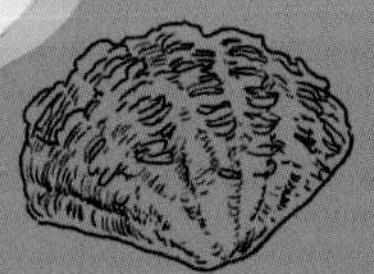

T. CROCEA AKA "BORING CLAM" BORES INTO THE REEF. (5–6 IN.)

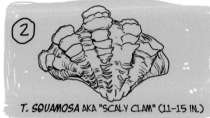

2

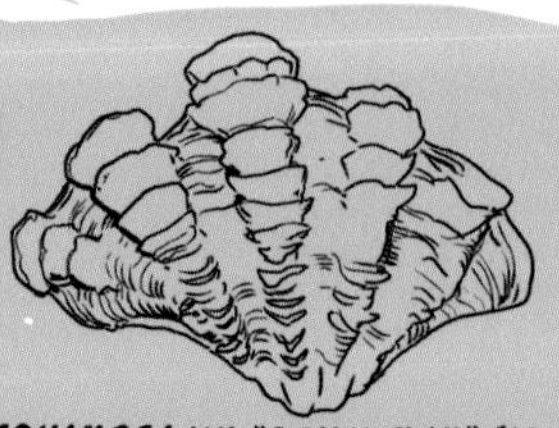

T. SQUAMOSA AKA "SCALY CLAM" (11–15 IN.)

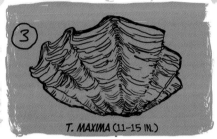

3

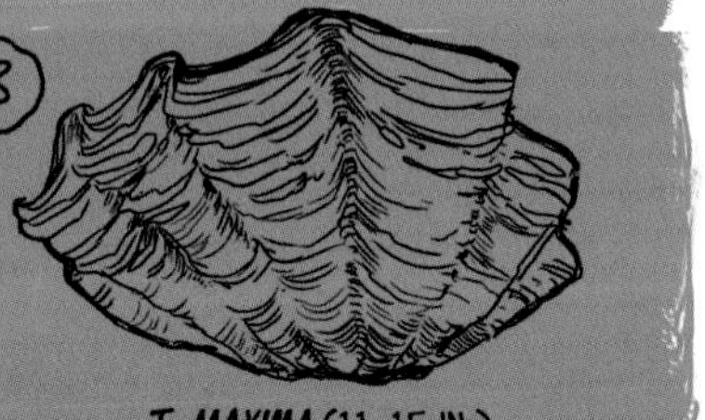

T. MAXIMA (11–15 IN.)

4

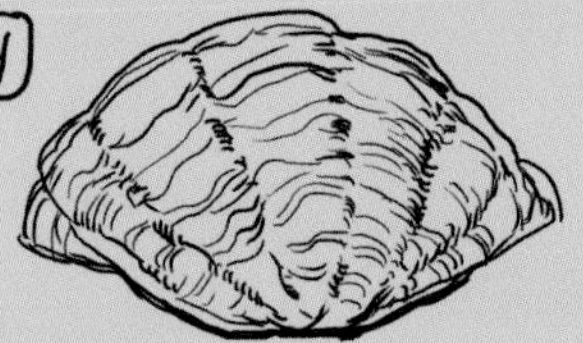

T. DERASA (19–23 IN.) AKA THE "DEVIL CLAM"

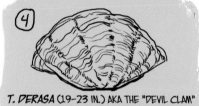

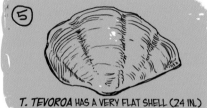

5

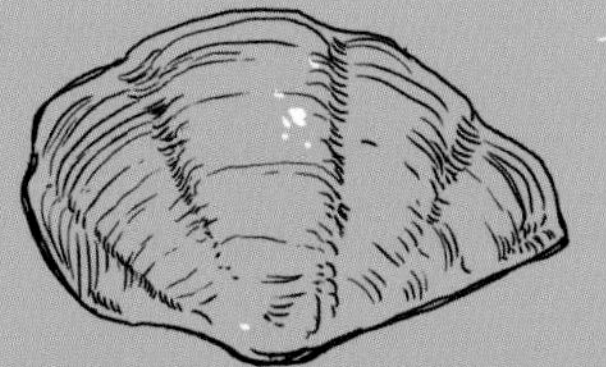

T. TEVOROA HAS A VERY FLAT SHELL (24 IN.)

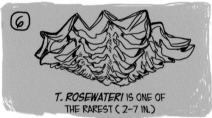

6

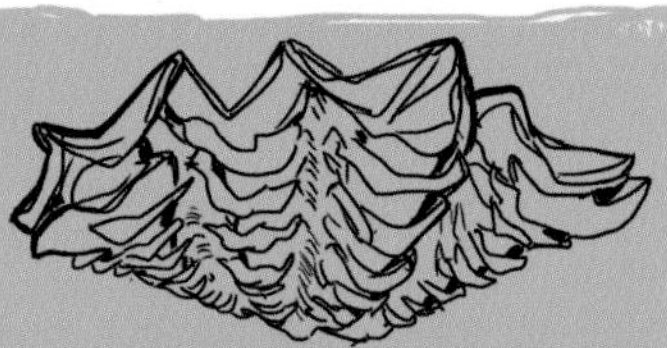

T. ROSEWATERI IS ONE OF THE RAREST (2–7 IN.)

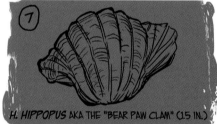

7

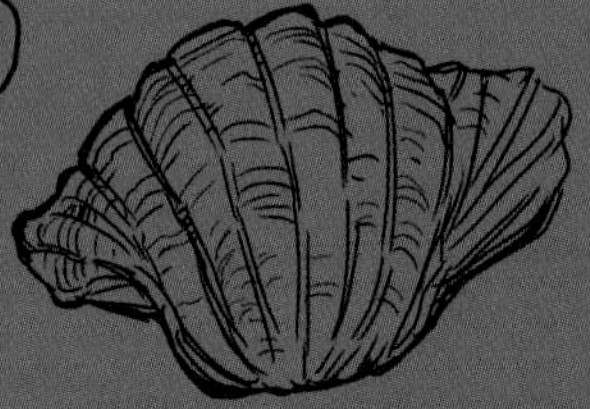

H. HIPPOPUS AKA THE "BEAR PAW CLAM" (15 IN.)

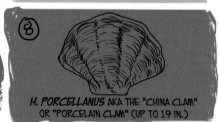

8

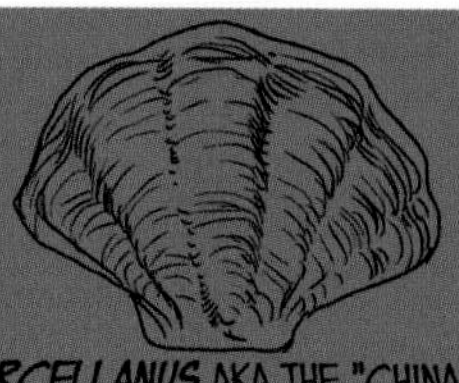

H. PORCELLANUS AKA THE "CHINA CLAM" OR "PORCELAIN CLAM" (UP TO 19 IN.)

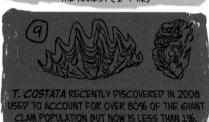

9

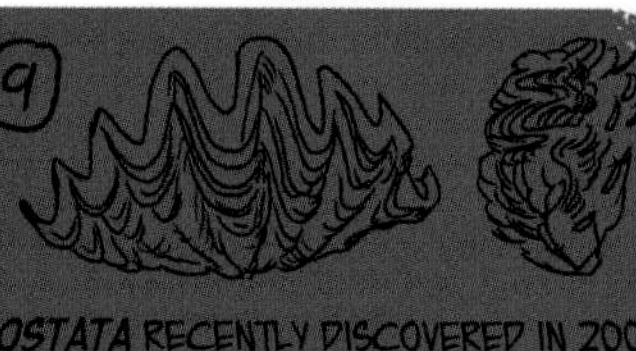

T. COSTATA RECENTLY DISCOVERED IN 2008 USED TO ACCOUNT FOR OVER 80% OF THE GIANT CLAM POPULATION BUT NOW IS LESS THAN 1%.

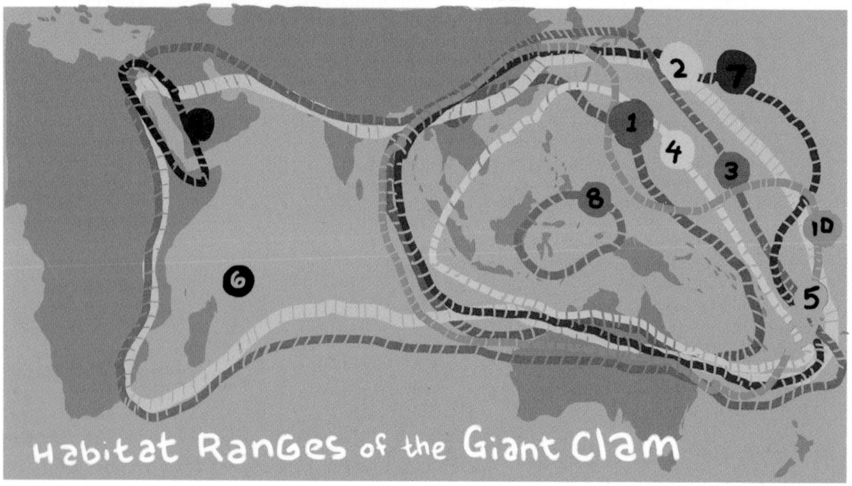
2
7
1
4
3
8
10
6
5
Habitat Ranges of the Giant Clam

10

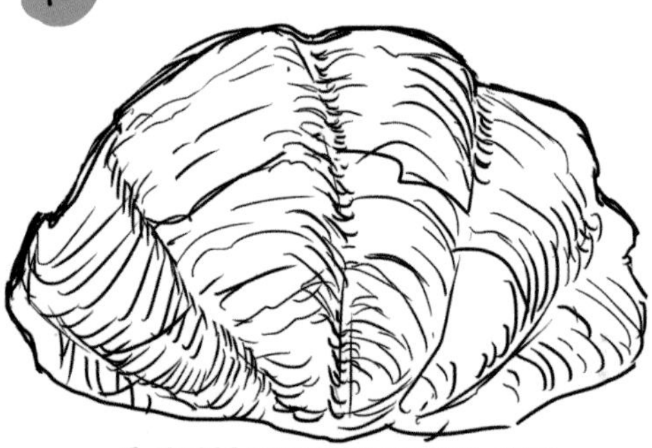

T. GIGAS, THE LARGEST OF ALL GIANT CLAMS, ALSO KNOWN AS THE "KILLER CLAM," CAN REACH THE SIZE OF 3–4 FT. AND LIVE 100+ YEARS (AND IS NO KILLER AT ALL).

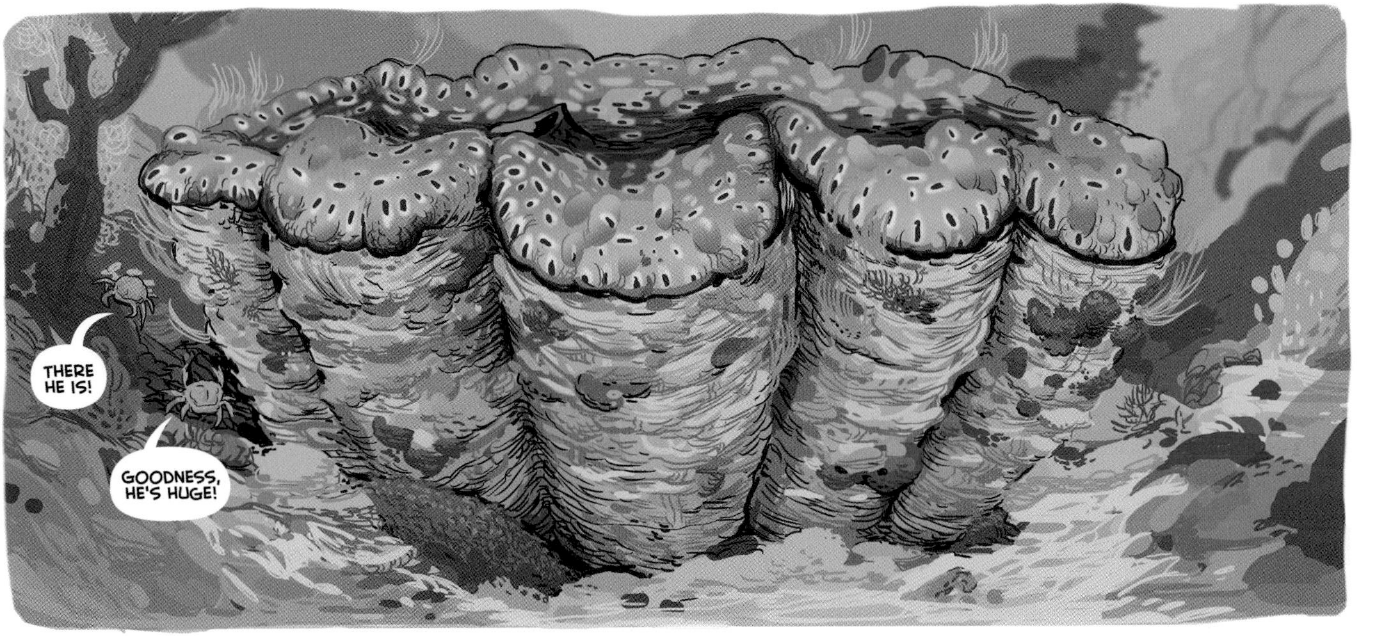
THERE HE IS!
GOODNESS, HE'S HUGE!

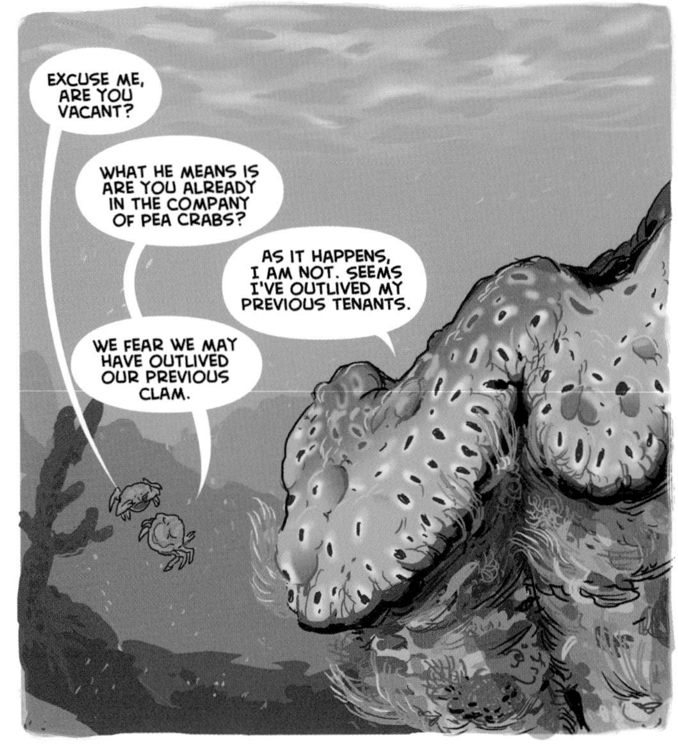
EXCUSE ME, ARE YOU VACANT?
WHAT HE MEANS IS ARE YOU ALREADY IN THE COMPANY OF PEA CRABS?
AS IT HAPPENS, I AM NOT. SEEMS I'VE OUTLIVED MY PREVIOUS TENANTS.
WE FEAR WE MAY HAVE OUTLIVED OUR PREVIOUS CLAM.

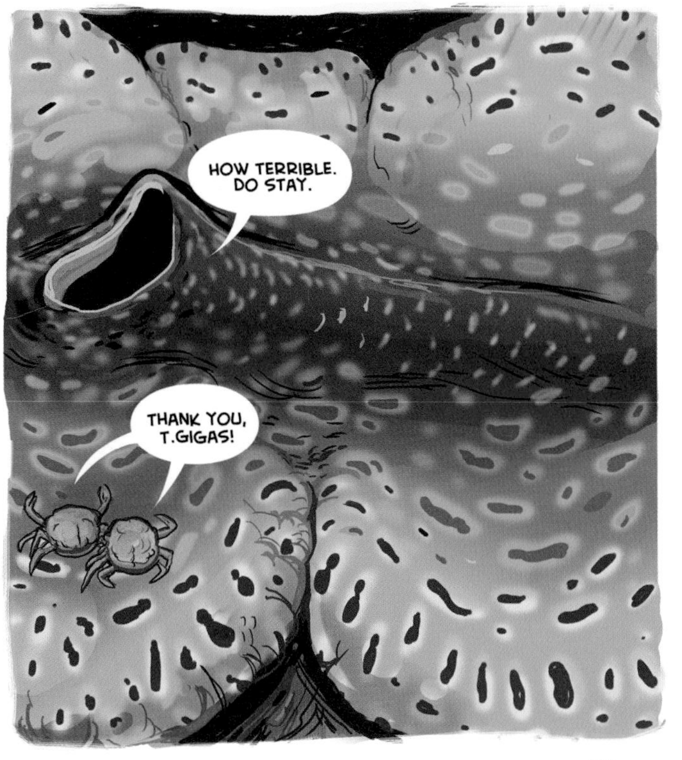
HOW TERRIBLE. DO STAY.
THANK YOU, T.GIGAS!

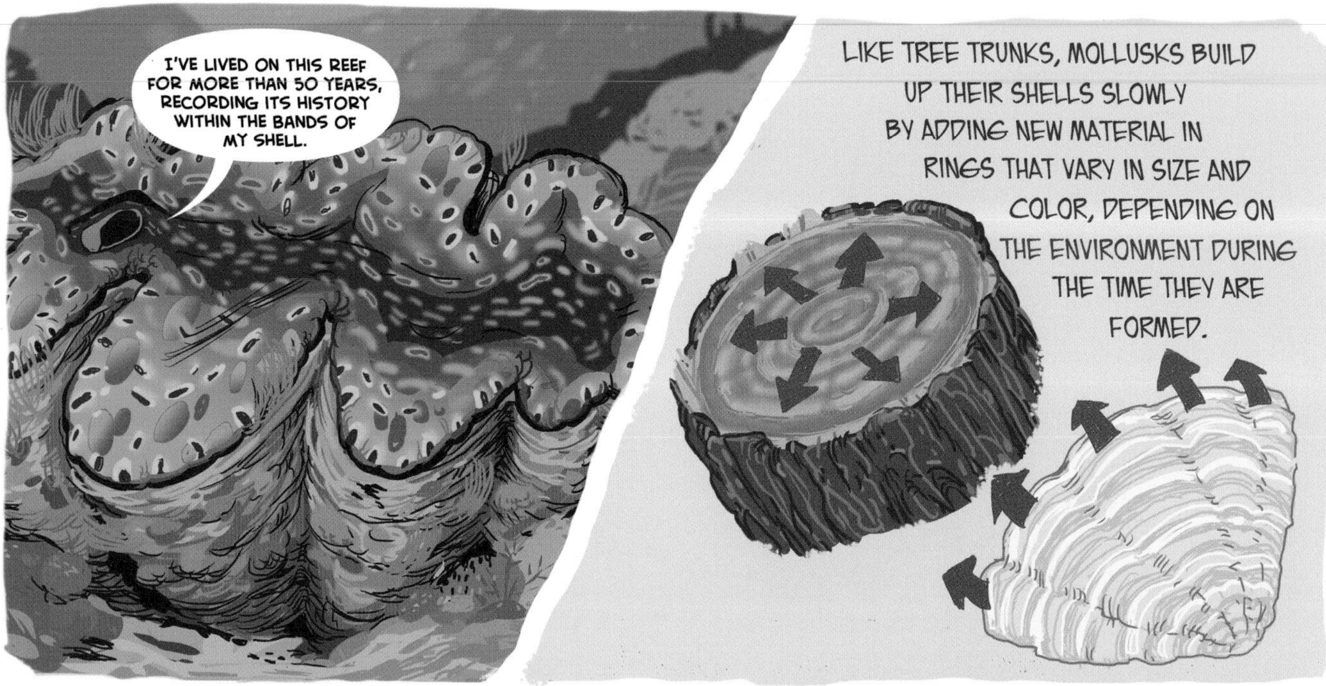
I'VE LIVED ON THIS REEF FOR MORE THAN 50 YEARS, RECORDING ITS HISTORY WITHIN THE BANDS OF MY SHELL.
LIKE TREE TRUNKS, MOLLUSKS BUILD UP THEIR SHELLS SLOWLY BY ADDING NEW MATERIAL IN RINGS THAT VARY IN SIZE AND COLOR, DEPENDING ON THE ENVIRONMENT DURING THE TIME THEY ARE FORMED.

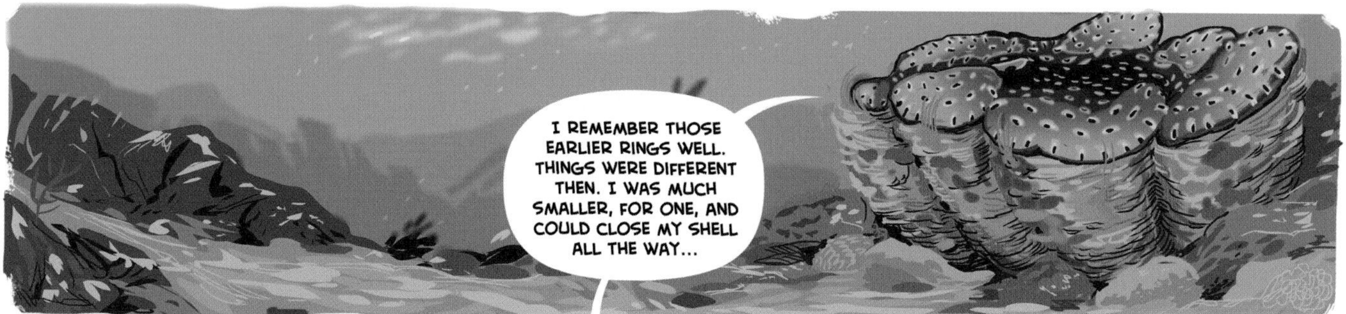
I REMEMBER THOSE EARLIER RINGS WELL. THINGS WERE DIFFERENT THEN. I WAS MUCH SMALLER, FOR ONE, AND COULD CLOSE MY SHELL ALL THE WAY...

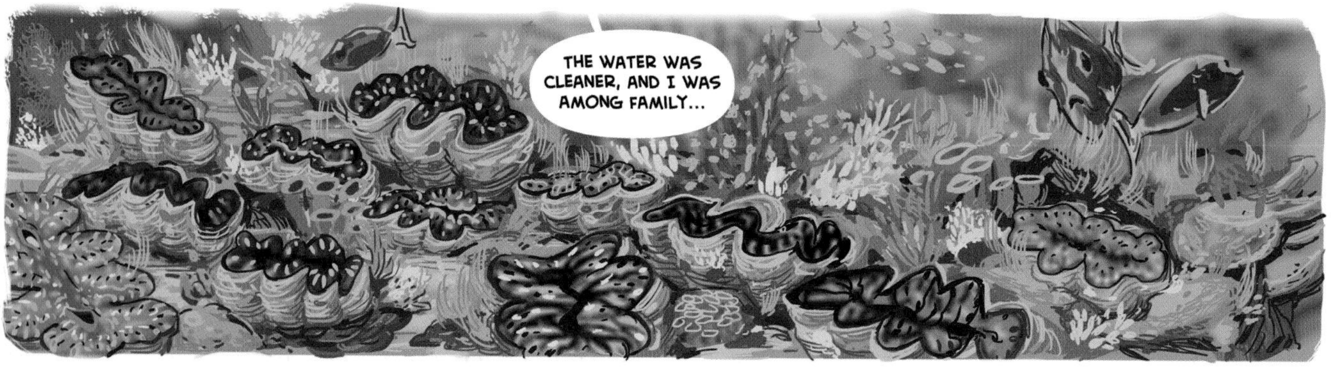
THE WATER WAS CLEANER, AND I WAS AMONG FAMILY...

MY COLONY AND I FILTERED THE WATER FOR THE CORAL, LENT OUR SHELLS TO THE SPONGES AND ALGAE, AND WATCHED OUT ON MANY LI'L FISH.

OUR EYES MAY NOT BE THE BEST AND THEY ARE VERY TINY BUT..

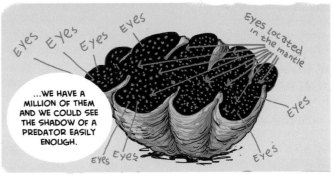

Eyes Eyes Eyes Eyes

Eyes located in the mantle

Eyes

Eyes

Eyes Eyes

...WE HAVE A MILLION OF THEM AND WE COULD SEE THE SHADOW OF A PREDATOR EASILY ENOUGH.

...WE'D RETRACT OUR MANTLES, CLOSE OUR SHELLS, AND TOGETHER WE LOOKED LIKE A PACK OF ANGRY MOUTHS...

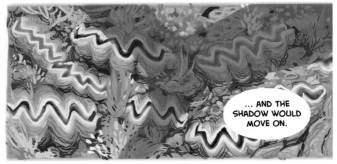

... AND THE SHADOW WOULD MOVE ON.

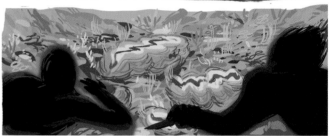

BUT NOT ALL SHADOWS PASSED BY US.

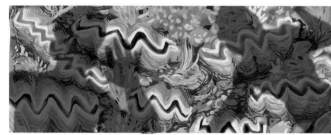

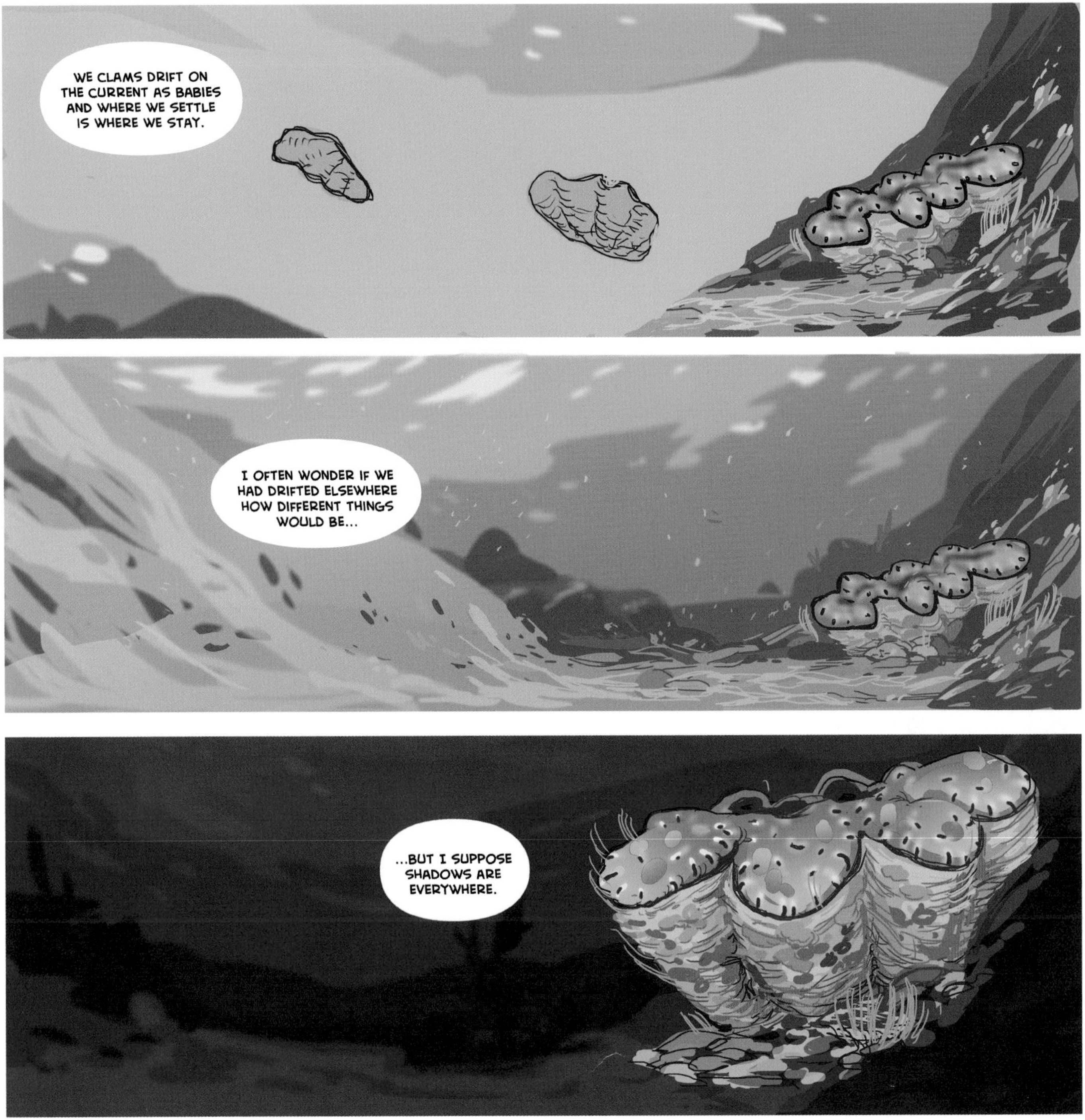
WE CLAMS DRIFT ON THE CURRENT AS BABIES AND WHERE WE SETTLE IS WHERE WE STAY.
I OFTEN WONDER IF WE HAD DRIFTED ELSEWHERE HOW DIFFERENT THINGS WOULD BE...
...BUT I SUPPOSE SHADOWS ARE EVERYWHERE.

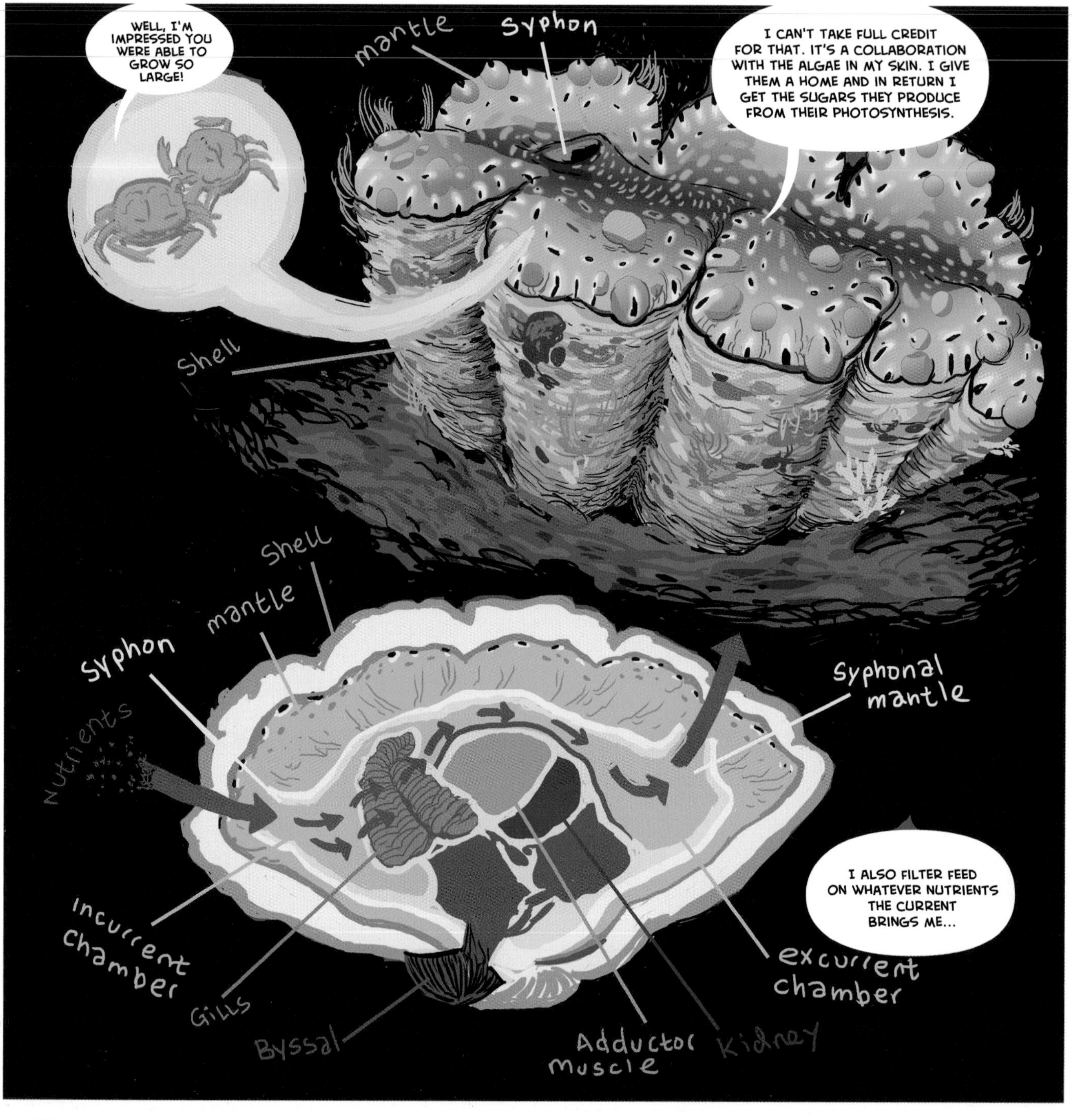
WELL, I'M IMPRESSED YOU WERE ABLE TO GROW SO LARGE!
mantle
Syphon
I CAN'T TAKE FULL CREDIT FOR THAT. IT'S A COLLABORATION WITH THE ALGAE IN MY SKIN. I GIVE THEM A HOME AND IN RETURN I GET THE SUGARS THEY PRODUCE FROM THEIR PHOTOSYNTHESIS.
Shell
Shell
mantle
Syphon
Nutrients
Syphonal mantle
I ALSO FILTER FEED ON WHATEVER NUTRIENTS THE CURRENT BRINGS ME...
Incurrent chamber
Gills
Byssal
Adductor muscle
Kidney
excurrent chamber

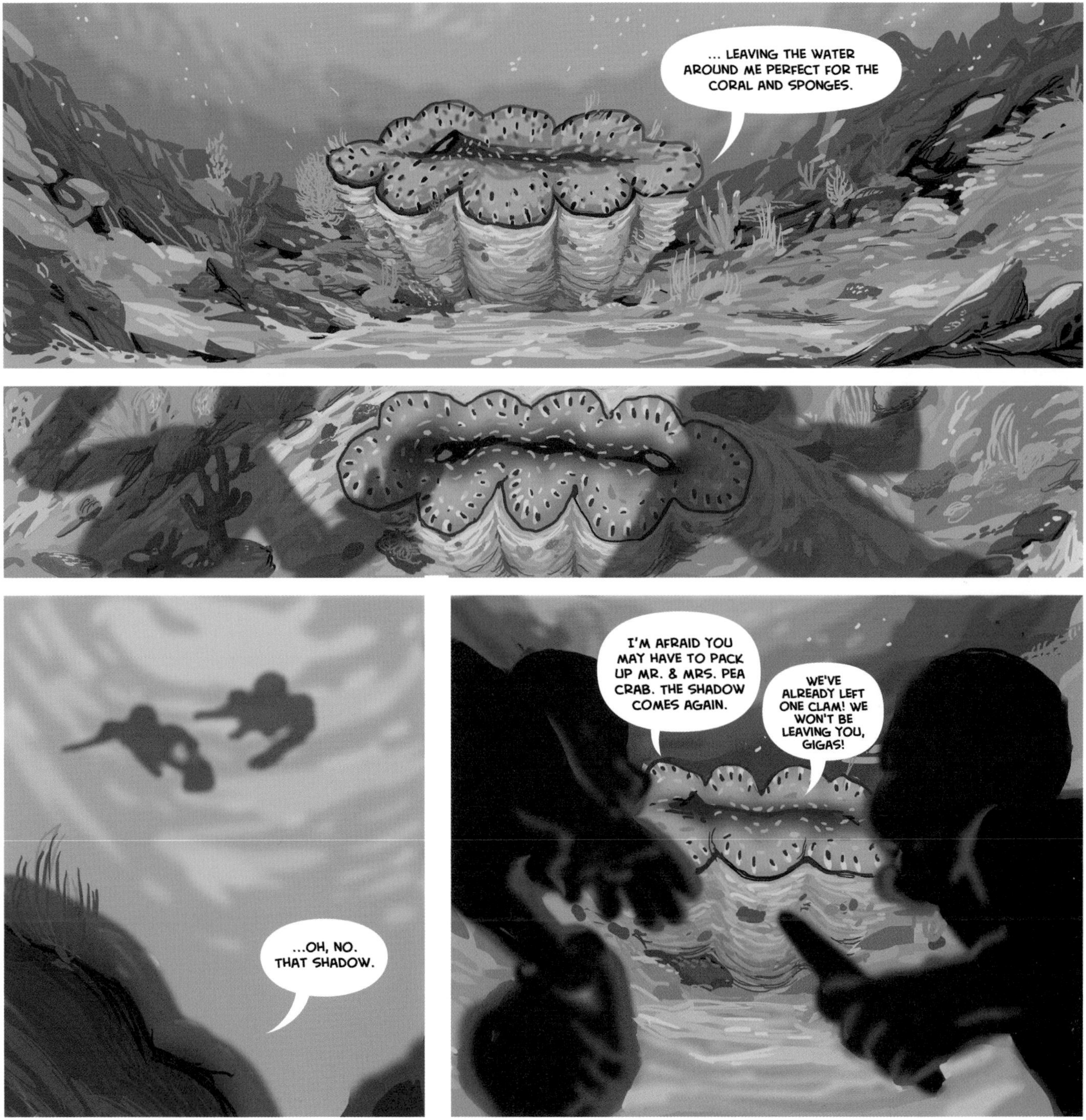
... LEAVING THE WATER AROUND ME PERFECT FOR THE CORAL AND SPONGES.
...OH, NO. THAT SHADOW.
I'M AFRAID YOU MAY HAVE TO PACK UP MR. & MRS. PEA CRAB. THE SHADOW COMES AGAIN.
WE'VE ALREADY LEFT ONE CLAM! WE WON'T BE LEAVING YOU, GIGAS!

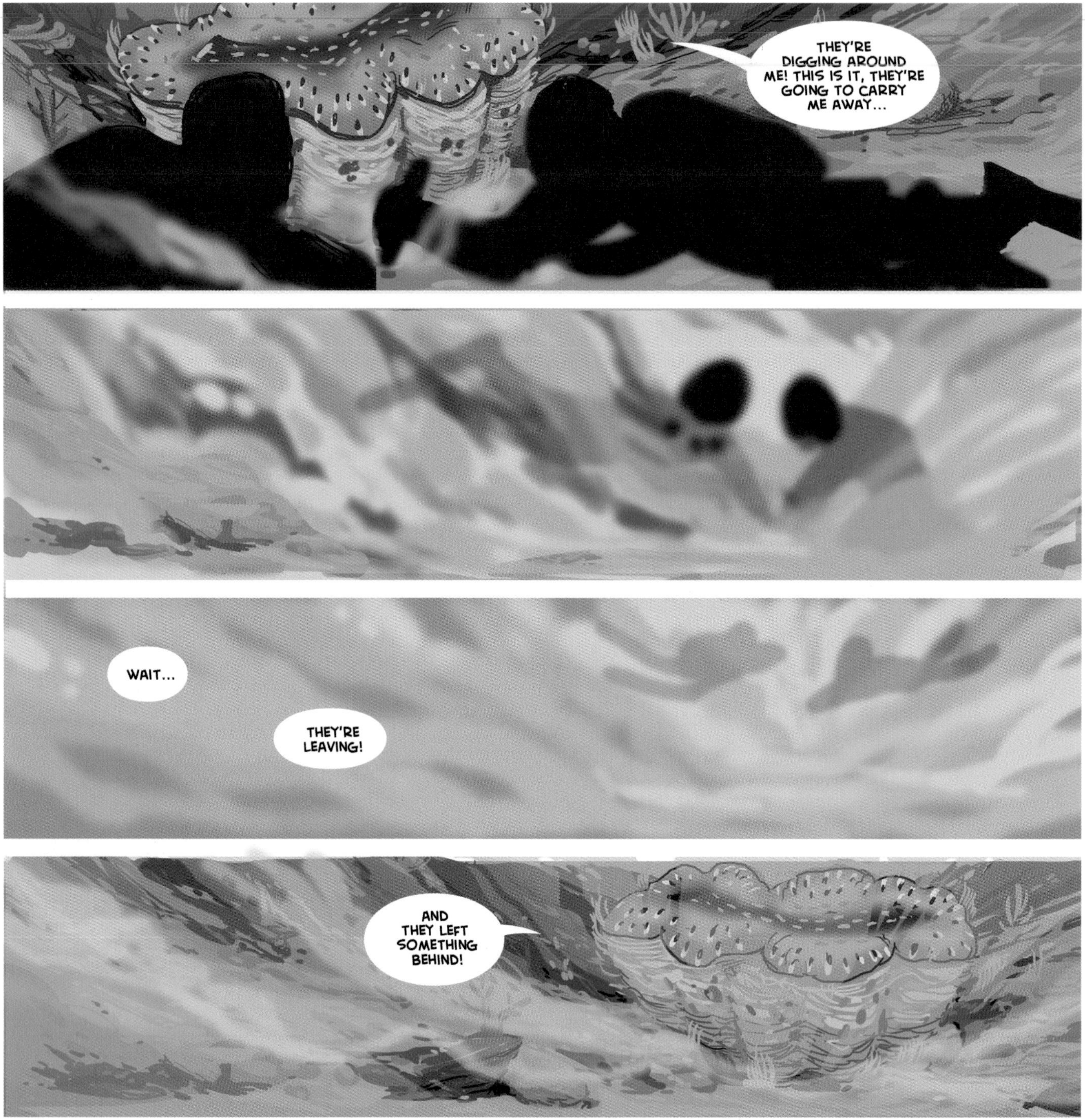
THEY'RE DIGGING AROUND ME! THIS IS IT, THEY'RE GOING TO CARRY ME AWAY...
WAIT...
THEY'RE LEAVING!
AND THEY LEFT SOMETHING BEHIND!

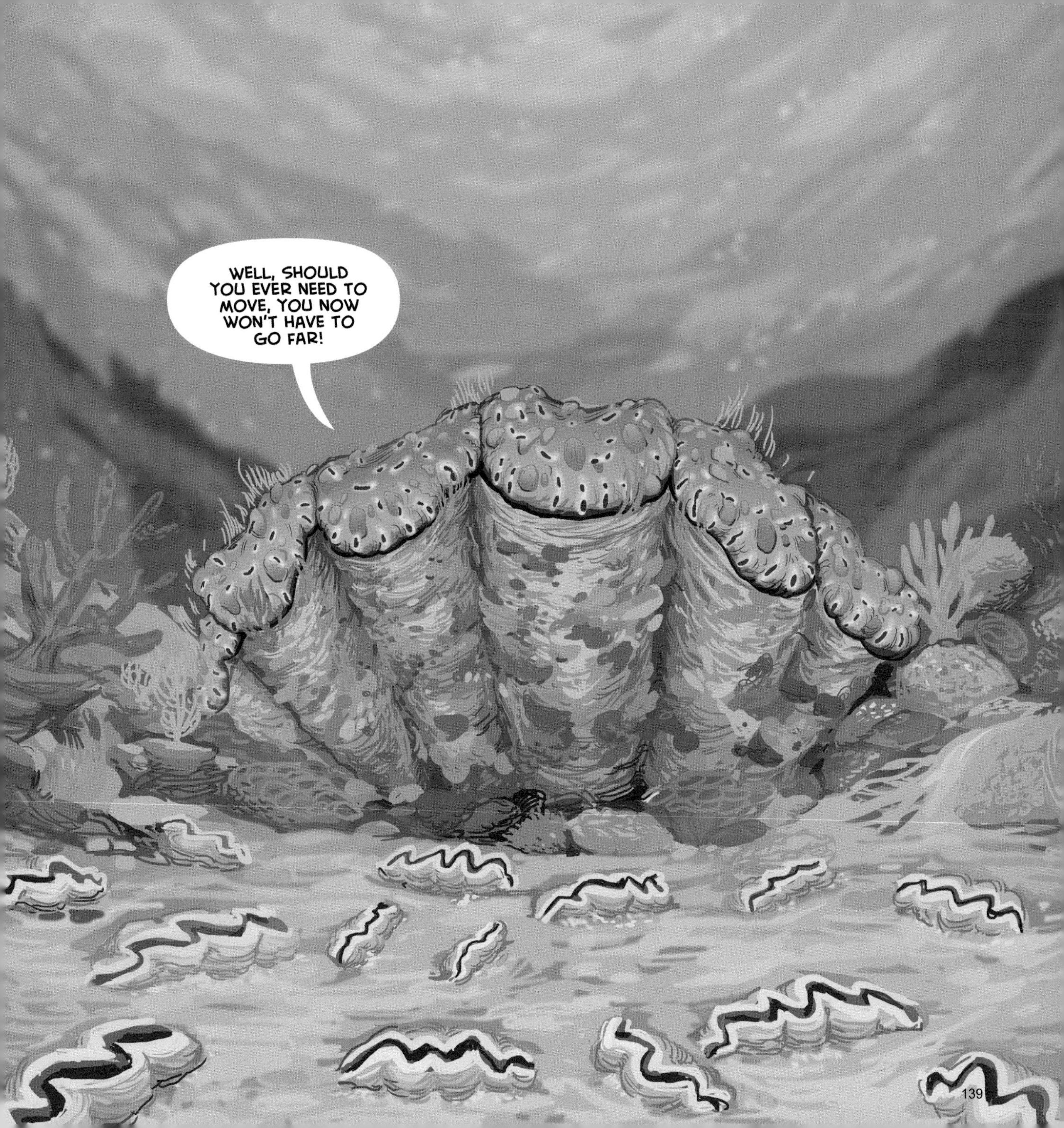
WELL, SHOULD YOU EVER NEED TO MOVE, YOU NOW WON'T HAVE TO GO FAR!

LIVING DANGEROUSLY

Despite having a habitat that spans the world, the hawksbill turtle is listed as critically endangered, with approximately 8,000 nesting females remaining in the wild. The combination of fishing gear such as gill nets and longlines plus the loss of coral reef systems threaten the turtles' existence throughout the ecosystems that provide their food and habitat. In many countries, hawksbill turtles are hunted for food and leather, and their bodies are used to make high-priced oils, perfumes, and cosmetics. Their beautiful shells are the primary source of the "tortoise shell" material found in some high-fashion accessories.

HAWKSBILL TURTLE

Research:
www.seaturtle.org/
www.pbs.org/wnet/nature/episodes/
voyage-of-the-lonely-turtle/
introduction/2503/
www.arkive.org/hawksbill-turtle/
eretmochelys-imbricata/

Read:
Harrison, Molly. "The Hawksbill Turtle" (2005). *The Kid's Times* 1(1): 1–3. NOAA's National Marine Fisheries Service, Office of Protected Resources. Free download: http://www.nmfs.noaa.gov/pr/pdfs/education/kids_times_turtle_hawksbill.pdf
Safina, Carl. *Voyage of the Turtle: In Pursuit of the Earth's Last Dinosaur* (2007). Holt Paperbacks.

HAMMERHEAD SHARK

In some parts of the world, shark finning and overfishing have reduced hammerhead populations by 99 percent in the past 30 years, according to the IUCN. At this rate, these animals may be extinct within the next 10 to 20 years. Unfortunately, hammerheads are not the only sharks to face this fate. With 70 million sharks killed each year for their fins, studies show that in the northwest Atlantic, all shark populations have been reduced by 50 percent over the past 30 years. Even worse, all sharks could be eradicated forever in our lifetime if steps are not taken to protect them—an alarming result that could have global consequences.

Research:
www.pewenvironment.org/uploadedFiles/FINAL_PEW_Shark Soup_Booklet.pdf
www.galapagospark.org
www.nmfs.noaa.gov/pr/species/fish/scallopedhammerheadshark.htm

Read:
Llewellyn, Claire. *The Best Book of Sharks* (2005) Kingfisher.
Mallory, Kenneth. *Swimming with Hammerhead Sharks* (2002). HMH Books for Young Readers.

ALBATROSS

The stunning albatross has, in one form or another, flown over the Earth's oceans for 50 million years. With an average life span of 50 years, these are also one of the largest flying birds alive today. In fact, an albatross's wingspan may reach an incredible 11 feet (3.4 m) across. Despite their power and size, albatross populations have suffered a dramatic decline during the last decade. As of 2009, 19 of the 22 species of albatross were officially considered to be vulnerable, nearly threatened, or critically endangered around the world. Their decline is mostly a result of human practices, including destructive fishing methods such as longlining.

Research:
www.birdlife.org/datazone/speciesfactsheet.php?id=3956
www.iucnredlist.org
animals.nationalgeographic.com/animals/birds/albatross

Read:
Coleridge, Samuel Taylor. "The Rime of the Ancient Mariner." (1798).
Whalley, George. *The Mariner and the Albatross* (1947). *The University of Toronto Quarterly* 16: 381-398, reprinted in Coleridge: A Collection of Critical Essays (1967). Prentice-Hall.

These gentle and majestic filter feeders are the largest rays in the world and cousins of sharks. Demand for the gills of manta and mobula rays has risen dramatically in the past 10 years for use in traditional Chinese medicine even though they were not historically used for this purpose. None of these purported medical claims are supported by science nor are they supported by traditional Chinese medicine texts. Researchers have found that the gill raker trade is conducted by the same networks responsible for the devastating trade in shark fins, which have turned to rays for additional profits as worldwide shark populations decline.

MANTA RAY

Research:
www.news.virginia.edu/content/university-virginia-engineers-are-designing-building-mechanical-ray-0
www.arkive.org/giant-manta-ray/manta-birostris/
www.abcnews.go.com/Technology/mechanical-manta-ray-bio-mimicry-engineers-copy-nature/story?id=17006976

Read:
Pennisi, Elizabeth. "Bio-inspired Engineering: Manta Machines" (May 27, 2011). *Science* 332.
www.sharkadvocates.org/cites_4sharks_manta_fact_sheet.pdf

BLUE WHALE

Even though it is the largest animal ever known to have lived, the blue whale's presence on this planet is severely threatened. Its once abundant population was demolished by whale hunters, who killed around 360,000 between 1900 and 1966, when the International Whaling Commission finally protected the species. There are now only between 10,000 to 25,000 of these magnificent animals remaining in the wild. They are still threatened by dangers, including collisions with ocean vessels and fishing gear entanglement.

Research:
animals.nationalgeographic.com/animals/mammals/blue-whale/
www.marinemammalcenter.org/education/marine-mammal-
    information/cetaceans/blue-whale.html
www.afsc.noaa.gov/nmml/education/cetaceans/blue.php

Read:
Nickin, Charles "Flip." *Among Giants: A Life with Whales* (2011). University of Chicago Press.
Bortolotti, Dan. *Wild Blue: A Natural History of the World's Largest Animal* (2008). Thomas Dunne Books.

With fewer than 400 remaining in the wild, the Mediterranean monk seal is one of the rarest animals on the planet. In better times, they lived on open beaches around the Mediterranean Sea. However, due to increasing human encroachment, they have increasingly retreated to rocky sea caves that are virtually inaccessible to people. These caves are a much more dangerous environment for the monk seal's young pups, and their hazards are one of the leading cause of death for the pups. Overfishing that has depleted their food supply and treacherous fishing gear that entangle and drown the seals further endanger this rapidly declining species.

MONK SEAL

Research:
www.nmfs.noaa.gov/pr/species/mammals/pinnipeds/
    mediterraneanmonkseal.htm
www.iucnredlist.org/details/summary/13653/0
www.monachus-guardian.org/

Read:
Riedman, Marianne. *The Pinnipeds: Seals, Sea Lions, and Walruses* (1990). University of California Press.
www.pelagosinstitute.gr/en/pelagos/pdfs/mediterranean_megaptera.pdf

The whale shark is the largest fish in the ocean, and a docile one at that. These gentle giants, reaching more than 40 feet (12.2 m) in length, are filter feeders, which means they have no teeth and only eat plankton. Even though there is no exact count of how many of these fish there are, they are still considered a highly vulnerable species. Many commercial fisheries target whale sharks for their fins, prompted by the global shark fin soup trade. On the black market, a single whale shark fin can fetch more than $50,000.

WHALE SHARK

Research:
www.dailymail.co.uk/news/article-2084508/The-touching-scenes-friendship-Filipino-fishermen-worlds-biggest-fish-man-nature.html
www.scientificamerican.com/article.cfm?id=love-whale-shark
www.smithsonianmag.com/science-nature/Swimming-With-Whale-Sharks.html

Read:
Taylor, Geoff. *Whale Sharks: The Giants of Ningaloo Reef* (1994). HarperCollins.
www.doc.govt.nz/Documents/about-doc/concessions-and-permits/conservation-revealed/sharks-mango-in-nz-waters-lowres.pdf

SEAHORSE

Seahorses are fascinating—almost magical—marine creatures. With an independently moving head that resembles a horse, a tail like a monkey, and skin that can change colors like a chameleon, these tiny creatures are unlike other ocean dwellers. Unfortunately, they share many of the same dangers that threaten other ocean creatures. Up to 20 million are trapped and traded each year to make traditional Chinese medicines. Hundreds of thousands of seahorses are also sold for the aquarium trade, which primarily supplies North American consumers. Most of these seahorses are juveniles, and they usually die within a short period of time. They are further threatened by overfishing, bycatch, and the habitat destruction caused by coastal construction.

Research:
animals.nationalgeographic.com/animals/fish/sea-horse/
www.montereybayaquarium.org/cr/seahorses.aspx
www.theseahorsetrust.org/seahorse-facts.aspx

Read:
Turner, Pamela S. *Project Seahorse* (2010). HMH Books for Young Readers.
www.montereybayaquarium.org/PDF_files/teaching_activities/Seahorse_Similes.pdf

The Atlantic bluefin tuna is considered one of the most highly evolved fish species, yet overfishing to meet the demands of the sushi trade have brought it to the brink of extinction. With bodies that can easily grow to more than 1,000 pounds (454 kg) at full maturity and that can accelerate at speeds equal to sports cars, bluefin tuna are among the fastest and largest bony fish in the oceans. According to the IUCN, over the last 40 years, the Atlantic bluefin's numbers have plummeted by 70 to 80 percent. Despite efforts from conservation groups, the United Nations recently rejected a US-backed proposal to ban bluefin exports.

BLUEFIN TUNA

Research:
animals.nationalgeographic.com/animals/fish/bluefin-tuna/
www.pewtrusts.org/our_work_detail.aspx?id=963
worldwildlife.org/species/bluefin-tuna

Read:
Ellis, Richard. *Tuna: A Love Story* (2008). Random House.
Earle, Sylvia A. *The World Is Blue* (2009). National Geographic.

CORAL

While most people don't realize it, coral is a sea animal. In fact, coral are vital to the ocean's ecosystem, and provide a habitat for more than 25 percent of all marine life. Coral reefs provide a safe place where millions of other sea creatures—both known and still to be discovered—hunt, breed, and spawn. And while these animals join together to form massive structures that can resist powerful ocean waves, they are also fragile and very sensitive. Ocean acidification, destructive fishing practices such as bottom trawling and dynamite threaten coral throughout the world's oceans.

Research:
www.mnn.com/earth-matters/translating-uncle-sam/stories/
    whats-killing-allthe-coral
www.oceanservice.noaa.gov/podcast.php
http://www.visitmaldives.com/kr/the-maldives/location-and-
    geography

Read:
Sheppard, Charles R.C.; Davy, Simon K.; Pilling, Graham M.
    The Biology of Coral Reefs (Biology of Habitats) (2009).
    Oxford University Press, USA.
Spalding, Mark D.; Green, Edmund P. *World Atlas of Coral
    Reefs* (2001). University of California Press.

MANATEE OR DUGONG

With a resemblance to land mammals, and in fact distantly related to elephants, the manatee is a gentle vegetarian giant of the sea. Sometimes called sea cows, the manatees favor shallow, marshy waters along the coasts of the Caribbean Sea, the Gulf of Mexico, the Amazon Basin, and across the Atlantic Ocean in West Africa. The world's largest population of manatees lives in Florida, but even there, fewer than 3,000 survive in the wild. Countless have perished due to climate change—in the winter of 2010, a freeze killed many manatees as well as other Florida sea creatures. Other threats are toxic algae caused by human pollution, loss of habitat, and boating collisions.

Research:
www.fws.gov/northflorida/manatee/manatees.htm
www.savethemanatee.org/default.html
www.defenders.org/florida-manatee/basic-facts

Read:
Colin, George; Lawder, Bertram. *In Search of Mermaids: The Manatees of Guiana* (1964). T.Y. Crowell.
Pittman, Craig. *Manatee Insanity: Inside the War over Florida's Most Famous Endangered Species* (2010). University Press of Florida.

The giant clam lives in the warm waters of the South Pacific and Indian Oceans. This kind of clam only gets one chance to find a nice home because once it fastens itself to a spot on a reef, it remains there for the rest of its life. These bottom-dwelling behemoths are the largest mollusks on Earth. They are capable of living more than 100 years, and can grow to a size of more than 4 feet (1.2 m) in length and weigh more than 500 pounds (227 kg). Even though it is illegal to sell these creatures around the world, they are still overharvested for their food and shells, and to be sold to aquariums. This trade has landed these creatures on the list of most-threatened marine life.

GIANT CLAM

Research:
animals.nationalgeographic.com/animals/invertebrates/giant-clam/
www.a-z-animals.com/animals/giant-clam/
animaldiversity.ummz.umich.edu/accounts/Tridacna_gigas/

Read:
Fatherree, James W. *Giant Clams in the Sea and the Aquarium* (2006). Liquid Medium.
Helsinga, Gerald. *Saving Giants* (ebook) http://store.blurb.com/ebooks/374835-saving-giants.

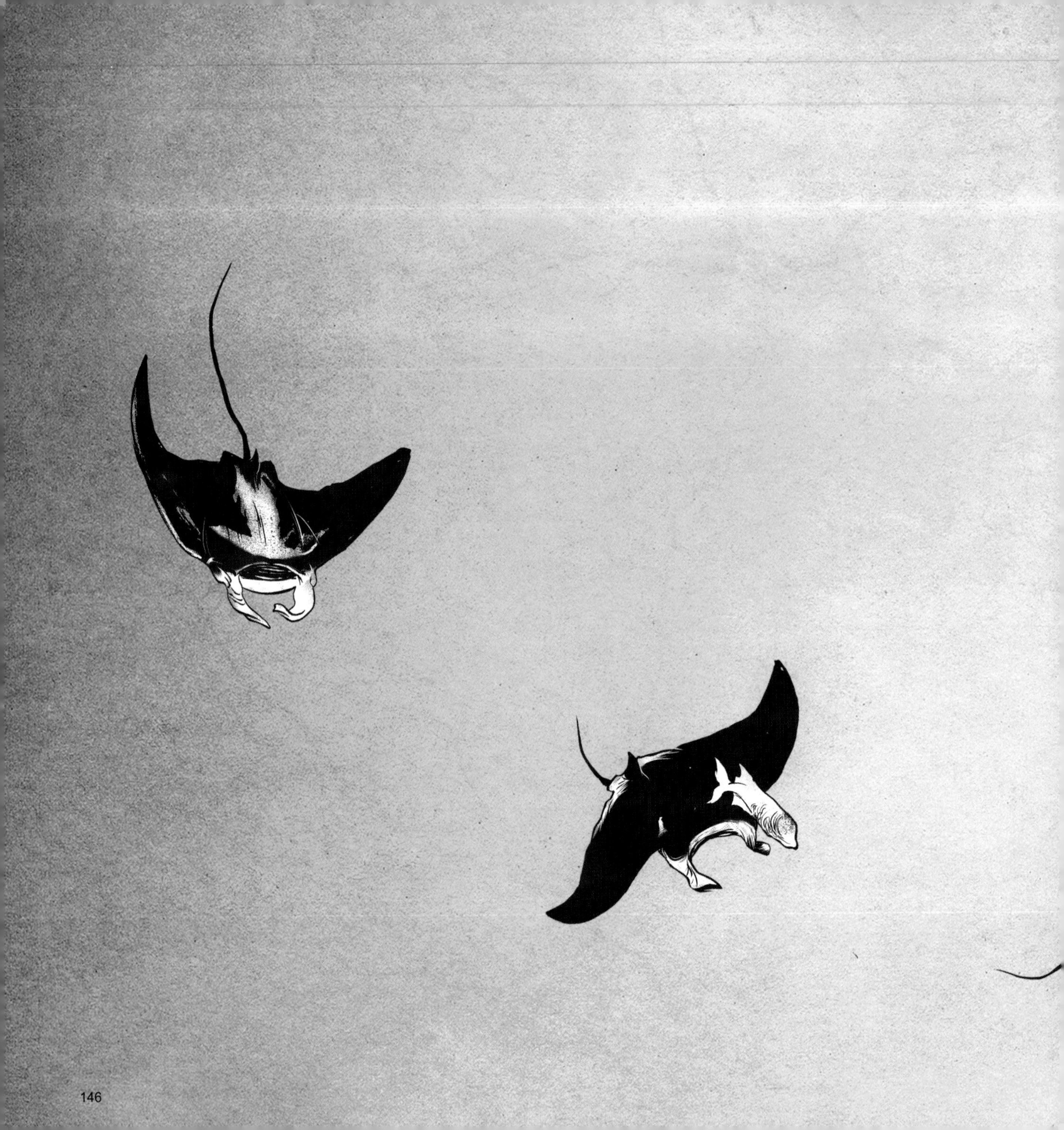

Writers and Artists

Brooke A. Allen is a human who creates comics in Washington, D.C. When she's not drawing comics, she's on a quest for national treasure. If anyone has any leads or a copy of the movie, feel free to contact her at brooklyn.a.a@gmail.com.

Jason E. Axtell is an educator and graphic illustrator from Virginia whose work combines elements from sequential art, graphic design, and the fine arts. His work includes the *Family Guy* comic book, coloring for the acclaimed graphic novel *Mr. Big*, and *Strays 'N Gates*, a collection of comic strips.

Steven Russell Black is a painter with an obsessive compulsion to champion the odd, fringe, or otherwise unappreciated. See more work at facebook.com/stevenrussellblack.

Michael Cowgill studied creative writing at the University of Evansville and George Mason University. He writes fiction, comics, and the occasional song in Falls Church, Virginia, and is a member of the D.C. Conspiracy. His comics work has appeared in *District Comics* and *Magic Bullet*. He hopes to one day meet a mantabot. You can find out more at michaelcowgill.com.

Matt Dembicki previously edited and contributed to the Eisner-nominated and Aesop Prize–winning *Trickster: Native American Tales: A Graphic Collection*. He also served at the helm of *District Comics: An Unconventional History of Washington, D.C.*, a Harvey Award–nominated anthology that was named as one of the best books of 2012 by the *Washington Post*.

DAVID ALLAN DUNCAN (who goes by Duncan) has been teaching drawing, sequential art, and comics history since 2003. He lives in a brown house in Georgia with his wife and son. He can be found at conventions and conferences around the country doing comics workshops, giving academic papers, and hawking his mini-comics. Check out gobnobble.com.

JF FRANKEL creates an eclectic bunch of comics and illustrations from his home in Berkeley, California. His previous marine biology comics include the *Water Column* trilogy, *Seafood*, *Trilobite*, and *Twilight of the Sea Cow*. See more of his work at jfnexus.com.

PAULINA GANUCHEAU is a freelance artist and designer working out of New Orleans. She can usually be found curled in a ball under her desk. Her weekly webcomic, *Zodiac Starforce* (with writer Kevin Panetta), can be found at zodiacstarforce.com.

PIERCE HARGAN grew up in Los Angeles. He graduated from college in 2012 and is pursuing his passion in Brooklyn, New York. This is his first short story. Visit him at piercehargan.com.

JAY HOSLER is a biology professor at Juniata College in Huntingdon, Pennsylvania. He studies insect behavior and neurobiology and has written and drawn comics about honeybees, Darwin, the eye, and evolution. When he isn't doing that stuff, he can be found goofing around with his sons, Max and Jack, and flirting shamelessly with his wife, Lisa.

ANDY K. is an illustrator and underground comic book artist based outside of Washington, D.C. His work is largely defined by his unique line work, characters, and vibrant colors. He has produced images for magazines, posters, album art, skate decks, comics, and much more. Visit andykart.com.

Pat N. Lewis is a cartoonist and illustrator living in Pittsburgh. His work has appeared in anthologies from BOOM! Studios, Top Shelf Comics, Graphic Classics, and McGraw-Hill. His first solo book, *The Claws Come Out*, was published by IDW Publishing. Currently, Pat is serializing his Reuben-nominated webcomic, *Muscles Diablo*, in *Where Terror Lurks!* at patnlewis.tumblr.com. Also visit patnlewis.com.

Steve Loya has been teaching and making his own art for more than a decade in northern Virginia. His work has been exhibited both locally and internationally and can be found in numerous digital and printed publications. Find out more about Steve's art at steveloya.com.

Dove McHargue is a freelance artist/writer working in the comics industry from his home in Savannah, Georgia. He spends the rest of his time as a faculty member at the Savannah College of Art and Design in the Sequential Art Department. Visit him at facebook.com/dovemchargue and imagetalker.blogspot.com.

Kevin Panetta is a comic book writer and comic store employee. He is currently living in Washington, D.C., but is considering moving to a volcano if this writing thing doesn't work out. His weekly webcomic, *Zodiac Starforce* (with artist Paulina Ganucheau), can be found at zodiacstarforce.com.

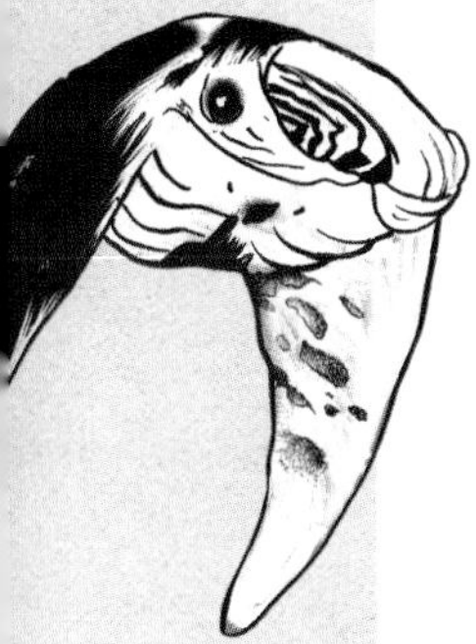

Tammy Stellanova is an illustrator, jewelry maker, and comic artist with a background in biology. You can view more of her artwork at tammystellanova.com.

Tom Williams lives and plays in Columbus, Ohio. He's done work for Dark Horse, Image, IDW, and Oni Press. Visit him at opencrashcomics.com.

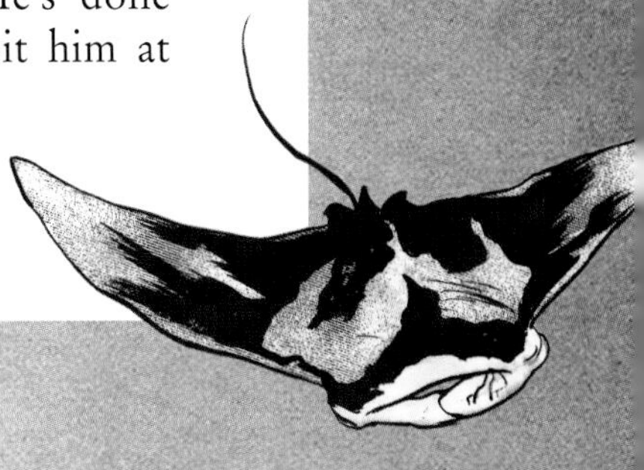

ABOUT PANGEASEED

PangeaSeed is an international organization that brings together members of the art, science, and environmental activist communities. Together we work to raise awareness and educate the public about the critical need for ocean conservation.

Originally organized to protect sharks, which have been victims of relentless harvesting to the point where these great predators are now in peril, PangeaSeed has expanded its mission to work for the protection of the planet's oceans and marine life. To accomplish this, the organization encourages environmental activism and sustainable consumption choices. While the organization is based in the United States, it works closely enough with its generous international network of supporters to have a global impact. And what an impact it is having! In Japan, PangeaSeed was the first organization to raise public awareness about shark conservation and preservation.

Ideology of PangeaSeed

There is an old saying, "A picture is worth a thousand words." At PangeaSeed, we take this to heart, then take it a step further.

In addition to encouraging volunteer activism and research, PangeaSeed uses art, music, film, and photography to create a sea change within the global community and promote an understanding of the need to preserve and protect the world's oceans.

A common thread throughout the team at PangeaSeed is that these artistic mediums transcend borders and race, as well as cultural and linguistic boundaries, to unite communities. It is essential to do this if we are to inspire the healing action we need to solve the time-sensitive issues our planet is facing.

We believe art and activism can spark positive change within individuals and their communities. No matter how large or small the effort, we are all morally responsible to take action and make better decisions for future generations and the natural world.

PangeaSeed has been fortunate enough to collaborate with influential artists from around the world to raise awareness on behalf of sharks and other endangered marine species. These incredibly talented individuals are the trendsetters who shape and communicate the zeitgeist that exists across cultures. By harnessing the incredible talent of these artists, we aim to increase awareness and educate many about the terrible effect people are having on oceans and about the marine animals that face certain extinction if we do not act now.

www.PangeaSeed.org

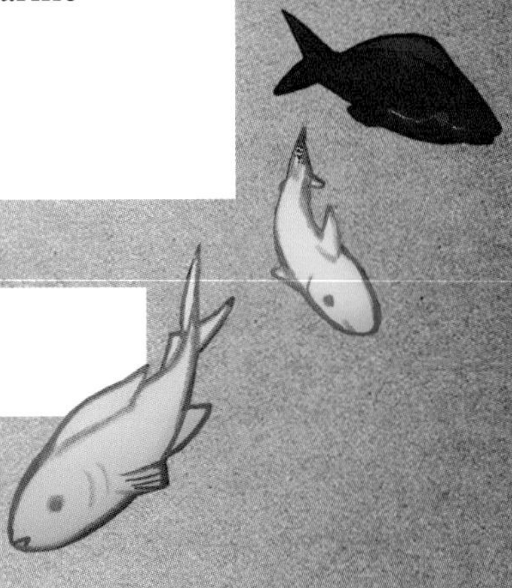

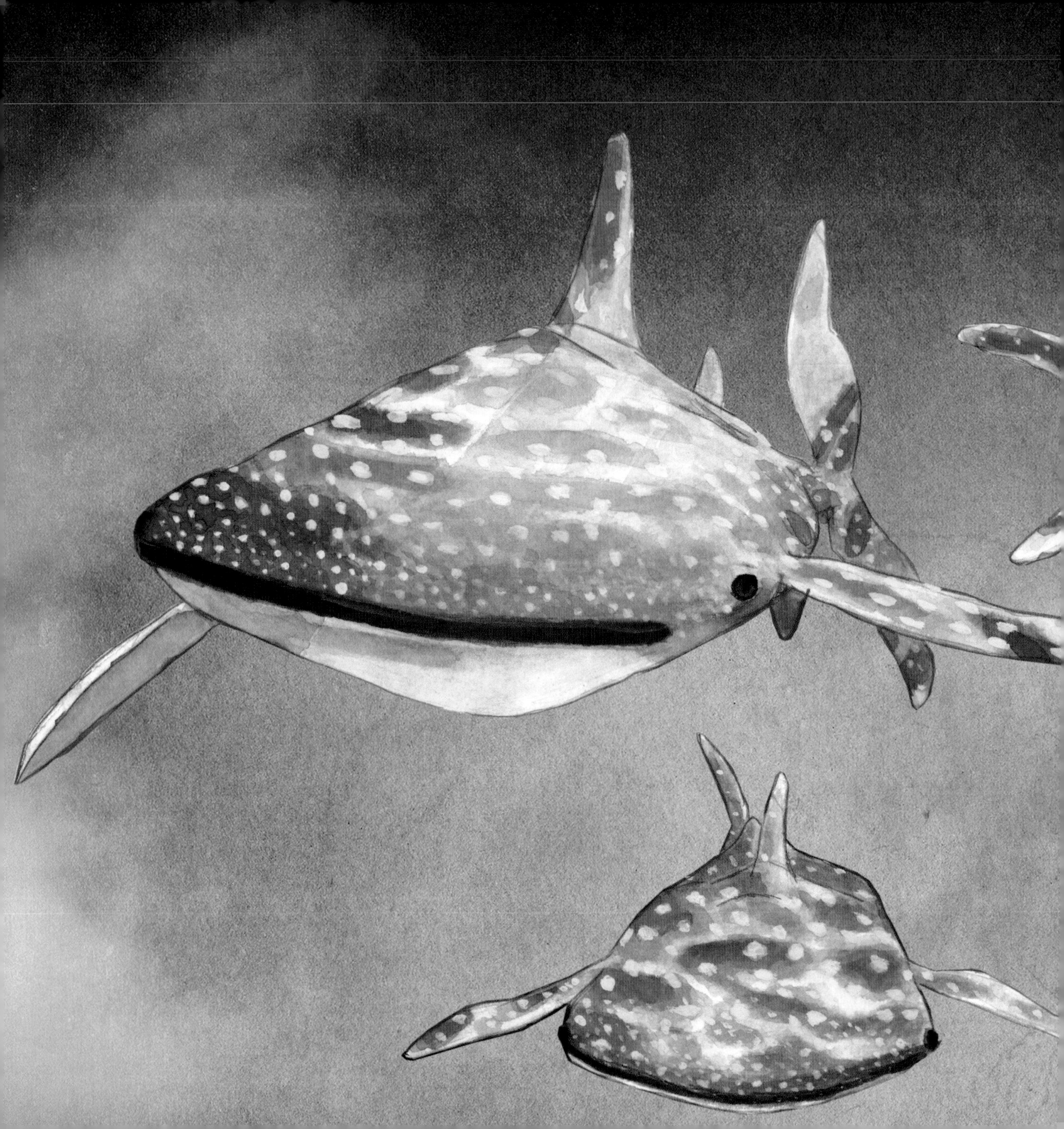

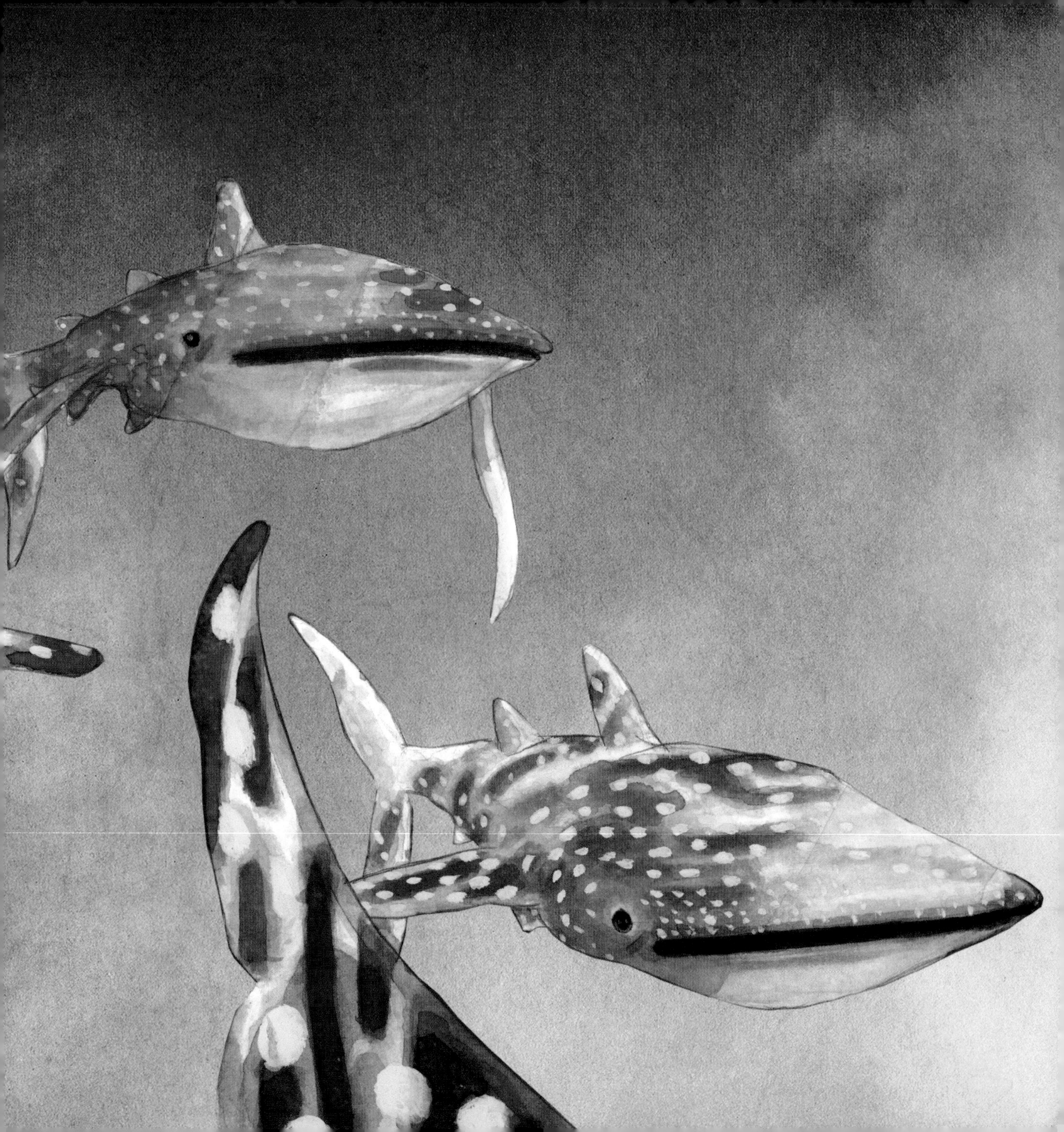